THE SUPREME COURT OF ONTARIO

THE HONOURABLE MR. JUSTICE CAMPBELL

OSGOODE HALL
TORONTO, ONTARIO M5H 2N5

For Dick Chaloner,

A great public servant.

Archie Campbell

April 2002

THE LAST DAY, THE LAST HOUR

The Currie Libel Trial

On 11 November 1918, the last day of the Great War, the Canadian Corps, led by Sir Arthur Currie, proudly liberated Mons after more than four years of German occupation, reversing the loss of the town by the British in August 1914. But the push to Mons in the last weeks of the war had cost many lives, and long after the war ended Currie was blamed by many, including the flamboyant Sam Hughes, the former minister of militia, for needlessly wasting lives. When the charge against Currie appeared in the Port Hope *Evening Guide* in 1927 in an editorial written by W.T.R. Preston, a veteran of a lifetime of journalistic and political wars, Currie was incensed. Against the advice of his friends he decided to sue for libel, and retained W.N. Tilley, KC, the leading lawyer of the day, to take his case.

This book reconstructs the events leading up to the trial and the trial itself, one of the most sensational in Canadian history. The cast of characters includes not only Currie, Tilley, Hughes and Preston, but also Frank Regan, the scrappy defence lawyer, Hugh Rose, the austere judge who tried the case, and many other prominent legal, military, and political figures of the 1920s.

The Currie case represented an unusual attempt to unravel and understand a major military operation within the confines of the trial process. Professor Sharpe's fascinating account demonstrates the dramatic potential of the adversary trial, as well as the hazards, uncertainties, and strains of litigation.

ROBERT J. SHARPE teaches civil procedure and constitutional law at the University of Toronto.

'The Return to Mons,' by I. Sheldon-Williams. Canadian troops entering
the Grand'Place on the morning of Armistice Day. On the left is a squadron
of British Lancers who took part in the retreat from Mons in 1914. The
Town Hall is in the centre, and Belfry is in the background at the right.

The
Last Day,
the Last Hour

The Currie Libel Trial

ROBERT J. SHARPE

Published for The Osgoode Society by
The Carswell Company of Canada Ltd

To my mother and father

Canadian Cataloguing in Publication Data

Sharpe, Robert J.
The last day, the last hour

Includes bibliographical references and index.
ISBN 0-459-32831-X

1. Currie, Arthur, Sir, 1875–1933 – Trials, litigation, etc.
2. Trials (Libel) – Canada.
3. Mons, Battle of, 1918.
I. Title.
KE237.C87S48 1988a   345.71′0256   C88-095253-9
KF224.C87S48 1988a

Picture credits: Canadian War Museum – 'The Return to Mons,' Acc. no. 8969; Public Archives of Canada – *General Arthur Currie*, PA1473, *General Sir Sam Hughes*, C20240, *William Thomas Rochester Preston* C6626; City of Toronto Archives – *Sir Arthur Currie* G & M 13157G, *W.N. Tilley and R.H. Parmenter*, G & M 13158G, *Frank Regan and W.T.R. Preston* G & M 13162G, *Mr Justice Hugh Rose* G & M 13161G; National Library – *Toronto Telegram 17 and 18 April 1928*

Maps: G.W.L. Nicholson *Canadian Expeditionary Force, 1914–1919* (Ottawa: Queen's Printer 1962). Reproduced with permission of the Minister of Supply and Services Canada.

Contents

Foreword

THE OSGOODE SOCIETY

The purpose of The Osgoode Society is to encourage research and writing in the history of Canadian law. The Society, which was incorporated in 1979 and is registered as a charity, was founded at the initiative of the Honourable R. Roy McMurtry, at that time attorney-general of Ontario, and officials of the Law Society of Upper Canada. Its efforts to stimulate legal history in Canada include the sponsorship of a fellowship, research support programs, and work in the field of oral history and legal archives. The Society publishes (at the rate of about one a year) volumes that contribute to legal-historical scholarship in Canada and that are of interest to the Society's members. Included are studies of the courts, the judiciary, and the legal profession, biographies, collections of documents, studies in criminology and penology, accounts of great trials, and work in the social and economic history of the law.

The current directors of The Osgoode Society are Brian Bucknall, Mr Justice Archie Campbell, Douglas Ewart, Martin Friedland, Jane Banfield Haynes, John D. Honsberger, Kenneth Jarvis, Mr Justice Allen Linden, James Lisson, Brendan O'Brien, Peter Oliver, James Spence, and Richard Tinsley. The attorney-general for Ontario and the treasurer of the Law Society of Upper Canada are directors ex officio. The Society's honorary president is the Honourable R. Roy McMurtry. The annual report and information about membership may be obtained by writing The Osgoode Society, Osgoode Hall, 130 Queen Street West, Toronto, Ontario, M5H 2N6. Members receive the annual volumes published by the Society.

'The Last Day, the Last Hour: The Currie Libel Trial' is the second publication in The Osgoode Society's trials series. Books about trials readily capture the attention of a public interested in the drama of courtroom confrontation, and they offer an opportunity to present often complex legal issues in an appealing and readable format. In their reconstruction of past legal and judicial methods, they also serve to highlight the changes in law and procedure that have occurred over time.

In his study, Professor Robert Sharpe has achieved all this and more. In 1927 an Ontario newspaper carried a column alleging that Sir Arthur Currie, in the final hours of the First World War, had shown reckless disregard for the lives of his troops in the pursuit of vainglory. Such rumours had been circulating for years, and Currie proceeded to meet them by initiating a highly risky action at law. There was much poignancy and some irony in the circumstances. A colleague had once said that he had 'an almost fanatical hatred of unnecessary casualties.' Currie evidently saw this trial as representing in a sense the final battle of the Canadian Corps. Like so many previous battles, however, this one exacted a high price, as Robert Sharpe so effectively illustrates in his reconstruction of this famous Canadian trial.

In relating these events with such skill, Robert Sharpe has added a significant new dimension to our understanding of our legal past.

Brendan O'Brien
President

Peter N. Oliver
Editor-in-Chief

Preface

This book is an account of a great Canadian trial. The Currie case represented an attempt to unravel and understand a major military operation within the confines of the adversarial trial process, and it presents a wonderful cast of characters – legal, military, and political. For several weeks in 1928 the case captured the attention of the whole country.

I have not attempted to base this narrative on any particular theme or theory; rather, I have written the book as a story, doing my best to describe the trial and the events which produced it. There are, however, themes implicit in the story itself.

The Currie trial undoubtedly played an important role in shaping the public's perception of the First World War. The case was tried ten years after the armistice was signed; it coincided with a flood of novels, plays, memoirs, and biographies, all struggling to comprehend the impact upon modern consciousness of the cataclysmic events of the war.

The Currie trial demonstrates the dramatic potential of the adversary trial. But the case also reveals the hazards, uncertainties, and strains of litigation, and perhaps even the limitations of the trial process as a means of discovering the truth.

The Currie case also provides an opportunity to reflect upon the law of defamation, not only as it appears to potential litigants, but from the broader perspective of reconciling the conflicting claims of the need to protect personal reputation on the one hand, and the desirability of free and open discussion of important public issues on the other.

I wish to thank the Osgoode Society and the Connaught Fund Legal Theory and Public Policy Programme, Faculty of Law, University of Toronto, for their grants to support my work. I have benefited from the comments of many friends and colleagues, and in particular I wish to thank Professors Craig Brown, Martin Friedland, Jack Hyatt, William Kaplan, Desmond Morton, Stephen Waddams, and Garry Watson. I also wish to thank Gus Richardson, Valerie Edwards, Gregory Reif, and Neil Fenna, who provided valuable service as summer research assistants. I am especially grateful to Peter Oliver, editor-in-chief of the Osgoode Society, for his helpful suggestions and for being so supportive of this project from the beginning. I owe special thanks to Kathleen Johnson for her fine work in editing the manuscript. Finally, I wish to thank my wife, Geraldine, not only for her many helpful suggestions and comments but also for her patience and encouragement.

General Sir Arthur Currie, commander of the Canadian troops
in France, June 1917.

General Sir Sam Hughes, Canadian minister of militia and defence

William Thomas Rochester Preston, 1927

Sir Arthur Currie walking to Victoria Hall, Cobourg, April 1928

W.N. Tilley (right) with R.H. Parmenter, Cobourg, April 1928

Frank Regan (right) and W.T.R. Preston outside the courthouse in Cobourg,
April 1928

Mr. Justice Hugh Rose (left) escorted to the courthouse by Sheriff J.D. Nesbitt,
Cobourg, April 1928

ALLEGED LIBEL THAT IS BASIS OF GEN. CURRIE'S SUIT

The Evening Guide.

PORT HOPE, ONT., MONDAY, JUNE 13, 1927

Price: 2 Cents

WAREHOUSE AT COBOURG?

DOMINION DAY COMMITTEE TO MEET

General Meeting Will Be Held Tuesday Evening In The Department of Agri-

CARS CRASH AT DALE SUNDAY
WOMAN REMOVED TO HOSPITAL

Adam Douglas, Driver of Car That Caused Accident, Summoned To Court and Fined For Reckless Driving and Had License Suspended for Two Months

MONS

Issue of Port Hope "Guide" of June 13, 1927, containing article on "Mons" for which the former Commander-in-Chief of the C.E.F. is suing for $50,000. Portraits (left to right) are: W. T. R. Preston, defendant, writer of article; Frank Regan, counsel, and F. W. Wilson, defendant, publisher of "Guide."

Toronto *Telegram*, 17 April 1928

Their verdict will decide Sir Arthur Currie's $50,000 libel against the Port Hope Guide

Above is the jury chosen in Sir Arthur Currie's $50,000 libel action against the publishers of the Port Hope Guide, the outcome of an article published in that newspaper charging the former commander-in-chief of the Canadian Corps with needless sacrifice of life at Mons on Armistice Day, November 11, 1918. Left to right (top) are: A. F. Sauch, farmer, Clarke Township; A. Belch, farmer, Darlington Township; E. Ashton, farmer, Darlington Township; W. H. Hycke, farmer, Percy Township; J. H. Winfield, musician, Port Hope; W. J. Gummer, farmer, Percy Township; James Swarbuck, miller, Clarke Township; (lower) G. F. Morrissey, agent, Alnwick; W. J. Sarginson, mill hand, Darlington Township; W. T. Duncan, gardener, Seymour Township; W. H. Patterson, farmer, Cavan Township, and G. Anderson, gentleman, Cobourg. (Pictures by Evening Telegram staff photographer.)

Toronto *Telegram*, 17 April 1928

Plaintiff in $50,000 Libel and Witnesses Who Were Called Yesterday

Above are shown Sir Arthur Currie, former commander of the Canadian Corps in France, who is suing for $50,000 libel, based on an article published in the Port Hope Guide, charging needless loss of life in the Canadian Corps during the last day of the war, Nov. 11, 1918. 1. Morley Drake, 18th Batt., Stratford, who testified of fighting on the last day. 2. W. J. Smith, Lindsay, 4th Engineers, who told of seeing one dead Canadian in Mons, Nov. 11th. 3. Albert Mason, 58th Batt., York County gardener, who saw a member of the Princess Pats lying dead in the streets of Mons, Nov. 11th. 4. Sir Arthur Currie on his way to court. 5. L. J. M. Calder, D.C.M., who will likely be called later in the trial. 6. John McKay, Toronto signaller, who testified his knowledge of the armistice early on the morning of Nov. 11th. 7. R. McPherson, M.M., a witness who will be called later in the trial. 8. Col. J. A. Currie, Toronto, former commander of the original 15th Batt. 48th Highlanders, who was threatened yesterday with arrest for contempt of court, and was today put out of the court room by order of Justice Rose. 9. Wm. Tedrman, sergeant-major of the 32nd Batt., who saw four dead Highlanders of the 42nd Batt. in the streets of Mons, Armistice Day. 10. R. Hodgson, a witness who will testify later. 11. Wm. Woodlock, Port Hope, painter, who heard the German convoys had gone through the Hun on Nov 10th. 12. Col. Orde. 13. Col. F. L. Armstrong. 14. Col. A. F. Duguid, of the historical records department, Ottawa.

Toronto *Telegram*, 17 April 1928

In the above layout, snapped by The Telegram staff photographer, the principal figures in Sir Arthur Currie's $50,000 libel action against the Port Hope Guide are shown in and arriving at the court room, where the trial is being heard before Mr. Justice Rose. Upper left, is Sheriff Nesbitt. In the centre group, seated, left to right, are: W. T. R. Preston, author of the article on Mons on which the libel is based, T. F. Hall, K.C., and Frank Regan, counsel for the defence, and F. W. Wilson, proprietor of the Port Hope Guide. Upper right, W. N. Tilley, K.C., counsel for Sir Arthur Currie, arrives at the court. Lower left, Mr. Justice Rose and (right) Col. Daley, secretary to Sir Arthur Currie, arriving for the trial. In the centre is Sir Arthur Currie, former commander-in-chief of the Canadian Corps in France.

Toronto *Telegram*, 18 April 1928

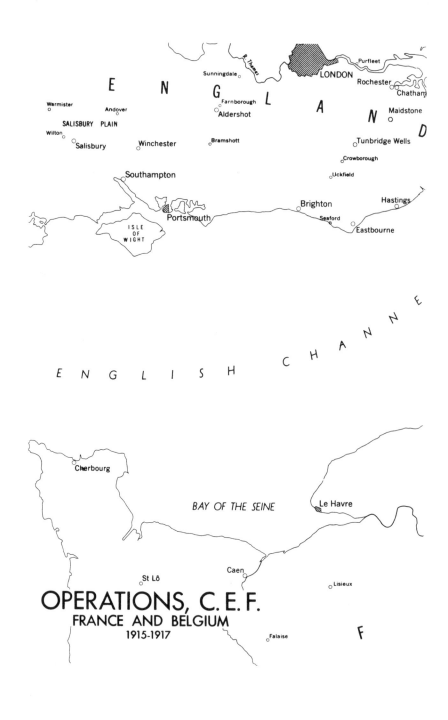

OPERATIONS, C.E.F.
FRANCE AND BELGIUM
1915-1917

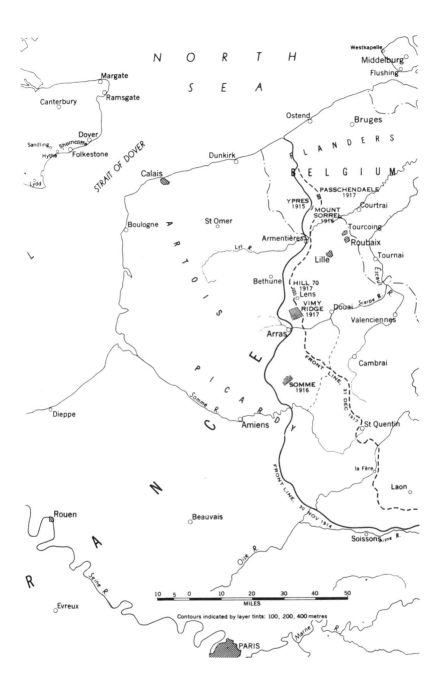

NORTH SEA

Westkapelle
Middelburg
Flushing

Margate
Ramsgate
Canterbury
Dover
Shorncliffe
Sandling
Folkestone
Hythe
Lydd

Ostend
Bruges

STRAIT OF DOVER

Calais

Dunkirk

FLANDERS

BELGIUM

PASSCHENDAELE
1917

YPRES
1915
MOUNT
SORREL
1915

Courtrai

Boulogne

St Omer

Armentières

Lyr R.

Tourcoing
Roubaix

A R T O I S

Lille

Tournai

Escaut R.

Bethune

HILL 70
1917
Lens

VIMY
RIDGE
1917

Scarpe R.

Douai

Valenciennes

Arras

FRONT LINE, 31 DEC. 1917

Cambrai

P I C A R D Y

Somme R.

SOMME
1916

Dieppe

Amiens

St Quentin

FRONT LINE, 30 NOV 1914

la Fère

Laon

Rouen

Beauvais

Soissons Aisne R.

F R A N C E

Oise R.

Seine R.

10 5 0   10   20   30   40   50
MILES

Contours indicated by layer tints: 100, 200, 400 metres

Evreux

Marne R.

PARIS

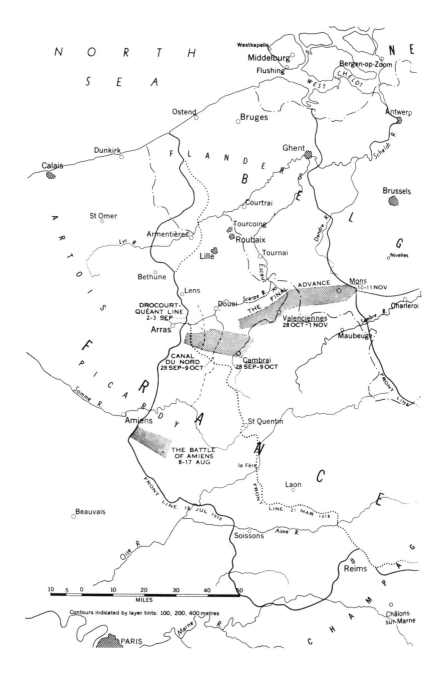

NORTH

SEA

Westkapelle
Middelburg
Flushing
Bergen-op-Zoom

N E

WEST SCHELDT

Ostend
Bruges
Antwerp

Scheldt R.

Dunkirk
Calais

FLANDER
B

Ghent

St Omer

Courtrai

Brussels

Armentières
Lille

Tourcoing
Roubaix
Tournai

E
L
G

Lys R.

Escaut R.

Dendre R.

Nivelles

ARTOIS

Bethune

Lens
DROCOURT-
QUÉANT LINE
2–3 SEP
Arras

Douai

Scarpe R.

THE FINAL ADVANCE

Mons
10–11 NOV

Charleroi

Valenciennes
28 OCT – 1 NOV

Maubeuge

Sambre R.

F

P I C A R D Y

CANAL
DU NORD
28 SEP–9 OCT

Cambrai
28 SEP–9 OCT

A

FRONT LINE

Somme R.

Amiens

THE BATTLE
OF AMIENS
8–17 AUG

St Quentin

N

la Fère

FRONT

C

Beauvais

FRONT LINE. 18 JUL 1918

Laon

LINE. 21 MAR 1918

E

Oise R.

Soissons

Aisne R.

Reims

G

A

P

Contours indicated by layer tints: 100, 200, 400 metres

10 5 0   10   20   30   40   50
MILES

Marne R.

PARIS

C   H   A   M

Châlons-
sur-Marne

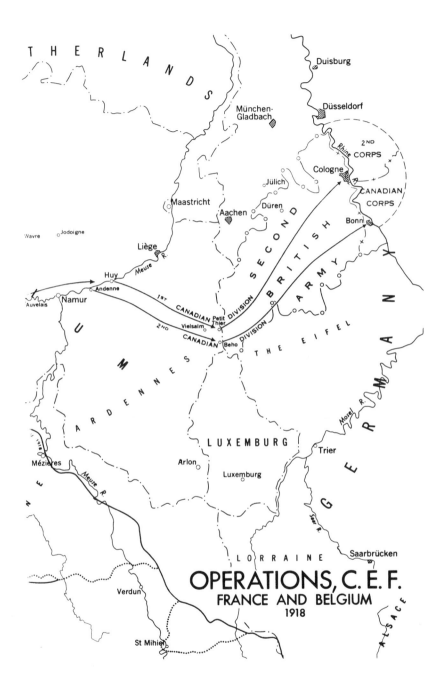

OPERATIONS, C.E.F.
FRANCE AND BELGIUM
1918

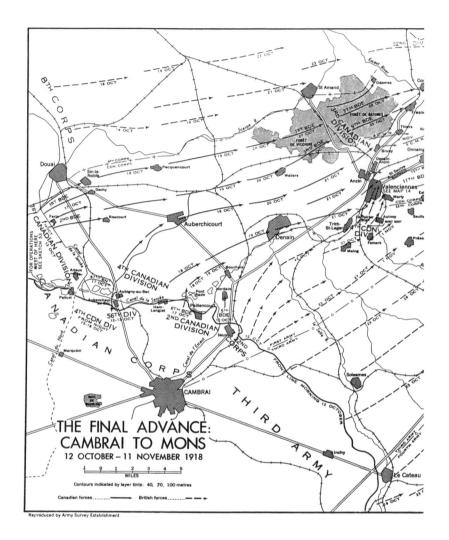

THE FINAL ADVANCE:
CAMBRAI TO MONS
12 OCTOBER – 11 NOVEMBER 1918

1 0 1 2 3 4 5
MILES

Contours indicated by layer tints: 40, 70, 100 metres

Canadian forces......... ━━━━━━▶   British forces......... ━ ━ ━▶

Reproduced by Army Survey Establishment

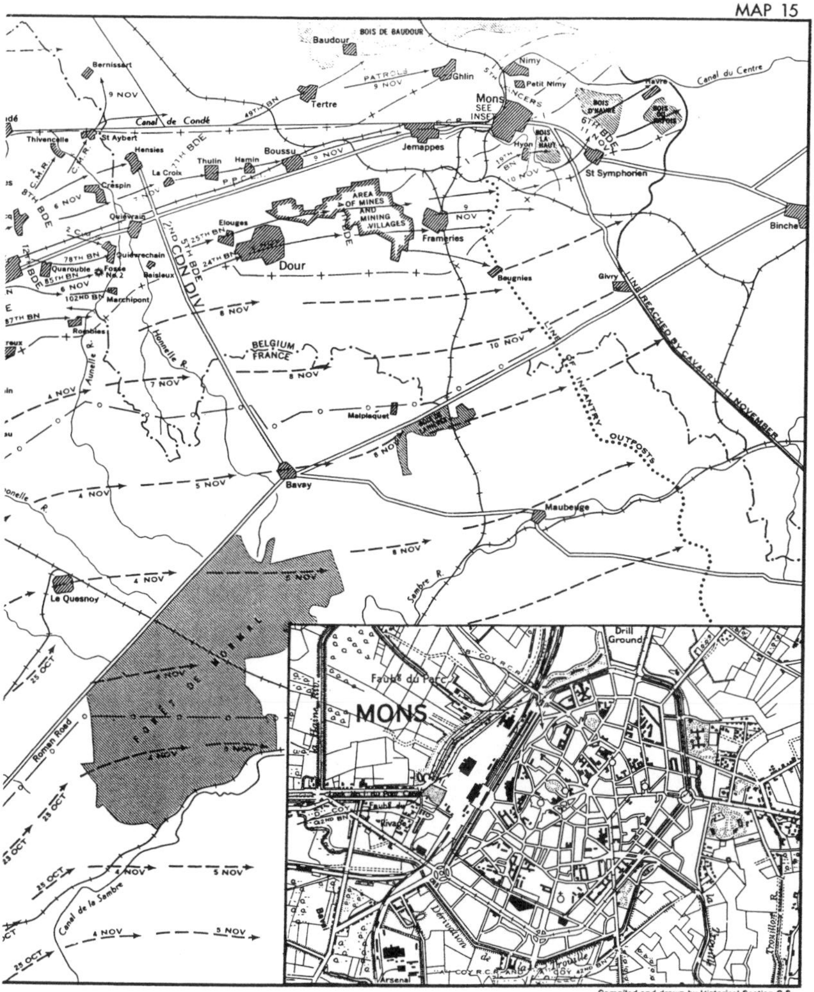

MAP 15

Compiled and drawn by Historical Section G.S.

The Last Day, the Last Hour

1

Mons

Mons is a pleasant Belgian town. It is the capital of the industrial province of Hainault and the centre of the Borinage coal-mining district. Situated on a hill, it dominates the surrounding countryside, which is marked here and there with slag-heaps from the coal mines. From miles away one can see the seventeenth-century baroque belfry rising from the castle ruins at the town centre. There are many other fine buildings, both public and domestic. St Wandru, the Gothic collegiate church, though it lacks a tower, has a splendid interior with fine statues, windows, and paintings. The streets of Mons, many of which are still cobbled, curl towards the town centre and the Grand'Place.

Virtually all of the town's inhabitants are French-speaking, and the town itself has a very French aspect. By contrast, the magnificent fifteenth-century Gothic Hôtel de Ville at the centre of town is entirely Flemish in design. Today, Mons bustles with traffic and commerce. One has the impression that despite the modern shop-fronts and the autoroute that now occupies the place of the boulevard which formerly defined its outer limits, the town still bears a resemblance to the Mons of 1918.

Mons is fifty kilometres southwest of Brussels and about twenty kilometres from the French border. It has been the site of many wars and battles. It lies in the path so often used by Spanish, Dutch, German, French, and English armies. The town was besieged, conquered, or occupied by foreign armies many times during the religious wars of the sixteenth century, during the wars of the Spanish and Austrian succession in the seventeenth century, and during the Napoleonic wars of the late eighteenth and early nineteenth centuries. Marlborough took the town just before his last great battle at Malplaquet, a few miles to the south.

It was at Mons that the British Expeditionary Force first fought the Germans in August 1914. Germany had demanded free passage for its troops through Belgium on 2 August and had declared war on France on the next day. On 4 August, German troops entered Belgium. British demands that the Germans leave Belgium went unheeded, and Great Britain's declaration of war followed.

The small Belgian army could not stop the German advance. On 7 August Liège fell to the Germans, and the first British troops landed in France. The French decided upon an all-out attack; the British agreed that their small but well-trained and well-equipped force would lend its support. On 21 August the British entered Belgium and made for Mons. They were directly in the path of the German advance. It was the first British military engagement on the continent of Europe since the Battle of Waterloo, which had been fought not far from Mons ninety-nine years before.

The British were outnumbered at Mons by vastly superior German forces, but they fought courageously for two days. The Kaiser referred to the British force as a 'contemptible little army,' and the veterans of the first battle proudly and defiantly carried the nickname 'Old Contemptibles' for the rest of the war. The first two Victoria Crosses of the war were won in that battle. The British stalled but could not stop the German advance. Casualties were heavy, but they were only a taste of what was to follow. Five thousand Germans were killed, wounded, and missing. The British sustained 1,500 casualties, including 763 fatalities.

For more than four years Mons remained under German occupation. Not until the very end, on 11 November 1918, was the invader expelled by the advance of the Canadian Corps under Lieutenant-General Sir Arthur Currie.

The liberation of Mons by the Canadian Corps in 1918 was greeted with great pomp and ceremony.[1] The mayor, Jean Lescarts, had been taken hostage by the invading German army in 1914 and forced to issue a humiliating proclamation calling upon the citizens of the town to co-operate with the conquering forces. On 11 November 1918 he lost no time in issuing another proclamation, copies of which were quickly pasted up throughout the town:

To the inhabitants of Mons.

After fifty-one months of suffering caused by the iniquitous, merciless and insolent occupation of the German Army, at last the City of Mons is delivered by the heroism of the British Army, which at the hour of the armistice, completed its series of victories at the very place where, on August 23, 1914, it came into contact with the enemy.

The Third Canadian Division, at the cost of heavy sacrifices, penetrated the City at 3 o'clock this morning, thus revenging with brilliant success the retreat of 1914. Glory and praise to it!

The armistice is signed, the German Army has surrendered, brute force is annihilated and justice and law triumphant [my translation].

General Currie, the commander of the Canadian Corps, described the events of the day in his diary.

Shortly after midnight, the 42nd batallion found a weak spot at the station, west of Mons, and entered the city. Some fighting took place through the streets, where I saw dead bodies later in the day. The German machine gunners defending the position were all volunteers, and remained at their posts until they were either killed or captured. At 4:30 in the morning the 3rd Division was able to report the complete capture of the Town ... At 7:30 in the morning a wire came from the Army informing us that the armistice was to come into effect at 11:00 a.m. when hostilities would cease.[2]

Currie made a formal entry into Mons in the afternoon of 11 November. A squadron of Fifth Lancers, a British cavalry unit that had seen action at Mons in 1914, formed the escort. Currie noted in his diary that 'each member of the squadron wore the Mons Medal' and that the commanding officer, now a lieutenant, had been a trooper in the first battle of Mons.

Currie was accompanied by a number of senior officers, including Major-General Frederick O.W. Loomis, commander of the Third Division, and Major-General Edward Morrison, commanding officer of the Canadian Artillery. Morrison, a journalist as well as a solider, later wrote that it had been tacitly understood that before peace was restored the Canadians should take Mons, the place in which the war had started for the British. Morrison described the scene he witnessed in Mons on the afternoon of 11 November:

The fight of the night before had been no bloodless victory. The enemy's dead were thick in the suburbs, and especially around the station, where they had made their last stand. The Canadian Infantry had made it a point of honour, notwithstanding the cautions against casualties, to drive the enemy from Mons before the 'cease fire' sounded, and they succeeded at a price. They had not been urged to the fight, but rather forbidden and restrained, but it is one of the wonders of the war how men will die for an idea. Their triumph would not have been so sweet had they not celebrated it in the Grand'Place de Mons. The entry of the Corps Commander with his staff mounted preceded by an escort of cavalry and followed by his battle standard, was a magnificient climax to the day of rejoicing. He literally rode into the captured city along the streets garnished with the enemy dead.[3]

Currie was met by enthusiastic civic officials at the Grand'Place, where a large number of troops representing all units of the Third Division were on parade. The Belgian national anthem was played, and after the troops had marched past Currie was invited into the municipal chamber to sign the town's formal register.

Later in the day, a formal proclamation was issued 'in remembrance of the liberation of the City after heroic fighting by the Third Division of the Canadian Corps of the First British Army.' Currie and several other officers were made honorary citizens of Mons.

At the ceremony on the afternoon of 11 November, during the reception at the Hôtel de Ville, Currie presented the town with his lance and pennant. On 12 November the Prince of Wales came to Mons, met with Currie, and signed the official register as Currie had done.

Another proclamation was issued on 12 November announcing a special funeral to be held the next day for Canadian soldiers killed within the limits of Mons and inviting all to attend the ceremony to honour the fallen men. Le Collège des Bourgmestre et Échevins de Mons conveyed a message of thanks to Currie for the town's liberation from German occupation. Special mention was made of the fact that 'à prix de leur propre vie' Canadians had taken the town by fighting 'corps à corps' and without shelling and destruction. Medals were struck and presented to the victorious Canadians – small ones about the size of a quarter for the men, much larger and more elaborate ones for the officers, and a gold one for Currie. A few days after the armistice, a local artist, Anto Carte, painted a portrait of Major-General

Loomis, commander of the victorious Third Division. Place de la Bavarie, where the Canadians entered Mons, was renamed 'Place du Canada.'

The Canadian victory at Mons was commemorated time and time again. In January 1919 General Loomis returned to present the town with a standard, which had the Union Jack in the upper left corner and the Canadian coat of arms in the centre surrounded by pennants listing the great Canadian battles at Ypres, Somme, Vimy, Passchendaele, Amiens, Arras, Cambrai, and, of course, Mons. The city fathers granted Loomis the right to display the crest of Mons in his coat of arms. In August of that same year, Lieutenant-Colonel Wilfrid Bovey, who had served on Currie's headquarters staff, came to Mons to make an official presentation of two Canadian eighteen-pounder guns, said to be the guns that fired the last shots of the Great War. Bovey told of the pride Canadians had felt in capturing Mons on Armistice Day, and suggested that the men were happier about recapturing Mons than they were about the armistice itself. 'Our dead sleep at Ypres, at St Julien, at Passchendaele, at Mons, and the soil in which they lie will always be dear to our hearts.'4

Each year, Currie received a letter from the mayor of Mons on Armistice Day. One year he replied, 'Your message of congratulation warmly appreciated. Please do not for a moment think that the Canadian people look upon the loss of their sons now buried in Belgium as a vain sacrifice, but as a bond which will unite our two countries.'5

The Mons War Museum was created by the City in 1930 to recall the battles of August 1914 and November 1918 and to remember how life was lived under the German occupation. A role of honour lists the 763 British soliders who fell in 1914. The Canadian collection is perhaps the most substantial. It 'concentrates on the events of the battle of Mons on November 10 and 11, 1918 and the liberation of the City at the dawn on armistice day by the Third Canadian Division.' It too has a roll of honour, a 'memorial to the 85 officers and men of the Canadian Corps who were killed in the liberation of Mons.' Several of these men are buried in the Mons communal cemetery, where the graves of many other Allied troops are also to be found. The graves of others, including the unfortunate George Lawrence Price, a Canadian private in the Sixth Infantry Brigade who was killed only minutes before the armistice, can be found in the beautiful St Symphorien cemetery a few miles outside the city, where they lie near fallen British comrades and German foes.

In November 1935, in a ceremony to commemorate the two battles of Mons, earth was taken from the graves of every British and Canadian soldier and placed at the foot of the belfry in Mons. Mons is the last of the great Canadian battles inscribed in the Vimy memorial, which was unveiled in 1936 by Edward VIII.

In the park of the Château in Mons, a monument was unveiled in 1952 by Field Marshal Lord Alexander of Tunis, the British minister of defence who had fought at Mons in 1914. Earth taken from the ground near the 1935 memorial was encased in the monument. Its inscription reads as follows:

Here the forces of the British Empire fought their first and last battles of the 1914–18 War.

On the 23rd and 24th August, 1914, the British Expeditionary Force commanded by Sir John French with supreme courage held the advance of overwhelmingly superior German forces.

On armistace day, 1918, after sixty hours of heavy fighting, Canadian Divisions entered Mons.

British and Canadian regiments have erected this tablet to the glory of God and to commemorate these events.

The Canadian capture of Mons was also commemorated on 12 June 1927 at the at the entrance to the Hôtel de Ville.[6] An honour guard of Belgian and French civil and military officials and Canadian ex-servicemen watched Lieutenant-General Sir Henry Burstall, commander of the Second Canadian Division, unveil an eight-foot bronze plaque presented by the Canadian Battlefield Memorial Commission. It bore the Canadian standard, the dominion coat of arms, and the following inscription: 'Mons was recaptured by the Canadian Corps on 11th November 1918. After fifty months of German occupation, freedom was restored to the city. Here was fired the last shot of the Great War.'

The Honourable Rodolphe Lemieux, the speaker of the Canadian House of Commons, had travelled to Mons for the ceremony. Lemieux's own son had been killed in France in August 1918. He delivered what a reporter described as an impressive oration, commending the Belgians for their patience during the occupation and their energy in post-war reconstruction. Despite the bitterness of the conscription crisis, which was still fresh in many minds, Lemieux reminded his audience that Canada, like Belgium, 'found its moral unity in harmonious diversity.' Recalling the spirit of 'justice, right and liberty' in which the Canadians entered Mons in 1918, he predicted that 'the world would never forget that the parting cannon shot on behalf of right oppressed and peace recovered through victory, was fired by Canadian soldiers. When the grandchildren of Belgians of today read the inscription they would but need to cast a glance at the battlefields nearby to learn that it was written in the blood of brave men.'

Lemieux recalled the Canadian triumphs of the last hundred days of the war and the advance led by the Corps commander, Lieutenant-General Sir Arthur Currie, from Arras to Cambrai, on to Valenciennes, and finally to Mons on the eve and day of the armistice. No one, certainly not those present, could forget that the Canadian advance had been costly, and Lemieux repeated the words spoken at the public funeral held on 13 November 1918 for the men of the Canadian Corps who fell in the fighting for the town. Extending their sympathy to the relatives of those who were killed, the grateful officials of Mons and the province of Hainault had assured all that 'the memory of these noble sons of Canada, whose bodies now rest in Belgian soil would be not only perpetuated in stone and bronze, but also by the more enduring tradition which each father would transmit to his son, each mother to her child, throughout the years to come because, in Mons, the name of Canada would ever remain synonymous with honour, loyalty and heroism.' That simple ceremony in June 1927 triggered one of the most sensational trials in Canadian history—a trial in which the integrity and competence of Canadian military leadership was challenged.

Some time before noon on the day following the unveiling of the plaque at Mons, in the office of the Port Hope *Evening Guide*, a small-town Ontario daily newspaper, the owner and publisher, Frederick W. Wilson, and a seventy-six-year-old veteran of many journalistic and political wars, William Thomas Rochester Preston, read the Toronto *Globe*'s account of the ceremony. Both men were well aware that not everyone viewed the capture of Mons as a source of pride. There were men who had been involved in the fighting, including local veterans, who had resented being pushed into battle yet again on the very eve of the armistice. Preston was working on a book of political memoirs, and had ready access to the details of the serious allegations made just after the war in the House of Commons by Sir Sam Hughes, minister of militia until 1916. Hughes had charged that Currie ordered the attack on Mons after he knew the armistice had been signed, 'thus needlessly sacrificing the lives of Canadian soldiers.'[7]

The *Evening Guide* would be on the street at five o'clock in the afternoon. Wilson knew of Preston's interest in the war and in Mons in particular, and he suggested that he write something for the paper that day. Preston went home and returned sometime before four o'clock with the draft copy. Wilson suggested one or two minor alterations. The manuscript was handed to the typesetter, and appeared as an unsigned editorial on the front page of that evening's paper.

MONS

Cable despatches this morning give details of the unveiling of a bronze plaque at the Hôtel de Ville (the City Hall) at Mons, commemorative of the capture of the City by the Canadians on November 11th, 1918. This is an event which might very properly be allowed to pass into oblivion, very much regretted rather than glorified.

There was much waste of human life during the war, enormous loss of lives which should not have taken place. But it is doubtful whether in any case there was a more deliberate and useless waste of human life than in the so-called capture of Mons.

It was the last day: and the last hour, and almost the last minute, when to glorify the Canadian Headquarters staff the Commander-in-Chief conceived the mad idea that it would be a fine thing to say that the Canadians had fired the last shot in the Great War, and had captured the last German entrenchment before the bugles sounded eleven o'clock, when the armistice, which had been signed by both sides would begin officially.

Canadian headquarters sounded the advance upon the retreating Germans, unsuspecting that any mad proposal for further and unnecessary fighting was even contemplated. The men were sent on in front to charge the enemy. Headquarters, with conspicuous bravery, brought up the rear. The fighting may have been more severe than was expected. Certain it is the Germans did not take the attack lying down.

Of course the town was taken just at the last minute before the official moment of the armistice arrived. But the penalty that was paid in useless waste of human life was appalling. There are hearts in Port Hope stricken with sorrow and mourning through this worse than drunken spree by Canadian Headquarters. Veterans who had passed through the whole four years of war lie buried in Belgian cemeteries as the result of the 'glories of Mons.'

Headquarters Staff assembled in the centre of the town as the eleven o'clock signal sounded that the official armistice was effective from that hour. Along the route that they had carefully and with safety made their way to the centre of the town, passing the dead and dying and the wounded, victims of their madness. It was common talk among the soldiers that while the staff were congratulating themselves upon the great victory and enjoying the pride upon having 'fired the last shot in the Great War,' a sergeant advanced and whispered to one of the Staff that unless they withdrew immediately to a place of safety, they would not be allowed to leave the place alive, as the guns of the indignant Canadian soliders were already trained on them. In less time than it takes to tell the story, Headquarters got into motors and were fleeing for their lives.

It does not seem to be remembered that even Ottawa, neither by government nor Parliament, gave Sir Arthur Currie any official vote of thanks, or any special grant as an evidence of the esteem of appreciation of his services. And this is the only case of the kind in connection with any of the high commanding officers of the war. He was allowed to return to Canada unnoticed by officials of the government or of Parliament and permitted to sink into comparative obscurity in a civilian position as President of McGill University. The official desire to glorify Mons, therefore, deserves more than a passing or silent notice. Canadian valour won Mons, but it was by such a shocking useless waste of human life that it is an eternal disgrace to the Headquarters that directed operations.

Sir Arthur Currie knew nothing of the Port Hope *Evening Guide*'s attack for several days. Currie had left military life in 1920 to become principal of McGill University. In mid-June 1927 he was preparing to leave on a two-month trip that would take him to a meeting of the Institute of Pacific Relations in Honolulu, and, had it not been for some journalistic rivalry, he might well have left the country without hearing of the matter. Peter Brown, the proprietor of the Port Hope *Times*, the *Guide*'s competitor, sent Currie a copy of the Mons article and invited the retired general to respond in the columns of the *Times*. The situation presented Brown with an attractive opportunity: an article or letter written by someone of Currie's stature responding to Preston and the *Guide* would make for an unusually exciting issue of his small-town paper.

Currie was incensed when he read the *Guide* article. Rumours of impropriety and needless loss of life in the taking of Mons had been current across the country since the war's end. Currie remembered 'the propaganda indulged in during the closing months of the war' and thought that 'the same gang' was at work again when he saw the *Guide* article.[8] Although he had been deeply hurt by these attacks against him, Currie had refrained from answering them directly. Sam Hughes had spoken in Parliament, where he enjoyed absolute immunity from suit. Here at last was an open, direct, and public statement that Currie could attack. 'I think,' he said bluntly, '[that] the time has come to stop it.'[9]

Stronger action than a reply in the Port Hope *Times* was called for: Currie wanted a forceful public vindication of his action. He politely declined Brown's invitation to write something for the *Times*, but asked Brown to send him twelve copies of the *Guide*. Brown, undoubtly disappointed that the *Times* would not carry Currie's reply, pressed Currie to take action against his rival: 'I sincerely trust that you will not allow a slur of the kind as published in the *Guide* to rest on either your good name or the good name of the Headquarters Staff of the Canadian Expeditionary Force.'[10]

Currie began to map out his strategy. Already, however, friends and colleagues at McGill were urging him to let the matter die. What could a distinguished general and principal of a great university gain by engaging in a mud-slinging match with an insignificant small-town newspaper? Stephen Leacock[11] and others at McGill urged Currie to forget the whole thing. The old rumours would only be given new life if Currie took the article seriously. Currie, however, was determined to grasp the nettle. He consulted his solicitor, George H. Montgomery, a prominent Montreal lawyer. In 1927 Montgomery was the bâtonnier of the Montreal bar, and was about to add membership on the board of governors of McGill University to an impressive list of corporate directorships.

Currie wanted to know if it would be possible to prosecute the *Guide* for libel in the criminal courts. A libel is a statement that tends to injure a person's reputation or to expose him or her to hatred, contempt, or ridicule. There was little doubt that the *Guide*'s article did just that to Currie. Most libel cases are brought in the civil courts as suits for damages, with the person whose reputation has been injured as plaintiff and the author and publisher as defendants. A criminal offence known as defamatory libel does exist, though in modern times criminal charges for libel are rarely laid.

Initial inquiries suggested that Preston himself was the author of the offending article. He was, as we shall see, a well-known figure with a dubious reputation, and he presented Currie with a rather attractive target. Montgomery considered the possibility of launching a prosecution in the criminal courts.[12] Could Preston be charged with criminal libel? A criminal prosecution offered certain advantages over a civil suit for damages.[13] The case would be brought in the name of the Crown as prosecutor rather than in Currie's name as plaintiff; if the prosecution was successful, the result would be a formal conviction and a penalty of either a fine or imprisonment rather than an award of damages to Currie. It would be clear that Currie had decided to go to court to vindicate his reputation rather than to recover a large sum of money.

For many reasons, however, Currie and Montgomery decided to bring a civil action for damages in which Currie would be the plaintiff and Wilson and Preston the defendants. Currie himself could commence a criminal libel prosecution, but he might easily lose control of it because the attorney-general had the right to take over the conduct of the proceedings. Although this was rarely done,[14] the risk of having the case taken over by someone he could not direct, perhaps even someone unsympathetic to his cause, had to be avoided. There were other problems. Currie knew that Preston and the Port Hope *Evening Guide* were bound to rely on the broad defence available under the Criminal Code. The code provided (as it does now) that it is not an offence to publish any matter where the defendant, on reasonable grounds, believes the statements to be true, where the subject is one of public interest and the discussion of it would be for the public benefit.[15] In civil matters, however, an honest belief in the truth of the statement complained of is no defence: the defendant must prove the truth of what was published. In other words, a defendant in a civil case is faced with no-fault liability. Even if the defendant honestly believes that what was said was true, there will be liability unless the defendant can prove that the statement was true in fact. The defendant in a criminal case is not to be convicted and punished if he or she had an honest belief in the truth of what was published. The difference between the criminal and the civil standard was crucial to Currie. Although no reported case defined the scope of the Criminal Code defence,[16] Montgomery surely would have advised Currie to avoid risking a trial in which the issue could be what Preston and Wilson believed rather than the actual truth or falsehood of their statements.

Another and more immediate problem was that in order to charge Preston it would be necessary to have evidence that he was the author of the article. In a criminal prosecution Preston would benefit from the right to silence, and he could not be forced to admit his authorship. A criminal defendant is never required to testify. In a civil action, however, pre-trial examination for discovery is available, and Currie's lawyers would be able to require Preston to answer questions under oath before the matter reached the trial stage.

Currie asked Peter Brown, the editor of the rival Port Hope *Times,* to help him link Preston to the article. Time was short, since Currie was leaving for Honolulu in a week. Montgomery retained a Port Hope lawyer, Duncan H. Chisholm, who also made inquiries. Everyone in Port Hope knew that only Preston could have written the article, but the problem was how to prove it in a court of law. Wilson and the *Guide's* staff sensed trouble and were very guarded. Chisholm reported that the typesetter might be induced to say that Preston was the author, but that 'to accomplish this ... would require the expenditure of some money.'[17] He doubted whether satisfactory evidence establishing Preston as the author could be found quickly, and he agreed with Montgomery's suggestion that the best remedy might well be an ordinary civil suit in which the defendant could be forced to answer questions on discovery.

Currie himself began collecting his ammunition. He wrote to Colonel J.L. Ralston, the minister of defence in the Liberal government, himself a lawyer, who had served under Currie with distinction during the war: 'It has been intimated to me that this article was written by W.T.R. Preston, a well-known Liberal, I know, but a man of whom I do not think the party is particularly proud.'[18]

Currie asked Ralston and Colonel A. Fortescue Duguid, the official historian and director of the Historical Section of the Department of National Defence and the custodian of the government's war records, for the department's assistance in searching the official records of the operations during the last forty-eight hours of the war. 'I am getting very tired, Colonel, of listening to these libels about my conduct at Mons and I shall probably take action in this case.'[19] Currie needed to know the casualty figures and whether the department could find officers or men who were living near Port Hope who might have been responsible for spreading the story.

Currie was leaving for Hawaii in a day or so and had to make up his mind whether to sue. The law required that he give the defendants formal written notice of his intention to sue within six weeks of the article's publication date, and the lawsuit itself had to be commenced by issuing a formal writ of summons within three months.[20] A decision had to be made before he left, and, against the advice of many friends and colleagues, Currie instructed Montgomery to proceed with the lawsuit.

Reliable proof of Preston's authorship was still not forthcoming. Preston would say nothing. As Currie's local solicitor, Duncan Chisholm, put it, 'he is too cunning a fox for that.'[21] The typesetter was being enticed by Brown to come to work for the *Times*; Chisholm hoped he might then provide the original copy of the article in Preston's handwriting. In the end, however, these efforts proved fruitless, and without reliable evidence that Preston was the author of the article, Currie could not risk naming only him as defendant. Montgomery decided to count on the discovery process for actual proof of Preston's authorship, but to sue Wilson as well, since there could be no doubt that he was the publisher. Before he left for Honolulu, Currie gave instructions to Montgomery to retain a Toronto lawyer, William Norman Tilley, KC, one of the leading advocates of the day, and to take whatever steps were necessary to proceed with the lawsuit.

2

Arthur Currie, the Great War, and the Canadian Corps

Arthur Currie was born on a farm near the town of Strathroy, Ontario, on 5 December 1875, the third in a family of seven children.[1] He grew up on the family homestead founded by his grandfather John Corrigan, an Irish Catholic, and his grandmother, an Irish Anglican, who had emigrated in 1838 to escape religious strife. Upon their arrival they became Methodists and changed their name to 'Curry.' Arthur Currie modified the spelling of his surname in 1897.

Currie was delicate and often ill as a child. He was a good student and was especially interested in literature. His plans to pursue a professional education in either law or medicine were cut short for financial reasons upon his father's death when Currie was fifteen. He took teacher training, which in those days was often seen as a stepping-stone to one of the professions, but he was unable to secure a job and returned to high school to gain an honours certificate and university entrance. In May 1894, at the age of nineteen, Currie was doing well at his studies, but he left suddenly for British Columbia after a quarrel with one of his teachers shortly before his final exams.

Currie intended to seek his fortune in the railway boom in the west. Unfortunately, economic prospects were less bright than he had hoped, and once again he turned to teaching. He qualified as a teacher in British Columbia and was hired at a salary of sixty dollars per month in a village twenty miles north of Victoria on the Saanich Peninsula. In 1896 he got a job teaching at the Victoria Boys' Central School. The next year Currie began what was to be a distinguished military career when he became a part-time soldier in the British Columbia Brigade, Canadian Garrison Artillery, a militia unit known as 'the Fifth.'

Although he was thought to be a good teacher, Currie was restless and discouraged by the bleak financial prospects of a life in the classroom. In 1900, after mulling over his future during an illness that confined him to hospital for several months, he decided to go into the insurance business. He had been offered a commission in the militia, but the expenses associated with the position were considerable. In addition, he wanted to get married. He joined the company of Matson and Coles as an insurance salesman. Sam Matson, an impetuous and aggressive businessman and a Conservative, took a strong liking to Currie, who was a modest young man and a strong supporter of the Liberal party. Despite their differences in temperament and politics, the two got on well and became lifelong friends.

Currie was married in August 1901 to Lucy Chaworth-Musters, the daughter of an English military officer. Lucy, who was the same age as Arthur, had been born in British Columbia while her parents were on a world tour following her father's retirement. Her mother died two weeks after her birth. Her father returned to England, leaving her in the care of Currie's aunt and uncle, who raised her as their daughter. Currie met Lucy at his aunt's home when he went to British Columbia in 1894.

By the time of his marriage, Currie was leading an active life. He was a Freemason, and served for two years as the president of the Young Men's Liberal Association of Victoria. He was even suggested as a possible candidate for the provincial legislature. In 1906 he rose to the rank of major in his militia unit; in 1907 he was made district deputy grand master of the Victoria District of Freemasonry; and in 1909 he assumed the command of 'the Fifth.'

As a businessman, Currie was not always successful. By 1904 he had taken over Matson's insurance agency, and in 1909 he entered a real estate partnership. At first, things went extremely well, and by 1911 he was making huge profits buying and selling real estate. In 1912, just when property prices began to turn downwards, he had everything invested in speculative land-holdings. The financial reverses he suffered in the next two years were to plague him throughout the war and even later.

Currie was an enthusiastic milita member. He attended every available instructional course put on by a detachment of the British army at Esquimalt and regularly ordered military textbooks from London.

By the time he assumed command of his regiment, he was attending militia events two or three nights a week and was constantly seeking new recruits. He was always to be found at Saturday afternoon rifle practice, and often attended the 6:00 AM practices as well. Under Currie's command, the regiment entered and won national shooting competitions.

Currie always displayed an independence of mind bordering on stubbornness. It was this quality that led to his first collision with Sam Hughes, the minister of militia and defence in the Conservative government that assumed office in 1911. In 1912 Currie's second in command, without Currie's knowledge or authority and contrary to standing orders, had given permission to the regimental band to play at a Tory function. Currie intervened, but a direct appeal was made to Hughes. Hughes ordered Currie to permit the band to play, but Currie remained adamant. When Hughes later came to Victoria, he threatened disciplinary action against Currie. Currie, however, remained steadfast: he told the minister that he would command his own regiment. Hughes, who was unaccustomed to such replies, placed his hand on Currie's shoulder and said, 'Well, Currie, I came out here to get your scalp but you're all right.'[2]

As the war approached, Currie's financial situation deteriorated badly. In 1913 he retired from the command of 'the Fifth' only to be enticed to take command of the Fiftieth Regiment Highlanders of Canada, which had been organized a year earlier. Sam Hughes's son Garnet, a graduate of the Royal Military College and a friend of Currie's, was a junior officer, and, probably with Sam Hughes's backing, persuaded Currie to assume the command.

The war broke out in August 1914, and Currie, then thirty-eight, was hesitant about the prospect of going overseas. By then he had two children (Marjorie, born in 1902, and Garner, born in 1911). He was depressed about his financial situation. Sam Hughes first offered him the command of the British Columbia military district. He turned this down. Hughes's response was to offer him the command of an infantry brigade at Valcartier in Quebec, the mobilizing point for the Canadian Expeditionary Force. Currie did not know what to do. His friends, including Garnet Hughes, urged him to accept. He agreed to allow Garnet to wire Sam Hughes and ask for more time to consider the offer, and to inform the minister about Currie's dire financial straits. Hughes granted him the time, and suggested that Garnet speak to Sam Matson, Currie's friend and business associate, about the financial difficulties.

As we shall see, the means Currie used to relieve the financial pressure was hardly orthodox and would later prove most embarrassing. It did, however, enable Currie to accept the command, and Garnet Hughes conveyed that news to his father.

In late August 1914 Currie left Victoria for Valcartier, where he was to assume command as lieutenant-colonel of the Second Provisional (Western) Brigade. In the words of his biographer, 'The amateur soldier who had never handled more than four hundred all ranks in peace time was now in command of four thousand in time of war.'[3] Garnet Hughes had preceded Currie east, and welcomed him to the confusion of Valcartier by offering him a corner of his own tent to sleep in for the first night. After less than a month at Valcartier, Currie and his brigade left for England at the end of September 1914.

Currie was a straightforward, serious officer. He demanded a lot from his men. His language was direct and often profane. The description of Currie's physical appearance by A.M.J. Hyatt is borne out by contemporary photographs:

He was a big man, over six feet tall and well over two hundred pounds. His size, which might have been impressive, made him conspicuous and awkward rather than big and dignified. He had a pear-shaped figure topped with a narrow head which looked even narrower because of his long, lugubrious jowls. According to a young soldier serving in the ranks, 'he always looked too heavy for his horse.' His uniform seemed uncomfortable for him, the tunic habitually bunching over the top of his Sam Browne belt, which, because of his large bottom half, appeared to encircle his chest rather than his waist. His forage cap was perched ludicrously on his head.[4]

The story of the role played by the Canadian Expeditionary Force in the Great War has often been told,[5] and need not be repeated here. However, a brief outline of the main events and of Currie's career will facilitate an understanding of the trial that is the subject of this book.

Canadian troops played an important part in the monumental effort required to overcome the Germans. The war exacted a notoriously high price for success, and Canada paid her share in suffering and death. Over 600,000 men were enlisted and 250,000 casualties sustained, 60,661 of them fatalities.

By the time Currie, then a brigadier-general, led his men ashore in France early in 1915, a pattern of stalemated trench warfare had been established. After the retreat from Mons, the war of movement and manoeuvre ceased and the opposing forces found themselves dug in on a line that eventually ran from the coast of the English Channel across Belgium and northern France through to Switzerland. The defences of trench, barbed wire, and machine-gun, amply supported by artillery to the rear, proved impenetrable to both sides. There they remained, two massive forces, separated by no more than a few hundred yards at many points, locked in a fearsome battle to the death.

Conditions in the trenches were gruesome. The landscape of the battlefield was a desolate sight. Little remained standing above ground. The surface, pock-marked with craters left by explosive shells, was littered with the bodies of fallen men. In the flat plains of Flanders, where the water-table was just below the surface, the trenches were frequently flooded and even the most rudimentary forms of sanitation were impossible. The air was filled with the stench of excreta and rotting human flesh. The trenches were infested with rats and lice, and, if those discomforts were not enough, the men lived in constant fear of being killed by a sniper's bullet or maimed by an enemy shell.

The events of the four years of the war have been categorized and classified into battles, but there is a terrible sameness to them. Nothing like the Great War had ever been experienced before. In its carnage, suffering, and utter frustration it was unprecedented. The military 'experts' had neither the means nor the ingenuity necessary to crack the enemy defences. Gains of a few hundred yards that cost thousands of lives came to be regarded as major triumphs. Often the ground gained at so dear a price would be lost again within a day or so.

A typical attack early in the war began with a heavy artillery barrage, intended to soften the enemy line, pounding the barbed wire and machine-gun emplacements. As the barrage was lifted towards the enemy's rear, the men were sent 'over the top' in successive waves to attack the enemy trenches. Enemy machine-gun posts that had survived the artillery barrage would literally mow down the attackers as they advanced. Those who evaded the machine-guns were often stalled by heavy barbed wire, and those who cut through might face hand-to-hand fighting upon reaching the enemy trench. Even if the first line of the enemy trench was taken, there were reserve lines that would have been reinforced as soon as the artillery barrage served notice that an assault was coming. At the Somme on 1 July 1916, in a single day, more than half of the 110,000 British troops who attacked were lost. A year later at Passchendaele, near Ypres, 370,000 British troops, including almost 16,000 Canadians, were killed or wounded, many of them seemingly swallowed up in the mud, in three and a half months of desperate fighting.

The Canadian Expeditionary Force fought throughout the war as part of the British army. The First Division, sent from Valcartier in 1914 and first into the line at Neuve Chapelle in April 1915, was a standard British formation of 18,000 men, a self-contained fighting force made up of three infantry brigades supported by artillery, engineers, medical services, and a supply system. A British officer, Lieutenant-General E.A.H. Alderson, commanded the First Division; three Canadians, including Currie, commanded each of the brigades.

The Canadians were put to the test in the spring of 1915 at the 'second battle of Ypres' when the Germans unleashed a major assault and initiated the use of poison gas. In September Currie was promoted to the rank of major-general and took command of the First Division. Alderson was elevated to the command of the newly formed Canadian Corps, which was made up of three divisions.

The autumn of 1915 was relatively quiet for the Canadians. Currie was busy reorganizing his division after the heavy losses suffered in the spring, when the Second Division, under Major-General Richard Turner, saw action at St Eloi, a controversial operation in which Turner, a favourite of Hughes, was thought to have made serious errors of judgment that lost him the confidence of Alderson and Sir Douglas Haig, commander-in-chief of the British army. In May, Alderson became inspector-general of the Canadian troops in England, and another Englishman, Lieutenant-General Julian Byng (who later became Canada's governor-general), was appointed commander of the Canadian Corps.

The Corps remained in Flanders through the summer of 1916 and saw action at the battle of Mount Sorel in June. In August the Corps was removed south to the Somme to take part in the bloody offensive that was already under way.

In these early engagements, despite his lack of previous combat experience, Currie impressed his superiors as a competent and efficient officer capable of assuming greater responsibilties. Although he was not particularly imaginative, he did plan each engagement with meticulous care and demanded the very best from his men.

Late in 1916, Currie learned that Prime Minister Robert Borden hoped that he would agree to assume the role of military adviser to Sir

George Perley, the first overseas minister in London. Currie was wary of political involvement, however, and he feared that his active military career would end if he took the post. He resisted the prime minister's overtures, and in the end General Turner agreed to accept the job on the understanding that he would later be given the command of the Corps in France when it came time to appoint a Canadian.[6]

The great triumph of Vimy Ridge occurred early in 1917, when, for the first time, four Canadian divisions fought together. The attack was carefully planned and highly successful. Vimy Ridge became a source of intense national pride, a symbol that Canada was coming of age as an independent force through her contribution to the Allied effort.

In June, Byng was promoted from commander of the Canadian Corps to army commander. He suggested that it was time for a Canadian to take over the Canadian Corps and that Currie was fully qualified to do so. Haig agreed that Currie was the most competent candidate; but in London, Turner pressed his own claim. The British had lingering doubts about Turner's ability, and favoured Currie. Borden and Perley also favoured Currie, but they had to contend with those, especially Sam Hughes, who supported Turner. Finally, amid controversy and intrigue, Currie was given command of the Canadian Corps. Turner maintained his seniority, but remained in London as general officer commanding the Canadian Expeditionary Force. Despite Turner's title, Currie was the winner.[7]

Currie's first major engagements as Corps commander were difficult and costly, but his reputation as a field commander grew. In the summer of 1917 Currie persuaded his army commander, General Henry Horne, to alter the plan of attack at Hill 70 and Lens and to adopt what proved to be a successful strategy. The losses, though heavy, were fewer than expected. In the autumn of 1917, at Haig's insistence but very much against his own wishes, Currie engaged the Corps at Passchendaele in the 'third battle of Ypres,' one of the bloodiest and most futile engagements of the war. In the end it was the Canadians who, after sustaining 15,654 casualties, seized the ridge of land that had been Haig's objective from the start.

Sam Hughes had insisted upon the formation of the Fifth Division in England. Instead of going to France to fill the depleted ranks of the existing formations, reinforcements remained in England waiting to go into action as the Fifth Division. Hughes dreamt of a self-contained Canadian army with his son Garnet in command of one of its divisions. Hughes was replaced as minister of militia in November 1916, but the Fifth Division stayed in England. Towards the end of 1917, the question of reinforcements had become critical.

Indeed, even if the volunteers who made up the Fifth Division had been sent to France, the Corps would still have been undermanned. The only answer seemed to be conscription. In the bitter and divisive federal election of 1917, conscription was the central issue. Currie was committed to the introduction of compulsory military service, for he believed that even more men would be needed in 1918. He feared that if Canadian reinforcements were not made available it would mean the end of the Corps as a fighting unit. The situation was so serious that at Borden's suggestion, and despite his wariness of politics, Currie made public statements supporting compulsory military service.[8] He was dismayed, perhaps naïvely, to find that his intervention provoked a response. Currie was labelled as the military correspondent of the Borden government and accused by some of the anti-conscription Liberals of incurring excessive casualties, thereby making conscription a necessity. The operations of the Canadian Corps came under close scrutiny, and at one point some Liberals, including Sir Wilfrid Laurier, spread the rumour that Currie was to be relieved of his post on account of the excessive casualties sustained at Passchendaele.[9] Currie was incensed, and wrote to Sir George Perley, Borden's overseas minister:

You know how I have striven to keep clear of politics, but both sides seem determined to mix me up in it. I do not consider that it is fair that in the propaganda issued by the Government my name should appear so prominently. When it does, the Opposition of course consider it good political tactics to throw mud, and some mud always sticks when thrown. To have gone through what anyone who has been here for three years has had to go through, and to have given the very best that is in one to the service of your country, would almost justify one in hoping that your own countrymen would not refer to you as a murderer.[10]

As the election approached, Currie considered becoming more directly involved: 'If I thought the situation in Canada was serious enough to possibly prejudice the successful operation of the Military Service Act I would be disposed to tell the people of Canada how serious the situation is, even if by so doing I had to give up my present position.'[11]

W.T.R. Preston was in London during the 1917 election, where, as we shall see, he played a prominent role on the Liberal side. It is quite likely that Currie would have known of his activities and that Preston was well aware of the charge of excessive casualties laid against Currie. When Currie went to London on leave in December, he reported: 'The air of London I found, as usual, to be filled with rumours and suspicion. I learned there, for the first time, just how bad my own health was. I also learned that I had become very unpopular with the Commander-in-Chief and the Army. I was told that the Canadian Corps was not working harmoniously with the higher authorities at all. I was also told ... that I was the one who had proved to be absolutely reckless regarding the lives of the Canadians.'[12] Currie was deeply stung by the charges, but they were only the beginning. Convinced in his own mind that he was the blameless victim of political intrigue, Currie decided to stick to soldiering as the election approached, and though he remained firmly committed to conscription, he maintained an anxious silence.

At the front the stalemate continued, and many wondered if the war would ever end. Then, in March 1918, having negotiated an armistice with the Bolsheviks in the east, the Germans launched a major offensive that continued into the spring and summer. The Germans made significant gains. There were days when the Allied command feared that the Germans could not be stopped.

In the crisis, Haig felt it necessary to order a deployment of the Canadian forces, which temporarily broke up the Corps as a unit. Currie pushed hard for the immediate reunification of the Corps, much to the annoyance of Haig, who was preoccupied with the serious threat posed by the Germans. Currie felt that the Canadians were most efficient as a corps, and by April he had reclaimed three of his four divisions. In Haig's opinion, Currie suffered from a swollen head.[13]

From August on, the war took a different course. The Germans steadily lost ground and the Allied forces were able to measure gains in terms of miles rather than yards. The Canadian Corps played what was perhaps its most significant role in the last hundred days of the war. The Corps was the spearhead when Amiens was taken in August. Later that month, the Corps broke through at Arras. By September an Allied victory seemed possible. Gains were steady, but the fighting was fierce and desperate. The Germans knew they could be annihilated if the Hindenburg defensive system cracked. The Canadians broke through at the Drocourt-Quéant Switch on 2 September. The Allied push continued, and the Canadian Corps made spectacular and heroic contributions in crossing the Canal du Nord and capturing Bourlon Wood at the end of September and Cambrai in early October. Currie later described the achievement of the Corps to Prime Minister Borden as follows: 'Between August 8th and ... October 2nd, the Canadian Corps had met and defeated 47 German Divisions, or one quarter of the German Army on the Western front.'[14] From the beginning of October it seemed clear that the war could not last much longer, but the Germans were still fighting desperately. The Canadian Press correspondent J.F.B. Livesay described the fighting at Cambrai 'beyond question ... the most savage and sustained in which the Canadian Corps has ever engaged.'[15] From Germany there were daily reports of low public morale, rioting, and the awareness of imminent defeat. The political situation deteriorated rapidly in Germany, and in early October the Germans sent a note to President Woodrow Wilson requesting that he initiate armistice discussions. Still, the London *Times* warned its readers on 8 October that the enemy could not be allowed to retreat without pressure and that 'there has never been harder fighting on the Western front than in the last few days, and this hard fighting will continue.' Calls for punishment and retribution were heard. In many quarters the German peace initiative was regarded with the utmost suspicion. Unconditional surrender became the objective – now was not the time to stop. Political leaders in France, Britain, and the United States expressed optimism, but stressed the need for a final effort that would bring about a lasting peace. Most felt that peace would have to be dictated, not negotiated.

Sir Douglas Haig warned his officers and men on 7 October that 'at the present time, false rumours are being circulated to the effect that peace is at hand, with the evident object of discouraging the troops and diverting them from the great task they are pursuing of overthrowing their enemies.' Haig repudiated the rumours, and urged a continued fight for a decisive result in the near future.[16] On 9 October President Wilson replied to the German peace note with a refusal to discuss terms so long as German forces were upon Allied soil. On 12 October, the day of the Canadian success at Cambrai, the Germans issued an evasive reply to Wilson in an attempt to find the most favourable terms upon which to begin peace discussions. Wilson continued to insist upon German withdrawal from occupied territory, thereby relieving Canadian and British fears that the Germans might escape unconditional surrender by driving a diplomatic wedge between the Americans and the Allies or by convincing the politicians to agree to militarily unacceptable terms.

Currie's diary entries during this period show that he knew that the end of the war was at hand. At the same time, however, he thought it necessary to keep up the push. Currie sent a cable to the prime minister in mid-October observing that 'unless Germany is decisively crushed now and reduced to military impotency, there will not be ensured the peace and happiness of civilization, the safety of mankind will be in danger, the security of our national existence will be jeopardized and the heritage of our children will be forever prejudiced ... Complete victory is within our reach. Let us have it so that the blood of our bravest and best shall not have been shed in vain.'[17] The Canadian government believed that the war should continue 'until the Kaiser and his clique disappear as a factor in German nationality.'[18] Major-General Sydney C. Mewburn, the Canadian minister of militia and defence, observed: 'I do not take much stock in this peace talk. Our answer to the German Government's note should be to redouble our efforts.'[19] There was talk in Ottawa of demanding indemnification from Germany for the cost of the war when Prime Minister Borden announced in mid-October that he would be going to London to take part in the expected peace discussions.

The British army had not forgotten that for Britain the war had started at Mons. Already it was said that Mons would be reached before the end. On 25 October, as the Canadians came within a mile of the Valenciennes-Metz railway, the London *Times* report of further British and Canadian successes was entitled 'On the Way to Mons.'

The exchange of diplomatic notes between the Germans and the Americans continued, with President Wilson insisting upon terms that would enable the Allies to enforce any agreements that were entered into and preclude a renewal of hostilities on the part of Germany. By the end of October it became clear that there would be no peace until the Allied military command was satisfied that Germany had been beaten finally and decisively. But the end could not be far off, and though the pursuit of the retreating Germany army produced some fierce combat, most troops believed that they would soon be fighting their last battle. The number of casualties in the last one hundred days was appalling. Currie regretted the number of Canadians lost during this last push, but observed, 'You cannot meet and defeat in battle one-quarter of the German army without suffering casualties.'[20]

General Erich Ludendorff, the German commander-in-chief, resigned on 27 October, and within a day or so Austria-Hungary appeared ready to surrender unconditionally. The Supreme War Council of the Allied powers met in Versailles to discuss the terms of an armistice.

Turkey surrendered on 31 October, and the armistice with Austria-Hungary was settled by 4 November, the day after the Canadians had taken Valenciennes. That same day it was announced that terms of an armistice acceptable to all Allied powers had been agreed upon at Versailles. The Germans were instructed to apply to Marshal Ferdinand Foch, the French commander who was to co-ordinate the strategic direction of all Allied forces for what were expected to be the last and decisive days of the war. In the light of the rapid deterioration of their military and political situation, the Germans were thought to have no choice but to accept whatever terms were offered. On 5 November it was reported that a commission of senior military officials had been appointed in Germany and dispatched to the western front to discuss the terms of the armistice. Orders were given to permit the German delegates to pass through the line to enable them to meet with Foch.

Rumours began to circulate that an armistice had been signed. One such rumour was published in the newspapers and caused wild celebrations in Montreal, Toronto, and other Canadian cities. On the morning of 7 November Canadian Corps headquarters received a message that the German representatives were on their way. The Montreal *Gazette*'s correspondent reported that when an officer at Valenciennes who was in touch with headquarters heard the news he drew a sudden breath and said, 'Then it is the end. The last battle has been fought. It is too wonderful to believe.'[21] That same day Currie noted in his personal diary, 'It begins to look as if the end is coming fast.'[22]

The German delegation passed through the line on the evening of 7 November and was advised of the Allies' terms on Friday, 8 November. The Germans were presented with an ultimatum. They had seventy-two hours, until Monday, 11 November, at 11 o'clock, to accept or reject the stiff terms. Foch refused their request for a provisional cessation of hostilities.

On 9 November the *Times* war correspondent with the Canadian and British forces wrote, 'I believe there will be positive disappointment among the troops if the armistice is declared before they have captured Mons.' That same day, in a proclamation to Germans living abroad, the imperial chancellor asked expatriates not to abandon faith in the Fatherland, but conceded that 'forsaken ... by its allies, the German people could no longer carry on the struggle against the growing superiority of its enemies.'[23]

Although victory seemed inevitable, the Allied strategy was to maintain contact with the Germans to make their retreat as difficult as possible and to ensure that they were not given time to dig in for one last desperate stand. The Kaiser abdicated and fled to Holland on 9 November, and the German republic was proclaimed. The German delegates were having difficulty getting instructions, and there was speculation that the seventy-two-hour deadline might have to be extended. But the end came when the Allies' terms were accepted in the early hours of the morning of 11 November, and Foch immediately issued his armistice order:

To the Chief Commanders:

1 Hostilities will cease on the whole front commencing at 11:00 hours on the 11th November.
2 The allied troops will not go beyond the line reached by them at that time and date until further notice.[24]

This was received by the First Army command, which in turn sent the following order to Currie and the other Corps commanders: 'Hostilities will cease at 11:00 November 11. Troops will stand fast on the line reached at that hour which will be reported at Army HQ. Defensive precautions will be maintained. There will be no intercourse of any description with the enemy. Further instructions will follow.'[25]

On the morning of 11 November, the Toronto *Globe* proudly proclaimed: 'The closing achievement of the campaign fell to the Canadians. Just at dawn – a few hours before hostilities ended – the men from across the Atlantic crowned their heroic and historic war career by the capture of Mons. Where the "Little Contemptibles" of Britain started, the sons of her overseas Dominion finished. It was a glowing example of "come back." '

Other accounts written shortly after the event suggest that the taking of Mons held considerable symbolic significance for those involved. Currie himself recognized this in his congratulatory telegram sent just before 11:00 AM on 11 November to Major-General Frederick Loomis, commanding officer of the Third Division, whose men had first entered the town earlier that morning: 'Warmest congratulations on having recaptured the historic battlefield of Mons before the cessation of hostilities.'[26] It was a sentiment Currie repeated in his report on the operations of 1918 when he wrote, 'It is befitting that the capture of Mons should close the fighting records of the Canadian troops, in which every battle they fought is a resplendent page of glory.' General Horne, commander of the First Army, wrote to Currie on 11 November, congratulating the Canadian Corps for its 'splendid crowning effort' in capturing Mons at the last moment; recalling the retreat from Mons in August 1914 in which Horne had taken part, he added, 'I am glad to have had the good fortune to command the Army which took Mons back. I congratulate you and your fine troops with all my heart.'[27] The report of the First Army operations from 28 August to 11 November referred to the fact that 'the Canadians had the additional incentive of capturing Mons before the close of hostilities,' and the history of Princess Patricia's Light Infantry records the pride of the regiment in being 'in the position of honour as one of the battalions which led the British Army back to Mons.'[28]

Currie wrote to Prime Minister Robert Borden shortly after the armistice to report on the operations of the Corps during the last days of the war, and, when referring to Mons, admitted that he 'appreciated the national pride our country would have if we finished the war with that old battlefield in our possession.' The desire to take Mons before the end was qualified by the need to avoid casualties: 'We could have taken Mons on Sunday, November 10, but it would have cost too much to do so.' Still, his description of the town's capture indicated that there had been losses. 'We felt our way all Sunday, and shortly after midnight troops of the 42nd Battalion found an opening. They entered the city, fought through the streets where I saw dead bodies there the next day, and surrounded the enemy machine gunners holding the South. These machine gunners fought to the very last. By 4:30 in the morning we had cleared the city, and when the armistice came into effect at 11:00 o'clock in the morning we were five miles to the east of Mons.'[29]

The armistice was cause for wild celebrations in many quarters. The most gruesome, horrible war in history had finally come to an end. But for most men at the front, the end was almost too overwhelming to celebrate. The chaplain of the Fourth Canadian Infantry Brigade, Robert John Renison, found himself in Mons on 11 November, just after the armistice came into effect. Renison had often heard the men speak of the celebrations they would have when the ordeal ended; yet 'the end of the war came as an anti-climax. The men on that morning seemed too dazed to understand. There were men killed at the last moment. There were men who tried to cheer at 11 o'clock, but they seemed ashamed of their own voices. The band played, but not nearly so enthusiastically as on a mess night. It was too much to expect that an ordinary being could realize it all at once. The quietest day of the last year in France and Belgium was the day of the cessation of hostilities.'[30]

The four years of fighting took an appalling toll. On 15 November Canadians were told that the country had suffered over 213,000 casualties, more than 55,000 of them fatalities. The country was warned that these figures 'will likely have to be increased owing to the fact that the troops of the Dominion were engaged in heavy fighting at Mons up to the last minute of the war.'[31] Few Canadian families had not been touched. The final tally of those killed came to 60,661. Later in November the Militia Department issued a statement in Ottawa giving Canada's Roll of Battles. It began in 1915 with the second battle of Ypres and listed such great achievements as Vimy Ridge and Passchendaele in 1917, Amiens, Canal du Nord, and Cambrai in 1918. It ended with 'the advance and capture of Mons, 7th-11th November, 1918.'

Arthur Currie remained with the Canadian Corps in Europe for several months after the armistice, and as military adviser accompanied Borden to the Paris peace conference. That Canada was treated as an autonomous nation at the conference was attributable largely to the fact that the Canadian Corps under Currie had played such an important role in the last hundred days of the war.

Currie returned to Canada in August 1919. He accepted the position of inspector-general of the military forces of Canada, but soon realized that he had made a mistake. Although he had an impressive title, he had none of the power and authority of a general in the field. He found 'the going slow and somewhat irritating.'[32] He disliked holding a position that many saw as merely a reward for past services. Currie felt that he 'was in the same class as the man who runs an elevator in a public building.'[33] He resented the fact that 'our Parliament is the only Parliament of the Empire or its allies, which has not at least moved and passed and spread on its minutes a vote of thanks' to its wartime forces.[34]

Currie had been inspector-general for only a few months when the board of governors of McGill University asked him to become principal of that institution. Although he was concerned about his qualifications for the post – he had no university training of any kind – Currie accepted. He was offered an attractive salary, and he thought the position would give him an opportunity to be of service to Canada: 'I shall meet thousands of young men every year and I hope that I may be of some help in starting them on the main portion of life's highway with proper ideas of citizenship.'[35]

Even after he went to McGill, Currie continued to concern himself with the problems of ex-servicemen. He actively promoted the cause of better pensions for disabled veterans, widows, and orphans, and he played an important role in the work of the Canadian Legion. He unveiled innumerable war memorials, and he dealt patiently and effectively with a steady stream of requests from veterans asking for job recommendations and other help. The focus of his attention, however, was devoted to the affairs of McGill, one of Canada's greatest universities.

Because of his wartime service, Currie was a well-known (though not universally well-liked) public figure, and it was often suggested that he should run for office. He seems not to have aspired to an active political role. At various times both political parties sent out feelers. When Currie was spoken of as a possible successor to Borden in 1920, he made it clear that he was not interested. Later, in 1924, there was widespread speculation that he was about to attempt to wrest the Conservative party leadership from Meighen. Currie responded: 'I have had many offers to [enter public life] but have always been firm in my refusal.'[36]

Currie had an uneven relationship with the Liberals under Mackenzie King. When King was elected in 1921, Currie wrote to congratulate the new prime minister; he noted that King's victory had depended upon the overwhelming anti-conscription vote in Quebec, and warned: 'They have had their revenge and there must be no continuance of any vindictive spirit, or the reaction will be swift and sure.'[37] Currie actively promoted the appointment of his old commander and friend, Julian Byng, as governor-general.[38] In the constitutional crisis of 1926, Currie thought King's conduct immoral, 'execrable in the extreme and unworthy of any support.'[39] King was 'the most dangerous public man who has appeared in our country,'[40] an attitude undoubtedly reinforced when Byng privately remarked to Currie that 'of course' King had lied to him.[41]

Currie was too busy and happy at McGill and too distrustful of politics to give serious consideration to public office. There was also a darker side to Currie's public image that might well have soured his attitude to politics. From the last days of the war Currie was dogged by the suggestion that he had been responsible for unnecessary casualties, particularly in connection with the capture of Mons.

3

Sam Hughes: War of Rumours

It is impossible to delve into any aspect of Canada's involvement in the First World War without encountering the extraordinary Sir Sam Hughes. Hughes was Canada's minister of militia from 1911 to 1916, and although he had been dead for almost six years when the Port Hope *Evening Guide* published its attack on Sir Arthur Currie in 1927, Currie's libel trial was the final episode in an old fight between the general and his former minister.

On 4 March 1919 Sir Sam Hughes rose in the House of Commons to speak in the debate on the speech from the throne. Although he still sat as a Conservative, he was often critical of his former cabinet colleagues, and his interventions were watched with interest. The Toronto *Daily Star* said of Hughes: 'Around him already there is developing that atmospheric halo that comes with historical figures.'[1] Hughes condemned the Union government for everything from the cost of war loans to the assumption of extraordinary and, in Hughes's view, unnecessary powers under the War Measures Act: 'If we are going to have autocracy in time of war, let us have it in time of peace, too, and send for the Kaiser to run the country.'[2] When he described Sir Joseph Flavelle, a wealthy supporter of the Conservatives, as 'the owner of this Government,' Hughes provoked laughter from the Opposition benches that lasted for several minutes. He went on to challenge

Flavelle's record as chairman of the Munitions Board and to accuse him of profiteering. On military matters, Hughes boasted of his own foresight in predicting the war, and he extolled the effort and achievement of the Canadian 'boys.' But then, recalling a recent speech made by his old cabinet foe Sir Thomas White, who spoke of Canadian pride in having taken Cambrai and Mons, Hughes became bitterly critical. Cambrai was not worth a single Canadian life, Hughes asserted. 'It is a dirty, little, one-horse town, with narrow streets, an ideal spot for machine gun positions and booby traps. Why any man of common sense would send soldiers in there, unless it were for his own glorification, I cannot comprehend.'[3] Then he came to the subject of Mons:

Were I in authority, the officer who, four hours before the Armistice was signed, although he had been notified beforehand that the Armistice was to begin at eleven o'clock, ordered the attack on Mons thus needlessly sacrificing the lives of Canadian soldiers, would be tried summarily by court martial and punished so far as the law would allow. There is no glory to be gained, and you cannot find one Canadian soldier returning from France who will not curse the name of the officer who ordered the attack on Mons. What was in it? They did not take the town, which was only a little one-horse town anyway. It had no strategic value, and the attack was only a bit of bravado as the Canadians had already passed it. What should have been done was to go around these places and take the Germans prisoners, and then make the Germans go in and remove the booby traps instead of having our boys blown up in hundreds as they were in Cambrai.[4]

Hughes had said openly and publicly what had been whispered since the end of the war, lending to these charges whatever influence he still had as a former minister of militia. Although the shield of parliamentary privilege precluded any action in 1919, the libel suit Arthur Currie launched several years later against the Port Hope *Evening Guide* had its genesis that March day in the House of Commons.

Sam Hughes was born on a farm near Bowmanville, Ontario, in 1852.[5] Like Currie, he began his working life as a schoolteacher. Hughes studied law briefly with a Toronto solicitor, but returned to teaching until 1885, when he bought a small weekly newspaper, the Lindsay (Ontario) *Warder*, which he published and edited for twelve years. Hughes was anything but a dispassionate editor. One of his biographers, himself a small-town Ontario editor and a person sympathetic to Hughes, states that under Hughes's ownership the Lindsay *Warder* displayed 'editorial invective which would be considered unbelievable today.'[6]

Hughes ran unsuccessfully for Parliament as a Conservative in the riding of North Victoria in 1891, Sir John A. Macdonald's last election. He won a by-election in the same riding the next year, and represented North Victoria, later called Victoria-Haliburton, until his death in 1921. Hughes was an avid sportsman and a skilful lacrosse player. He was also an active member of the local militia. As a boy he was called out at the time of the Fenian raids, and in 1897 he was named lieutenant-colonel of the Forty-fifth (Victoria) Battalion. He was a non-smoker and a strong advocate of temperance.

Hughes was stocky and had a ruddy face, a firm square jaw, and bushy eyebrows. His manner of speech was plain and direct, and was often spiced with profanity. He was abrupt and sometimes insulting, even to the likes of the governor-general.[7] Hughes held high office in the Orange Lodge and was a staunch imperialist. In the 1890s, as a member of Parliament, he offered to raise and command a battalion of a thousand men to serve under Kitchener in the Soudan. According to an observer sympathetic to Hughes, his 'zeal and earnestness ... for all things British had made him a *persona non grata* with a considerable section of people, who looked upon him as a fanatical Orangeman, a visionary, and a wind-bag.'[8] He was a passionate and at times ferocious debater in the house, and few members of Parliament were neutral in their views on Sam Hughes.

When the Conservatives won the 1911 election and Robert Borden assumed office, he decided that Sam Hughes 'had earned promotion.'[9] Hughes had been a loyal Borden man, and he had a solid base of support in the Ontario Orange community. But he also had many important enemies in the Conservative inner circle, including Thomas White, Borden's minister of finance, and Borden hesitated before making the appointment because of Hughes's 'erratic temperament, his immense vanity.'[10] When he finally appointed Hughes minister of militia, the governor-general, Lord Grey, criticized the appointment. Borden sent for Hughes: 'I ... discussed with him his past vagaries, his lack of tact and his foolish actions and words on many occasions. He frankly admitted his faults and told me that he realized his impulsiveness but he would be more discreet in the future. However, discretion did not thereafter prove to be a dominant characteristic.'[11]

In 1911 Hughes took up his ministerial task with great enthusiasm.

He was convinced that war was imminent and that the empire was unprepared. His cabinet colleagues did not share his view of the need to prepare for war. They did not even consider Hughes's ministry to be an important one. Hughes was determined to prove them wrong. He appeared on public platforms across the country in his militia uniform, urging the cause of compulsory military training for home defence and the construction of drill-halls in every community. His message proved popular with militia officers, but was received with considerably less enthusiasm by officers of the permanent force, who felt threatened by this enthusiastic amateur. More than one member of the permanent force who directly incurred Hughes's displeasure was dismissed and replaced by a militiaman. On the political front, Hughes became something of a liability. Economic conditions were bleak in the early years of the Borden administration, and 'Drill Hall Sam's' demands for more money for the militia and armouries in every community and his preaching of imminent war with Germany seemed out of touch with reality and the serious problems that confronted the nation.[12]

In 1914, however, when Hughes's prediction of war came true, he had to be taken more seriously. He could no longer be dismissed as a raving fanatic. Mobilization began in earnest, and, in Borden's words, Hughes displayed 'astonishing energy,'[13] though that energy was not accompanied by the careful organizational skills necessary to mobilize an army. The minister rejected a carefully prepared mobilization plan designed by the senior British officer in Canada at the outbreak of the war. In its place he adopted a highly personalized scheme that allowed him to go directly over the heads of the permanent staff officers and appeal to the local militia. He later described it in romantic terms to the House of Commons:

There was really a call to arms, like the fiery cross passing through the Highlands of Scotland or the mountains of Ireland in former days. In place of being forwarded to the district officers commanding, the word was wired to every officer commanding a unit in any part of Canada to buckle on his harness and get busy. The consequence was that in a short time we had the boys on the way for the first contingent, whereas it would have taken several weeks to have gotten the word around through the ordinary channels.[14]

The assembly point was a hastily improvised camp at Valcartier near Quebec City, and in less than a month there were over thirty thousand men there. Hughes took personal charge of the inevitable chaos. He organized units, ordered equipment, and appointed officers on the spot. Borden acknowledged that Hughes's 'inexhaustible energy and resourcefulness were a great asset to Canada,' and that 'no other man could have accomplished during a similar period what he did achieve in the training and organization of the First Canadian Expeditionary Force.' But the prime minister also knew that Hughes could not resist the temptation to act as military commander as well as minister and that 'his intense vanity and rather vindictive temper which developed during this period contributed to the difficulty of the situation.'[15]

Many stories were told about Hughes's exploits at Valcartier. According to one, Hughes complimented an officer during an inspection: 'A fine unit you have here, Major.' When the officer politely pointed out that he was only a captain, Hughes responded enthusiastically, 'You are a major now!' Hughes toyed with the idea of taking an active command himself. He later explained to the House of Commons that while his 'heart's ambition was to go to the front ... my position here is much larger than it could possibly be in command of a mere division or corps at the front.'[16]

Thousands of volunteers were quickly raised by a recruiting system that has since been described as 'a confidence trick.'[17] Hughes insisted that the men be recruited and organized in Canada in local battalions. This scheme offered local worthies who were able to get a contingent together the hope of leading their own men into battle; the volunteers saw it as a promise that they would be fighting beside their chums from home. Once recruited and dispatched to England, however, these local units had to be broken up to reinforce existing formations. This dispersal was strongly resented by the recruits and their unemployed officers, though their resentment tended to be directed not at Hughes but at the staff officers in England who had to implement the painful breakups. Organization of the Canadian effort under Hughes's tenure was a shambles, but the anger of the men who were the victims of the disarray was directed at the 'inexperienced staff officers who covered their uncertainty with brusque officiousness.'[18]

Hughes combined his ardent pro-British and pro-empire sentiments with an equally strong sense of national Canadian pride. He was prepared to raise an army for the defence of the empire, but he insisted that his men go into battle as Canadian units with Canadian officers in control. He did not hesitate to make these views known, and he offered his advice to the British generals freely, often insisting upon a Canadian's appointment or promotion. The language he used to push his point was often extreme. On 30 November 1915 Hughes sent a wire to Max Aitken, later Lord Beaverbrook, a Canadian publishing and financial entrepreneur who had the ear of many prominent English politicians, and who at that time was performing rather uncertain duties as 'Canadian Observer.' Hughes instructed Aitken to protest emphatically against staff positions in the Canadian force being filled by British officers. 'There is altogether too much staff college paternalism and espionage abroad. If the feelings of returned soldiers were known another Boston tea party might be looked for.'[19] Prime Minister Borden was shocked when he saw a copy of the telegram, and he immediately wrote to Hughes reprimanding him for his language and for failing to clear the content of the message with his cabinet colleagues.[20] This rebuke did not stop Hughes. In a remarkable letter written only a few days later to Sir John French, commander-in-chief of the British forces, Hughes pleaded: 'My one desire is that our Colonial troops should be Officered by their own colonials.' Hughes again recounted the experience of the American Revolution, which, he implied, would be repeated. 'At the close of the Seven Years' War, the seeds of the Revolution which began a few years later, had been deeply implanted throughout the ranks of the Colonials who had taken part in that war.' Although Canada had agreed that a British general should command the First Division, Hughes argued that 'Steele, Turner or my brother John Hughes, or a dozen more that I could select in Canada, would have ... done, to put it mildly, just as well as the General Officer who was in Command.' Canadians had achieved remarkable gains, but, according to Hughes, resented and distrusted many of their British officers. 'The returned soldiers, I am sorry to say are nearly all permeated with a spirit similar to that engendered in the American Colonists long years ago.'[21] This was hardly the sort of communication a British field marshal was accustomed to receive.

Hughes's tenure was characterized by his highly personal style of administration. Lines of authority were fuzzy or non-existent. Senior Canadian officers in England lacked a clear mandate. The inevitable confusion was a constant source of frustration and annoyance for all, including the political powers in Ottawa, the British War Office, and those like Arthur Currie who were actually fighting the war. Desmond Morton amply documents the hopeless state of affairs under Hughes, and concludes that the disarray was not without design: 'By deliberately creating confusion among the Canadian commanders in England, the minister guaranteed that his own will would remain paramount.'[22]

For Currie and others in the field, one of the most troublesome issues was getting reinforcements from England to France, where they were desperately needed. In March 1915, only 60,000 of the 240,000 Canadians in uniform were in France. In 1916, 25,000 Canadians were training in England, but only 1,000 were made available for active service. General Edwin Alderson, then the Canadian Corps commander, became so desperate for men and so frustrated by the confusion in the Canadian organization that he made his request for reinforcements through British channels. Arthur Currie wrote to John Carson, a crony of Hughes who was then effectively in control in England, 'I almost feel as if it is no further use making complaints because the position is almost hopeless.'[23] While Hughes dreamt of a Fifth Division, and ultimately a Canadian army, Currie faced the immediate problem of reinforcing the depleted ranks of the existing formations.

Another bone of contention was the matter of appointments and promotions. Hughes insisted upon having his say in these matters, and took great pleasure in seeing that his friends got what they wanted; he was quite open in favouring his son Garnet. Officers in the field, like Currie, understandably took exception to Hughes's interference and often ignored his pleas. As we shall see, Currie clashed directly with Sir Sam on this most sensitive matter.

Hughes's passionate defence of the Ross rifle is notorious. As an Opposition member Hughes had been appointed to the Small Arms Board, which had approved the Ross rifle for use in the militia. As a marksman he admired the weapon's qualities as a target rifle. The overwhelming evidence, however, was that the Ross was unsuitable for combat conditions. It was far too sensitive to dust and mud, and it jammed when fired in quick succession. To Hughes, however, the Ross was a national symbol. An attack on the rifle's quality as a weapon was an attack on the technical and industrial capacity of Canada. He simply would not listen to criticism. Politically, the Ross could have been a major embarrassment to the Liberals. It was Laurier's government that had financed the rifle factory in the prime minister's own Quebec riding. But Hughes, a Tory, fought hardest in its defence. Loyalty to the Ross became something of a test of loyalty to Hughes, although after the war many of Hughes's admirers admitted the deficiencies of the Ross and faulted the minister for not having acknowledged them.[24] General Alderson was forthright in his criticism, and Hughes's response was vicious. He became convinced that Alderson was untrustworthy, biased, and incompetent. According to Hughes the rifle was faultless, and Alderson had been criminally negligent in allowing his men to use inferior English ammunition.[25] Hughes's hostility to Alderson was increased because the general had stood in the way of

Garnet Hughes's appointment. Hughes wrote to the prime minister that while his favourites Turner and Watson and his son Garnet were all 'recognized as practical soldiers and giants,' Alderson was a 'pigmy and an intriguer.'[26]

The Ross rifle was not the only piece of Canadian equipment Hughes championed despite its obvious deficiencies. He was outraged when thousands of 'MacAdam shield shovels,' an invention of his secretary, were found useless and sold for scrap. His insistence that 'his boys' wear Canadian-made boots that quickly disintegrated in mud earned him the nickname 'Sham Shoes.'[27]

As the war progressed, Borden's ambivalence toward Hughes gradually changed from unease to outright dissatisfaction. He tried to contain Hughes, but with little success. On several occasions Hughes insisted upon going to England, where he would issue orders and directives without constraint and certainly without consulting his cabinet colleagues. The prime minister wrote in his diary for 8 January 1915, 'On matters which touch his insane egotism he is quite unbalanced. On all other matters [he is] able and sometimes brilliant.'[28] Borden had 'difficulty during the year in keeping Hughes down to mere administration of his department,'[29] and the cabinet became increasingly intolerant of the minister's excesses. When Borden reprimanded Hughes on many occasions, Hughes's eyes would fill with tears and he would become contrite and promise to mend his ways. But he always reverted to his old habits. Hughes was becoming an embarrassment to Borden's government. The organization, or the lack of it, of the Canadian war effort was a disgrace, and the English authorities regarded Hughes as a buffoon.

Borden felt that he had to tread carefully, however. Hughes had a strong following in Canada. In the early days of the war he had become a national figure. He courted the press and held daily informal press conferences. The reporters attending these 'séances', as they came to be known, were provided with lively copy. Hughes remained something of a hero for his prescience with regard to the war and for the apparent success of his enthusiastic recruitment methods. Borden tried to limit his power and influence, but Sir Sam was a difficult man to tie down. By the summer of 1916, however, even Borden's patience had been tried to the breaking-point.

The Liberals had uncovered serious mismanagement, if not fraud, in the purchase of munitions supplies on the part of J. Wesley Allison, to whom Hughes had granted unchecked authority. Hughes foolishly remained loyal to Allison even when it became clear that his trust had been abused. Borden summoned Hughes back to Ottawa from one of his trips to England. On the day he appointed a royal commission to investigate these serious allegations, Borden recorded in his diary, 'It is quite evident that Hughes cannot remain in the Government.'[30] Two days later Borden speculated that Hughes might resign his post and go to the front. Although Hughes was exonerated of any personal fault by the royal commission, he had clearly shown serious misjudgment in trusting and standing by a man like Allison. Borden decided to create a Ministry of the Overseas Military Forces of Canada 'to curtail the activities of Hughes' and 'thus relieve the Government from the unfortunate results of Hughes' visits abroad.'[31] Borden appointed Sir George Perley as overseas minister in October 1916, and Hughes was effectively stripped of his power. Joseph Flavelle was now in charge of munitions, Sir Edward Kemp was chairman of the War Purchasing Board, and R.B. Bennett was responsible for manpower. F.B. McCurdy was in charge of the day-to-day operations of Hughes's department.[32] Hughes, bitterly disappointed, accused Borden of deceit. Borden seized the opportunity and demanded Hughes's resignation. Many considered Borden's action long overdue, but the prime minister later wrote that he had hesitated because he 'knew that Hughes had a considerable following, the force of which was an undetermined factor' and had waited until he was 'perfectly sure that his dismissal would not entail any serious danger' to the administration.[33]

Hughes was undoubtedly a failure as a minister, but he was an intriguing failure. Leslie Frost, who would become premier of Ontario, served with the Canadian Corps in the First World War and later represented Hughes's federal constituency in the provincial legislature. He described Hughes as 'an incredible man' to whom history had been unfair. While he admitted that Hughes was 'abrasive, impetuous with very strong and positive views,' Frost contended that Hughes's achievements, especially in the early days of the war, when he set about 'to awaken people from their complacency,' have been underestimated.[34]

Hughes's energetic and enthusiastic recruitment methods did produce remarkable immediate results, but they later created severe problems. His nationalism and proud amateurism undoubtedly appealed to many Canadians, especially in a war in which British generals earned few accolades. But his accomplishments were overshadowed by his personality and his excesses.[35] His stubborn adherence to his own hastily formed judgments on matters such as the Ross rifle was disastrous, as was his determination to advance the causes of his friends and to stick by those such as Allison who were so clearly unworthy of his trust. Sir Robert Borden, who had cause to know, described Hughes's moods: 'During about half of the time he was an able, reasonable and useful colleague, working with excellent judgment and indefatigable energy; for a certain other portion of the time he was extremely excitable, impatient of control and almost impossible to work with; and during the remainder his conduct and speech were so eccentric as to justify the conclusion his mind was unbalanced.'[36]

Even Hughes's admirers, awed by his energy and charmed by his generosity, acknowledged his faults. One sympathetic biography is entitled *His Faults Lie Gently*, and its author admits that Hughes was 'truculent, ruthless and bombastic ... arrogant, impetuous and eccentric.'[37] He was domineering and unable or unwilling to change his mind on anything. Brigadier-General Charles Winter, who served under Hughes as military secretary at militia headquarters, admired the minister's ability to get things done and to cut through red tape, but he admitted that Hughes used 'domineering' methods and that 'he was inclined often to forget that he was the Minister, an administrative officer of the Cabinet and not an executive military commander.'[38]

After he was dismissed from the cabinet Hughes remained on the government side of the House, but he often attacked his former colleagues, especially his old rival Thomas White and his successors in London, George Perley and Edward Kemp.[39] His bitterness was unconcealed and in various speeches he attempted to defend his record by discrediting the work of others who had criticized him. He felt that the ministry in London was top-heavy with bureaucrats, and he saw no need for a second ministry: 'If half of that army of employees had been behind Gough when the line broke at St. Quentin [during the German offensive of 1918] the German attack might have been checked ... Under the old system General Carson and thirty men did the work in England which is now being done by hundreds of men and a minister surrounded by his retinue.'[40]

Hughes did not make such statements without a purpose. He had not given up on returning to office, and he even thought that he might become prime minister. He continued to correspond with his friend Max Aitken, now Lord Beaverbrook, and on 8 December 1918 he wrote to ask for help from the press. The choice, he told Beaverbrook, was for him to form his own third party or to push out Borden, and 'then with the great bulk of the Tory party behind me and the tremendous following of the British speaking Liberal Party, I could either form a coalition or go to the country.'[41]

Although Currie owed his appointment in 1914 as a brigade commander to Sam Hughes, the two men often collided. Both were strong-willed and determined, and Currie certainly was never close enough to Hughes to earn the unquestioning loyalty that Sir Sam was inclined to accord his favourites. Currie often criticized policies favoured by Hughes, and Hughes was not one to take criticism kindly. Hughes's blind commitment to the controversial Ross rifle has been mentioned. Currie thought that the weapon endangered the lives of his men, and he said so as early as March 1915 in a report to a board of inquiry that was investigating the merits of the rifle.

The two men often differed on appointments and promotions. Despite his staunch imperialist views, Hughes was also a nationalist. He distrusted the British military establishment and was anxious to see the Canadian Corps become a truly national force led by Canadian officers. Indeed, had Hughes not held these views, it is unlikely that Currie would have been given the command of a brigade in 1914. Currie was sympathetic to the idea of a national corps, but he felt that there were simply not enough competent Canadians to assume all the positions. He did not want some of the amateurs produced by Hughes's recruitment methods put in command of men in the field. Ironically, it was Currie himself who did more than anyone to make the Canadian Corps a national force and a source of national pride, but his motivation was tactical. He simply thought that the Canadians fought better together as a unit. He was fiercely proud of the Corps' achievements, and complained after the war to Borden that the British did not always give the Corps the credit it deserved.[42]

The greatest source of the bitterness between the two men was the fact that Currie blocked the promotion of Hughes's son Garnet. Hughes had openly and unashamedly fostered his son's career. When the commander of the Third Canadian Division was killed at Mount Sorel in 1916, Hughes wired General Byng, then in command of the Corps: 'Give Garnet 3rd Division. Sam.'[43] Byng paid no attention, and was later berated by the minister on one of his trips to France.

Although Arthur Currie and Garnet Hughes were friends from their days in the militia at Victoria, Currie had reservations about Garnet's capabilities as an officer. In October 1915, when the Second Division was being formed, Sam Hughes insisted that Garnet be promoted to the command of an infantry brigade. The British command felt that more experienced officers were required for the untested troops of the Second Division, and transferred Garnet Hughes to Currie's First Division. Currie protested strongly and tried to block Garnet's appointment. He concurred only after weeks of pressure from Sam Hughes.

Later, when Currie was appointed commander of the Corps, the question of Garnet's advancement surfaced again. The Hughes faction in London had supported the appointment of Richard Turner over Currie. They had lost that battle, and politics seemed to require compromise. Sir Sam Hughes, who still sat in the house as a backbencher, had become a thorn in the government's side. Could he be quieted with the appointment of his son to the command of the First Division? Borden himself intervened in Garnet's favour. He wrote to Perley: 'If Garnet Hughes is acceptable for Division Commander, I would like to see him appointed, but I leave the question to your judgment.'[44] Currie was pressured to accept Garnet as a term of his own appointment, but he would not be swayed.

I refused to accept ... any conditions which I thought would embarrass me. Their main condition was that I should accept as my successor in the 1st Division Major General Garnet Hughes ... I was importuned, threatened and bullied. I was told that Garnet Hughes would get the 1st Division, that there was a combination in England and Canada for him, that neither I, nor any man could beat; that his father wanted him to get the position and that God help the man who fell out with his father.[45]

Currie insisted that the post go to General Archibald Macdonell, who was said to be 'one of the few Canadian generals to leave a favourable impression on the men in the ranks.'[46] Macdonell had been opposed by Sam Hughes when he was given a brigade command in 1916, and his promotion over Garnet must have been particularly galling.[47] Garnet was bitterly disappointed, and after a stormy session with Currie he shouted: 'I will get you before I am finished with you.'[48]

The dispute between Sam Hughes and Currie over Garnet Hughes's career was intertwined with another and much more important issue, the question of reinforcements. Sam Hughes's insistence upon recruiting and sending over complete battalions has already been noted. Although Currie was prepared, up to a point, to respect the identities of the battalions, he felt that it was more important to preserve formations that had already fought together. This meant that the units arriving from Canada would have to be broken up and placed with existing units, irrespective of promises made by recruiting officers. Currie's plan prevailed, much to the annoyance of Hughes and the volunteers who had been promised they would fight beside their friends.

To make matters worse, Hughes thought that Canada should put an entire army of two corps into the field, and just before his resignation he authorized the formation of the Fifth Canadian Division with Garnet Hughes in command. Currie badly needed men to reinforce the existing corps, which had suffered heavy losses at Passchendaele and Lens; yet men were being held back in England to fill the ranks of the Fifth.

The reinforcement problem was a general one in the British army, especially after Passchendaele. In January 1918 the British proposed that each infantry brigade be reduced from four to three battalions. If this system was adopted for the Canadian forces, only a few thousand additional men would be required to produce an army made up of two corps of three divisions each. Naturally enough, the Hughes faction favoured the scheme. The problem of finding work for the excess supply of officers would be alleviated, and the idea of a self-contained Canadian army would appeal strongly to nationalist sentiment. When Currie met him while on leave in London, Garnet Hughes was confident he would have his way: 'I'm prepared to put my cards on the table and wager you any odds you like that the 5th Division will go to France,' he told Currie.[49] Sam Hughes had even higher ambitions for his son. He wired his old friend, Lord Beaverbrook: 'Why not Garnet command Corps if change occurs.'[50]

Currie argued that there was no need for the Canadian Corps to adopt the British scheme, which in his view would injure the effectiveness and esprit de corps that had been built up. He thought that dividing the Corps would merely add a wasteful level of bureaucracy. It did not take 'a very great stretch of imagination'[51] to guess who would fill the newly created officer positions – those long on political influence and short on military experience and ability. Currie's plan was to add one hundred men to each of the forty-eight infantry battalions that then made up the Corps. Heavy casualties were expected to reduce fighting units, and the proposal would cause considerably less confusion than the major reshuffling required by the alternative scheme. With some help from Haig, Currie persuaded Sir Edward Kemp, the new overseas minister of militia, to allow the Fifth Division to be broken up. Again, Garnet Hughes pushed for a command in the field; but, to his intense annoyance and frustration, he remained in England at the War Office.

Despite these differences, Sam Hughes continued to speak well of Currie for some time following his resignation. On 30 January 1917, in a House of Commons speech urging the expansion of the existing forces, Hughes described Currie as a 'prudent and efficient officer.'[52] Before long, however, Hughes became convinced that Currie was a butcher with no regard for the safety of his men. By January 1918 he had begun a campaign against Currie on the matter of casualties. He wrote to the prime minister requesting a meeting to discuss a variety of matters, including 'Lens and somewhat similar massacres – and the object in each.'[53]

That same month it was rumoured that Currie was ill and had asked for leave from the front. Currie suspected that Hughes's crowd in London was at work. He complained to Lord Beaverbrook that the rumours of his poor health and the possibility of his being relieved of the command of the Corps 'were very persistent, and I have the firm belief that it was propaganda on somebody's part.'[54] In a letter to Harlan C. Brewster, the premier of British Columbia, Currie openly expressed the hurt he felt regarding the allegations of excessive casualties. 'No one regrets casualties more than I do ... Criticism, a public man like you has long since found out, is oft times very cruel.' As for the stories of his request for a furlough, Currie remarked: 'I may tell you that there are some who would like to have the position in which I now am, and I am quite certain that they are the ones who initiated this propaganda.'[55]

In the House of Commons on 6 May 1918 Hughes made a veiled attack on Currie by praising Richard Turner, the man who had been passed over when Currie was made Corps commander. Hughes suggested that Turner was wasted in London. He was, according to Hughes, a 'magnificent young officer ... who always kept in view the necessity of saving the lives of his men ... He would not send his men up against the machine guns as some officers do with reckless disregard for life.'[56] Although Hughes did not mention names, few could have doubted that Currie was one of the officers he had in mind. As minister of militia and defence, Hughes said, he had protested to the British 'against sending our Canadian boys up against machine gun positions without any protection.' The reminder of Hughes's former ministerial position lent an air of credibility to his very serious charges.

After the Canadian forces, under Currie, had taken Cambrai in September 1918, Hughes alleged in a letter to Prime Minister Robert Borden that there had been a 'useless massacre of our Canadian boys.' Linking Cambrai to 'the massacres at Lens [and] Passchendaele,' Hughes claimed that in these operations 'the only apparent object was to glorify the General in command, and make it impossible, through butchery, to have a Fifth and Sixth Division and two Army Corps.' He said that Cambrai should have been surrounded rather than attacked, and any general who had ordered otherwise 'should be tried by court-martial.' Hughes urged Borden to remove the 'incompetents' and avoid further slaughter.[57] In a letter to Max Aitken, Hughes expressed his concern with regard to Cambrai, Lens, and Passchendaele: 'Currie was a coward at St Julien and a damned fool ever since. He was the cause of practically having murdered thousands of men at Lens and Passchendaele and it is generally supposed the motive was to prevent the possibility of Turner coming back with the Second Army Corps, and to prevent Garnet from commanding a Division. The "Black-hand Gang" is the name returning officers give Currie, and the small crowd behind him. God pity the Canadians. Gallant fellows butchered needlessly.'[58]

When word of Hughes's charges reached Currie, he was, of course, upset. He complained to a friend: 'The people of Canada have as yet a very faint idea of what this Corps has accomplished, and some there are, apparently, who desire that the truth shall never be told, and what is told, is often times very much distorted ... To say that the casualties have been excessive is an easy thing to say; but I can imagine nothing meaner, more ungrateful and untrue.' He described Hughes as a 'liar ... at times insane, and apparently ... a cur of the worst type ... had that man had his way, the Corps would still be armed with the Ross rifle, which caused more unnecessary casualties by far than any other factor that I know of. Had he had his way, or had his friends their way, the several appointments in the Corps would not have been held by the best men, but by his friends. Merit would not have counted, but what would have placed them there would have been their willingness to lick his boots.'[59]

Currie was convinced that Hughes was simply annoyed at him for blocking Garnet's advancement. Warned that Hughes was likely to continue his efforts to discredit his record, Currie replied: 'We have always had a rumour producing factory in the Canadian Corps ... However much we dislike the mud slinging, I cannot see how I can stop it.'[60] A few months later, he wrote to a friend: 'I could explain why the propaganda has been carried on if I cared to wash dirty linen, but that is an operation in which I do not think the people of Canada are much interested, and it will not be indulged in by me.'[61] In the end, Currie seems to have discounted the threat Hughes posed: 'I have faced too many dangers and pitfalls in the last four years to be afraid of him ... If my record in this war can be tarnished by such as he, then I don't much care.'[62] Currie was confident that if the need arose he would find a champion. He suggested that if Hughes threatened to get out of hand, a firm statement from a senior minister describing the accomplishments of the Corps and refuting the charge of excessive casualties would clear the air.

In Ottawa, it was known that Hughes was not going to let the matter drop. Sydney Mewburn remained publicly silent, but he was concerend about the allegations. He cabled Sir Edward Kemp, who was still in London: 'There is some disposition to criticize General Currie on the ground that he incurred unnecessary losses in capturing Mons at a time when it was known hostilities were about to cease.'[63] Mewburn asked Kemp to supply him with accurate information regarding casualties.[64] Sir Thomas White mentioned in a speech the pride Canadians had felt in seeing their Corps take Cambrai and Mons, but he hardly delivered what one would call a spirited defence of Currie's record. Perhaps there was just no political mileage to be gained in supporting Currie; indeed, he may have been seen as a political liability. ·

Hughes's speech on 4 March 1919 in the House of Commons, which is quoted at the beginning of this chapter, was viewed as a deliberate attack on Currie. On the day after the speech the Toronto *Daily Star* published a front-page defence of Currie's tactics at Cambrai, suggesting that he had not ordered a frontal assault and that the advance had been aided by more than sixty tanks. Cambrai was hardly an example of a bloody-minded 'over the top' strategy that typified the war. But in another story published on the same day, the *Star* reported that many people were saying 'that the contentions of the former Minister of Militia are widely reflected among the soldiers coming home and those still overseas, and that particularly the final attack on Mons is bitterly resented.'[65] The more prevalent view was that Hughes had demonstrated a serious lack of judgment and that it was pointless to stir up the matter now; to do so would only cause unrest and further pain to those bereaved. However, now that Hughes had spoken publicly of 'the criticism which has been floating about Ottawa for several weeks, many people, members included, feel that the Government must deal with the matter.'[66] Some suggested that an inquiry into the question of war casualties was needed. Others thought that Hughes had become completely unbalanced. One editorial writer asked whether the inquiry 'should be a parliamentary, a military, or a medical one.'[67] Within a few days Hughes himself was calling for an inquiry into the casualties suffered at Passchendaele and Cambrai.[68] Most journalists regarded Hughes's allegations as outrageous, but there were those who thought there must be something to what the ex-minister had said.[69] A letter published in the Toronto *Telegram*, apparently written by a veteran and signed 'Cambrai,' stated that the casualties at Mons had numbered seven thousand, half of them fatal.[70] These figures were quickly refuted; some put the count at six, and some suggested that the truth was to be found somewhere between the two figures. Although the public reaction was overwhelmingly sympathetic to Currie, Hughes had clearly succeeded in giving prominence to what had been only a whispered rumour.

Currie was dismayed when no one in the government came to his defence, but he decided against making a public statement. A libel suit was out of the question, since Hughes was entitled to assert the absolute defence of parliamentary privilege. A week after Hughes had spoken, the casualty figures for Mons and Cambrai were still being debated in the daily papers. Colonel Cyrus Peck, who had served under Currie and had won the Victoria Cross, took his seat in the House for the first time on the day of Hughes's attack on Currie. Peck attempted to refute Hughes's allegations. He assured the House from his own experience that Currie was most solicitous of the safety of his men. He numbered the Mons casualties at seventy-five, adding that that figure might have represented losses incurred over several days and several miles of the front. If the attack on Currie did not stop, Peck threatened, 'there will be some gentlemen who will curse the day they were born.'[71] This remark started a rumour in Ottawa that a sensational document defending Currie and attacking his enemies was about to be released.[72]

The best Currie was to get from the government came weeks later with a guarded response from the minister of the overseas military forces, Sir Edward Kemp, to a challenge from Rodolphe Lemieux, later the speaker of the House of Commons and the man who unveiled the commemorative plaque in Mons in 1927. Replying rather weakly to Lemieux's suggestion that someone from the cabinet should refute Hughes's charges, Kemp said that he had already expressed 'unbounded confidence in General Currie' in an earlier speech.[73] Later that same day, in the course of defending his own record against Hughes, Kemp added that the commander of the Canadian Corps 'has made a high place for himself in history; he measures up to a proud standard as compared with other great generals of the war; he was ever considerate of the men under him, and always exercised patience and foresight in dealing with problems which came before him.'[74] Was this a staunch enough defence of the man the government had relied upon to lead the country's army? Currie and many others thought not. When Borden returned from Paris in July, he paid tribute in the House to the Canadian Corps. He then referred to the anti-Currie sentiment, which he described as unjust. Borden defended Currie, asserting that on more than one occasion, at risk to his own status and reputation, Currie had taken a stand out of concern for the safety of his men.[75] Again, Currie and others thought that this was too little, too late.

It would be wrong to suggest that Sam Hughes was the sole source of Currie's problems. Hughes was the most public and the most prominent individual to weigh in against Currie, but he was merely repeating stories he had heard. Currie's comrade and official biographer, Colonel Hugh Urquhart, noted that 'soon after the Armistice was declared, an attack was delivered against Currie's reputation. It swept through the Canadian Overseas Force and Canada with the speed of a virulent infection.'[76] Soldiers convalescing in hospitals overseas talked of excessive casualties and called Currie a butcher. Currie himself recorded in his diary as early as 17 November 1918 that there were 'some ... senior officers in England [who] spend most of their time visiting and condoling with the wounded; intimating to the latter that the casualties in the Canadian Corps have been altogether too high.'[77]

There seems to be no question that Currie had little rapport with the men in the ranks. He was jovial and popular with fellow officers, but he appeared stiff and abrupt to the ordinary soldier. Although he was concerned about their well-being, Currie did not really understand his troops. Even the sympathetic and devoted Urquhart recognized Currie's limitations in this regard, and he provides several examples. On one occasion when Currie heard some men singing, 'Oh my, I don't want to die, I just want to go home,' he took this as an indication of a lack of commitment to their task and asked their officer if they really meant it. The officer replied sarcastically, 'They have been singing that ditty to my knowledge for three years, and they have never gone home yet.'[78] Currie often said things in a way that made the troops resent him. At a critical stage in an engagement late in the war, his order of the day, issued to all members of the Corps, stated: 'To those who fall I say, you do not die but step into immortality.' While this was thought to be inspirational in some quarters,[79] the men who had fought long and hard and whose lives were on the line detested what seemed to them to be false heroics.[80] Earlier, at the Somme, Currie halted a battalion on its way out of battle and addressed the men formally: 'That is the way I like to see you, mud and blood.' The remark was undoubtedly well intentioned, but the men found it callous and insulting.[81] When he exhorted a battalion to go on using the word 'we,' grumblers were heard to say, 'Who does the fighting anyway, him or us?'[82] Urquhart concluded that the spirit of antagonism that dogged Currie at the end of the war resulted from his failure to understand his troops. Others had a more sinister explanation. A first-hand account asserts that one soldier who lost his brother shortly before the armistice threatened to shoot Currie or the 'next higher-up' at Mons on 11 November 1918.[83]

Currie, of course, was not the only general of the Great War to suffer criticism, particularly with respect to casualties. The common soldiers understandably resented senior officers who, as the troops saw it, put them into the squalor of the trenches to die while they enjoyed comfort and safety well to the rear. The soldiers did the fighting and the dying. The generals had servants to tend to their personal needs, were well fed and well paid, and got all the glory when glory was to be had.[84] Whether or not this is a fair picture of the stresses and dangers of generalship is beside the point: it is how the common soldier saw it.

The trench warfare stalemate of the Great War certainly did not provide a setting in which generals would be seen in a favourable light. They had no answer to machine-guns and barbed wire except massive human attacks by the infantry that were bound to result in an enormous loss of life. Attrition was perceived to be the way to victory. Commands born of this strategy necessarily seemed callous and unthinking. As Desmond Morton puts it, 'The problem was not that the staff officers were, on the whole, bunglers but that they were appallingly efficient because at the end of their minute calculations and detailed orders lay the unbridgeable abyss of no man's land with its guardian machine guns, barbed wire, gas, and artillery barrages.'[85]

Currie was certainly no military genius, but he did establish a reputation as a careful and sound tactician. Hyatt's study of Currie's military career concludes that Currie could be counted on to carry out a plan successfully with common sense and maximum efficiency. He would often criticize and improve upon a plan of attack. Lloyd George thought highly of him, and later wrote that Currie would have been considered for the post of commander-in-chief of the British forces had the war continued.[86] But Currie was not in a position to quarrel with the basic strategy adopted by the British, nor did he seem at all inclined to do so.

Currie received little in the way of public recognition for his war service. On Borden's initiative the cabinet discussed awarding Currie a special payment, as was done for the senior British generals (Haig got £100,000, Byng £30,000). At the same time, however, the government was resisting the demands of ordinary veterans for better pensions. The proposed special payment to Currie was strongly opposed, and nothing came of it.[87]

Currie received a cool reception when he returned to Canada. He arrived in Halifax by ship in August 1919, and though he was given a formal reception at the city hall, he had expected more. The reception in Ottawa was also disappointing. On Parliament Hill there were few cheers and even some hissing. Sir George Foster's speech was anything but effusive,[88] though Currie's speech at a banquet that night at the Château Laurier was well received.

Shortly after his return to Canada, Currie went on a speaking tour in his capacity as inspector-general of Canadian forces. He encouraged the public to accommodate to the needs of returned men. He was greeted by large and enthusiastic audiences. In Toronto he spoke at Massey Hall without a prepared text. His speech ended dramatically with an off-the-cuff response to Hughes's accusations: 'There are some who say I am a bullhead fighter, that I simply keep rushing ahead, but in the great Amiens drive, when we came up against the old Somme defences ... I pointed out that I thought that the battle had gone far enough.' When it came to Mons, Currie emphasized that the push to the end had been an order and that Canadians followed their orders. He told his enthusiastic and receptive audience that the Allied forces were instructed not to relax the pressure at the end while the armistice was being discussed. Mons was taken, he said, by the time the armistice was signed, and he pointed out that the city itself had not been shelled, which proved that there had been no planned attack. 'About 7:30 on the morning of November 11th we got the word that the armistice would come into effect at 11 o'clock and orders to that effect were immediately sent out and the fighting stopped.'[89]

The front page headline of the Toronto *Daily Star* that evening proclaimed 'ATTACK ON MONS NOT ORDERED BY GEN. CURRIE.' An editorial admonished those who listened to his detractors: 'The public must learn to base its criticism on facts, and not on the hearsay of individuals who were never in direct touch with the Corps Commander.' The next morning, the Toronto *Globe* said that Currie had 'effectively answered the cruel slanders' of Sir Sam Hughes; the ex-minister was described as an 'armchair critic three thousand miles from the field of battle.'[90] The Manitoba *Free Press* advised its readers that Currie had 'briefly but emphatically denied the charge which has been in circulation throughout Canada, that as commander of the Canadian forces, he sacrificed the lives of many Canadian soldiers the day the armistice was signed, by ordering the capture of Mons.'[91]

Within a month, however, Hughes was at it again. On 29 September 1919 he insisted that a report be prepared showing casualties by battalion in several of the major engagements, including Mons, along with the plans and conduct of each action. He proceeded to complain, in a rambling fashion, of some of the criticism and interference he had suffered as minister. He renewed his attack on Flavelle and argued yet again the case for a Canadian army of two corps, a dream which he thought had been shattered by excessive casualties. Once again he took up the cause of General Turner, suggesting that a 'great mistake was made' when Currie rather than Turner got the command of the Corps.[92] Hughes proceeded to discuss several of the engagements of the later stages of the war, repeating what he had earlier said about Cambrai. At several points he was challenged by Colonel Cyrus Peck and by Brigadier-General William Griesbach, another member of the House who had been involved in the fighting. Hughes concluded by returning to the subject of Mons: 'The Germans were retiring, and anyhow Mons was not a city of any great importance; I would not give the snap of my little finger for it. It is a nice little place, but to sacrifice the lives of Canadians on the eve of the armistice was quite out of place and more of a piece of bravado than an attempt to help the great cause of human liberty at an acceptable time.'[93]

Hughes's speech drew little reaction from the other members, who listened in stony silence. The fire and enthusiasm Hughes had once exhibited was gone, and many in the chamber and galleries had trouble hearing him. One reporter commented that 'it was almost pathetic to see "the greatest driving force in all history," the hero of many a dress parade, singing his old song to an empty gallery and a sleepy House.'[94] The Montreal *Gazette* deplored his renewed attack on Currie and suggested that Hughes was attempting to defend his own record by slurring that of another. 'It would have been better for Sir Sam Hughes, Parliament, and the country, if he had been content to let history judge of his war work and record than to have impeached the bravery, courage and judgment of the Canadian corps commander, General Sir Arthur Currie ... Sir Sam Hughes did a great work for the Canadian Militia and the Canadian Expeditionary Force, and it was unnecessary for him to attack a gallant soldier and great leader to emphasize his own contribution to Canada's war effort.'[95] Currie was still troubled by the stories: 'There are times when one feels it keenly that it is necessary to fight a battle in one's home land. I feel though that victory will come just as sure as it did to the old Corps in France.'[96]

Almost a year later, on 16 June 1920, Hughes delivered another rambling speech condemning Currie as a deceitful coward and alleging 'that many Canadians would be above the sod today if he had not carried out his tactics and strategy in relation to Cambrai.'[97] It was the last public pronouncement Hughes would make on Currie's conduct. It attracted little attention, and although Currie made no effort to answer it, he was distressed by Hughes's remarks and by the failure of the government to respond. 'It is hard indeed,' he wrote, 'that I must ... defend myself against the base calumny of a lying and dying rattlesnake. Should he ever be manly enough to prefer his charges outside the walls of Parliament where he is privileged I should take immediate action.'[98] Sam Hughes died in August 1921, but the rumours lived on. Currie remained silent until 1927, when he thought that he had found a way to vindicate himself.

4

A Case for the Defence?

Frederick W. Wilson, the proprietor and publisher of the Port Hope
Evening Guide, was sixty-seven years old when the Mons article was
published. He had come to Port Hope fifty years earlier with his father
to take over the *Guide*, one of the oldest newspapers in the country.
Wilson published the *Guide* in partnership with his own son, Donald.
Until the Currie case, the *Guide's* only brush with controversy had
come when its founder, William Firbie, purchased some type and
fixtures from William Lyon Mackenzie, the firebrand Toronto editor, a
hundred years earlier.[1]

In 1927 there were over one hundred daily papers in Canada, but the
number was declining in the face of increased competition from the
major publishers.[2] The Mons article in the *Guide's* issue of 13 June
1927 was the only item of national or international news. Accounts of
a local softball game and a swimming accident and notices of a variety
of social functions filled the few pages of this modest daily, which sold
for two cents a copy.

It is likely that Wilson had a long association with W.T.R. Preston,
the author of the Mons article. Both men were Liberals, and Preston
had published a rival Port Hope paper years earlier. But in temperament
and style the two men were very different. Wilson was 'of kindly disposition'; he wrote in a simple style, and treated his readers as a family.[3] He loved to quote from the great authors and poets, and was a

dedicated small-town journalist. Preston's disposition was more raucous, and, as we shall see, he had a controversial past.

Two weeks after the Mons article appeared, the *Guide* published a special 'Confederation Number' to mark 1 July.[4] The lengthy editorial extolling the virtues of life in small-town Ontario was surely the product of Wilson's pen rather than Preston's. Wilson made no apology for the *Guide*'s focus on local issues and local affairs:

> We cannot all go to the big centres to see and hear the great speakers and artists, but by use of the gramophone and radio we may hear the best without leaving our firesides.
>
> At Confederation and for many years before, the Dear old *Guide* was published (since 1831) and we have kept in touch with our friends daily since 1878, and we thank you all for continuing to believe in us and for giving us your support.
>
> The big events since Confederation, we leave you to read in our histories, we have endeavoured to deal more with local matters.

When he was notified of Currie's lawsuit, Wilson consulted another well-known Liberal, George N. Gordon, KC, who practised law in Peterborough, a town thirty kilometres north of Port Hope. Gordon had sat in the House of Commons from 1921 to 1925, and had earned the right to call himself a privy councillor when he served as Mackenzie King's minister of immigration for a month just before the government's defeat in 1925.

When Currie returned from Honolulu in the fall of 1927, a letter from Gordon awaited him. Gordon was less than forthright: he did not say that he was acting for Wilson, but simply tried to dissuade Currie from proceeding with his suit against the *Guide*. 'I trust, you will not think that I am impertinent if I suggest, that for a man of your outstanding prominence to get into a fight with a little country newspaper, is not likely to maintain the very eminent standing that you hold.' Gordon said that the local lights of Port Hope and the neighbouring area looked on the matter 'as a kind of baiting episode, and seemed to attach no importance to the incident, until it was rumoured, about this district, that you were taking the matter up seriously.'[5]

Currie remained firm. As he saw it, the *Guide* had picked a fight with him, which required retaliation. 'You speak of the matter as being a kind of "baiting episode," ' he wrote to Gordon. 'I see no reason why the Port Hope *Guide* should indulge in what you call "baiting" towards myself.'[6]

Gordon was concerned about what the suit might do to Wilson. He arranged a meeting with Currie and was given a full explanation of Currie's version of the Mons attack. Gordon was persuaded that Currie had the resources and the determination to overwhelm Wilson and Preston. He reported his meeting with Currie and advised Wilson and Preston to retract the statement at once. Indeed, he threatened to withdraw from the case if they declined to retract.[7]

Preston was spoiling for a fight, but Wilson was less certain. In early October, Gordon wrote to Currie suggesting that 'one of the parties' might consider a retraction and suggested that Currie's solicitor, George H. Montgomery, be asked to prepare a statement that would satisfy Currie.[8] Currie replied two weeks later; his terms were stiff, but he held out some hope that a settlement might be reached: 'The editor must know that he has done a grievous wrong, but he has made no attempt to correct this injustice. If he comes to Montreal I am willing to submit a statement which he should publish, but if he won't come then I propose to go to him with all the horse, foot and artillery I can command.'[9]

Gordon's response, like Currie's, was both conciliatory and threatening: 'It is just because I feel that you have not only been wronged but seriously so, that I feel I should do something to untangle the situation.' Gordon added a word about the uncertainty of a jury trial. Then, as if to distance Wilson from Preston, he said: 'If you knew the editor of this little paper, and something about the circumstances of this case, I think you would have a different view of him.'[10] The letter concluded with a postscript: 'Wilson just called and is going to Montreal to see you.'

The statement of claim was served on the defendants at about this time, and Gordon drafted the statement of defence on Wilson's behalf.[11] These formal documents, known to lawyers as the pleadings, set out the position of each party and define the issues of the case for the trial. The statement of claim repeated the full text of the *Guide* article, provided a one-paragraph summary of the military ranks Currie had held, and recited his post-war appointments as inspector-general of militia and principal of McGill University. The pleading identified the sting of the Mons article as being 'that the Plaintiff, while in command of the Canadian Corps and at a time when no military advantage could possibly accrue therefrom for his own selfish and dishonourable purpose and acting in disregard for the lives and safety of Canadians under his charge, ordered an advance for the purpose of securing an apparent but useless victory, hoping thereby to bring at the close of the war glory to himself and his staff.' As a consequence of the article, Currie 'had been and is greatly injured in his character and in his reputation as a military commander and as an officer and in his position and authority as Principal and Vice-Chancellor of McGill University.' The plaintiff claimed $50,000 in damages. How Currie, Montgomery, and Tilley settled on that figure is not clear. An award of that magnitude would have put Wilson and the Port Hope *Guide* into bankruptcy. The newspapers quickly fastened on the figure, and in the frequent front-page reports of the progress of the case to trial labelled it 'Currie's $50,000 libel case.' Currie did not want or expect to make money on the case. Indeed, he was advised that even if he won it was unlikely that he would get enough to cover the expense of bringing the case to court. Had he claimed less, however, it might have seemed that he did not consider the libel a serious one.

The defendants answered that the statements they had published were true, and they denied that Currie had suffered any damage. Specific reference was made to the 'records of the House of Commons.' Wilson and Preston pleaded that statements in the article 'were made in good faith, in the public interest, and without malice and that the said statements dealt with a subject matter on which there was a duty upon the defendants to disclose to the public,' and that 'the statements were a proper subject for discussion in the press.'

Unfortunately for Wilson and Preston, the law accords the press very limited protection for statements concerning public figures or matters of public interest. They did plead 'fair comment,' but the scope of that defence is limited. A defendant will succeed on the fair comment defence if the statement complained of is an expression of opinion on a matter of public interest, but only if the truth of the assertions upon which the opinion is based can be proved. Wilson and Preston could, for example, claim that the statement in the article that the loss of life at Mons was 'useless' was an expression of opinion on a matter of public importance protected by the fair comment defence. But unless they could prove that there had actually been loss of life, the opinion would lack the necessary foundation in fact. Similarly, their conduct was not excused in law because they were merely repeating what others, including Sam Hughes, had said. A report of the proceedings of Parliament is protected, but the *Guide* had not reported Hughes's statements; it had simply adopted them as its own, and therefore no privilege applied.

Even a journalist who has made reasonable attempts to verify his story will lose a libel suit if the truth of what was written cannot be proved according to the exacting standards of the law. Wilson and Preston could not defend themselves on the basis that the words of an ex-minister or the stories from returned veterans provided a reasonable basis for their belief in the truth of what they had published. The truth of each assertion would have to be proved by firsthand evidence.

The law of libel must strike a balance between protection of reputation and freedom of the press. By imposing what amounts to no-fault liability, the law strongly favours the protection of reputation. If Wilson and Preston were defending the Currie case today, they probably would argue that the protection of reputation has to be modified in the light of the right of freedom of expression and freedom of the press enshrined in the Charter of Rights and Freedoms.[12] Currie was, after all, an important public figure, and the subject of the Mons article was a matter of public concern. The military establishment had decided to make something out of the capture of Mons. Wilson and Preston believed that by bringing to the public's attention another side of Mons they had simply done their duty as journalists.

If Sir Arthur Currie wanted to set the record straight, Preston pointed out, he had other ways of doing it. Any newspaper in the country would have carried his refutation on its front page. Is the need to protect reputation so compelling that it justifies a set of legal rules that make the press liable unless the truth of every disparaging remark can be proved according to the exacting standard of the courtroom? Does such a rule unduly inhibit investigative journalism? Such questions were not taken seriously by lawyers or even by most journalists in 1927, and it seems to have been assumed that a rule more favourable to the press would merely encourage scurrilous attacks upon innocent public figures.[13]

The statement of defence was filed on behalf of both Wilson and Preston, but it was clear from the outset that Preston would insist upon representing himself, not only because he feared that Wilson might surrender, but also because he wanted to appear as his own lawyer at the trial.

Efforts to reach a settlement continued. Currie met with Wilson at McGill University on Saturday, 5 November 1927, at ten o'clock in the morning. The meeting lasted about one hour, and Currie did most of the talking. The tone was civil but hardly friendly.[14] Currie made it clear to Wilson that he was deeply disturbed by the article, which he considered vicious and untrue in every respect. He proceeded to explain, with the aid of a large map and copies of his actual orders, the disposition of the Canadian Corps and his own version of what had occurred at Mons. He emphasized that he had been given orders to advance to the high ground east of Mons and that the Allied strategy, determined by General Foch, had been to maintain pressure on the retreating German army right up to the last.

Currie asked Wilson where he had gotten his information for the article. Wilson mentioned the *Globe* article about the unveiling of the plaque, the Hansard reports of Hughes's speeches, and conversations he had had with returned men. Currie was scornful. He told Wilson that he had lived with these rumours for ten years and the publication of the charge in the pages of the Port Hope *Guide* gave him the chance to clear the matter up once and for all. He denied that there had been any real attack on Mons and claimed that not a single Canadian had been killed on 11 November. The Corps had maintained pressure on the retreating Germans and had accomplished its assigned task with minimal losses. Currie described his own entry into Mons not, as the article said, just after 11:00 AM, on November 11, but at 3:00 PM. He told Wilson that he had seen one dead German and no dead Canadians. Is it possible that Currie failed to review his diary entry for 11 November 1918, where he had written, 'Some fighting took place through the streets, where I saw dead bodies later in the day'?[15]

Wilson said little throughout the hour. Currie's story was certainly not the one he had heard before. Despite Currie's forcefulness, Wilson still wondered whether it was not time to give the ordinary soldier a chance to tell his side of the story. At the end of the interview Currie asked, 'And now, Mr Wilson, what are you going to do about it?' Wilson answered ambiguously, 'Sir Arthur, I intend to do just what I believe is right.'

Wilson returned to Port Hope and related to Preston what he had been told. Wilson was worried. He now knew that Currie was a formidable figure and that he was determined to see the case through to the end if necessary. Could they really prove the truth of everything Preston had written? The generals and senior officers would all be on Currie's side. Could Wilson find witnesses with the knowledge and the fortitude to stand up to their former commanders? Could he afford to litigate a case of this complexity? If he lost, he would have to pay not only damages but Currie's legal costs, which would easily run to thousands of dollars. Everything Wilson owned was at stake.

Preston remained undaunted, however. He relished the limelight, and knew that the case would be a true cause célèbre. But Preston recognized that Wilson was on the spot because of what he had written, and he suggested that Wilson withdraw and leave him to fight the case alone. Wilson considered doing so, but decided to carry on. As a journalist, he found it difficult to capitulate to Currie's demands. He became convinced that someone should stand up for 'the little guy.' The privates who had been on the firing line were entitled to tell their story and to have their share of the glory, if glory there was, in the taking of Mons.

W.T.R. Preston was no stranger to controversy. As a politician, journalist, and author he had been in the public eye for over forty years. When he wrote the Mons article Preston was seventy-six years old. He had just completed his second book, *My Generation of Politics and Politicians*, a highly personal and partisan account of Canadian politics from pre-Confederation days to the present. The emphasis of the book was on scandal and corruption, with numerous tales of bribery and election-rigging. Preston was a Liberal, and he relished Tory-bashing.[16] Few prominent Conservatives escaped his invective, from Sir John A. Macdonald to Arthur Meighen. Preston's assessment of Sir Robert Borden gives some idea of the book's flavour: 'If a burial service could be read over his political demise it would read, "He brought nothing into public life and he carried nothing out." As a matter of fact, he entered Parliament a comparatively poor man, and went out with a colossal fortune.'[17] Borden, like many others who were attacked by Preston, decided that the charge was unworthy of public refutation.[18]

Sam Hughes was one of the few Tories Preston liked. Preston wrote that Hughes had a 'vivid personality' and was 'a thoroughly good sort.'[19] True to form, however, Preston's praise for Hughes was not unreserved. He claimed that before being appointed minister, Hughes had received substantial annual payments from Sir Charles Ross to promote the rifle manufacturer's interests in Ottawa.[20] Preston's plain insinuation was that this transaction explained Hughes's staunch defence of the Ross rifle during the war. On another occasion, Preston stated that Hughes's habit was to speak first and think later.[21] Apparently, he did not think that this characteristic was at work with respect to Hughes's allegation about what happened at Mons, for, in addition to paraphrasing that allegation in the Port Hope *Guide* article, Preston repeated Hughes's remarks verbatim in *My Generation of Politics and Politi-*

cians. Strangely, Currie seems to have been unaware that he appeared in Preston's book even before the newspaper story was published.

Preston had close ties with the Port Hope area. A native of Ottawa, he had been educated at Victoria University in Cobourg, and his wife came from Port Hope. Preston published the Port Hope *News* for two years, until he left the town to become a member of the parliamentary press gallery in Ottawa as a representative of several Liberal papers, including the London *Advertiser* and the Montreal *Herald.*

Always active in the affairs of the Liberal party, Preston was the Ontario party's general secretary from 1883 to 1893. He became a familiar figure on election platforms across the province, delivering his spirited and partisan message and debating with some of the leading Tories of the day. In 1885 he ran unsuccessfully for the House of Commons in the riding of East Durham. In 1894 he became librarian to the Ontario legislature, though he seems to have been more occupied with politics than with books. In 1896 he ran for the House of Commons, this time in the riding of West Toronto. Again he lost.

Preston was implicated in the 1899 election fraud in West Elgin, when serious allegations were made against the Liberal 'machine.' Preston's congratulatory telegram to the Liberal victor, telling him to 'hug the machine,' was leaked to the press, and was thought by many to amount to a confession. The day after the disputed West Elgin election, the Laurier government appointed Preston inspector of immigration offices for Europe, and dispatched him to London with an annual salary of $3,000 and a generous travel allowance. His appointment created an uproar in the House of Commons, where he was vilified by Conservative opposition members who alleged that he had been spirited out of the country to avoid scandal.[22] In the end, however, the commission appointed to investigate the election was unable to find any personal wrongdoing on Preston's part, though its verdict seems closer to 'not proven' than 'not guilty.'[23]

Preston undertook his duties as an immigration commissioner with energy, and it seems that he was reasonably effective. Western Canada had to be populated, and Clifford Sifton, Laurier's minister of the interior, encouraged Preston to find the 'desirable' sort of emigrant from Europe. Even as an immigration commissioner Preston was in the public eye. He was a favourite target of the Conservatives in the House of Commons. Preston himself admitted, 'I know of no one outside of Parliament, and scarcely half a dozen in, who has been more subjected to criticism than I, in Parliament and out of it.'[24]

Judging from the criticism he attracted, it hardly seems that he was treating his job as a patronage sinecure. In September 1907 Robert Borden, then leader of the Opposition, cited Preston's work as at least part of the reason for the influx of immigrants who were taking jobs many native-born citizens wanted. Whatever his contemporary critics thought, Preston's overseas work earned him a place in standard modern reference works, which report that 'he played an important part in diverting toward Canada the flood of immigration that preceded the First World War.'[25] Preston also served as Canada's trade commissioner in Japan, and then moved to fill the same post at the Hague in 1910. The defeat of Laurier and the Liberals in 1911, however, spelled the end of his diplomatic career.

Preston's first book, *The Life and Times of Lord Strathcona*, was published in 1914. It was an account of the political and financial affairs of Donald A. Smith, later Lord Strathcona, a man who came to Canada as a poor Scottish boy and who left as a wealthy and powerful railway magnate. The book was published shortly after Strathcona's death. One can understand why Preston waited for his subject's demise and why five publishers refused the manuscript. Strathcona is portrayed as deceitful and conniving, and his success and fortune are attributed to his greed and his exploitation of the Canadian people. Preston contended that Strathcona had abused his public office as a member of the House of Commons by supporting and abandoning the two parties in turn, according to his own financial interests.

The book's publication prompted two libel suits in England, where Preston was living at the time. Ironically, Preston was the plaintiff in both cases. In the first, Preston sued the London *Daily News* on account of a highly unfavourable review that described the book as an attack of sustained malevolence. Preston argued his case without a lawyer. The newspaper won the trial, pleading the defence of fair comment. Preston's appeal, which he also argued himself, was quickly dismissed.[26]

In the second action, Preston claimed that he had been defamed by a cable dispatch written by F.A. McKenzie, a Canadian journalist working in London, and published in an Ottawa paper. McKenzie's article stated that Preston had been prompted to write the book because of his differences with Stratchona, and concluded by quoting a passage from the *Daily News* review: 'There is no doubt a suitable name for this sort of thing in Canada. In England it is known as mud-slinging.' Preston's libel action attracted widespread attention in England and Canada.[27] He denied any animosity towards Strathcona, and insisted that he was merely trying to write a serious history of the political life of the times. He maintained that his purpose was a patriotic desire to repress a Canadian tendency to political corruption. Preston told the jury that he attributed his defeat in two attempts to gain a seat in the House of Commons to the large sums of money the Strathcona interests had poured into the coffers of his opponents. McKenzie, pleading his own case, apologized for squabbling in a courtroom with a fellow Canadian while others were fighting the war, but insisted that Preston's book was a malicious and venomous attack on an honourable man and that he could not in conscience retract what he had said. The trial ended inconclusively when the jury was unable to agree on a verdict.

Preston remained in England and corresponded regularly with Sir Wilfrid Laurier, providing the Opposition leader with spicy accounts of the British political scene and gossip about the war.[28] He seems never to have had a harsh word to say about Currie. Preston was often critical of the Canadian government's war administration, but he was reluctant to find fault with Hughes. 'Don't put all the blame on him. His colleagues are equally at fault.'[29] When the shell scandal broke, Preston observed: 'I am sorry Hughes is implicated, apparently. I had hoped that he was free from this sort of thing.'[30]

Preston came into the public eye again when he was named one of three Liberal scrutineers to supervise the overseas vote in the 1917 conscription election.[31] Shortly before the election, legislation was passed to ensure that the troops overseas were given the vote, a factor hardly designed to help the chances of the anti-conscription Laurier Liberals. While many English-speaking Liberals were deserting the party, Preston remained loyal and fiercely partisan. He actively sought his appointment as scrutineer. 'There is no sacrifice I am not prepared to make, and there is no work too hard for me to undertake.'[32] Preston was incensed by the Union government's tactics, and thought that the arrangements for soldier voting were 'calculated to win the election for the government by fraud.'[33] He told Laurier, 'I would join the rioters before I would allow any conscription act to be administered by that gang of political pirates in Ottawa.'[34] Preston, no stranger to the unsavoury side of elections, found plenty to occupy himself with in the 1917 campaign. He clashed with General Sir Richard Turner and Garnet Hughes, who were openly partisan in the Conservative cause, and he so annoyed one officer that he was arrested and held overnight. He complained loudly that the military authorities were actively helping the Tories and hindering the Liberals. This was hardly surprising, since many officers saw conscription and the need for more men as a matter of life and death for those already in the trenches. Preston did, however, report to his leader that General Currie had intervened to put a stop to improper electioneering at the front.[35]

Preston advised Laurier on how to appeal to the troops and how to get his message past the censor. He urged Laurier to promise the men that their jobs would be guaranteed upon their return from the front and that a soldiers' relief fund would be established through the imposition of an 80 per cent tax on wartime profits. 'Give me this platform,' he wrote to Laurier, 'and I'll willingly run in the most ultra-Tory constituency in the Dominion and I'll win.'[36]

The Union government appealed directly to the troops. 'We regard the winning of the War as the supreme issue, and are resolved to leave lesser matters in abeyance while the united energy of the Canadian people is directed to that end.'[37] Preston considered this to be a shameful example of flag-waving for partisan purposes, and he responded on behalf of the Liberals with some strongly worded pamphlets directed to the troops. He accused the Borden Conservatives of corruption and profiteering:

While you, with true British courage and amazing fortitude have faced, and are preparing to face, appalling conditions and stupendous sacrifices, political vultures at home have been fattening, and are preparing to fatten still more, upon public expenditure and public necessities. Colossal fortunes have been amassed by Government pets through exorbitant profits, who have made no personal sacrifices nor suffered any personal inconveniences. The political hangers-on at Ottawa have been raking in the gold while you and your comrades were being raked by German shells.[38]

He accused the military of sending Liberal sympathizers to the front and even to certain death in no-man's-land.[39] In the end, the Liberals were soundly defeated. After the votes were counted, a disappointed but indignant Preston wrote to Laurier that 'the evidence that is accumulating here of fraud, perjury and every conceivable kind of election malpractice is simply overwhelming.'[40] He advised his leader that 'when the accumulation is complete you will be staggered at the enormity of the offences which have been committed.'[41] Whatever the truth of these extravagant allegations, there unquestionably were irregularities in the voting, and Preston armed himself with material he could use for his partisan speeches for years to come.[42]

Preston returned to Canada and to politics in April 1918. He settled in Port Hope and became the president of the Durham Liberal Association. In 1921 he again ran unsuccessfully for Parliament, this time in the riding of Durham. Between 1921 and 1923 he was asked by the federal government on several occasions to act as chairman of labour conciliation boards. In 1923 he was commissioned to investigate freight rates on the Great Lakes. His report was characteristically controversial and strongly worded. He found that American interests had established a monopoly and that excessive rates were being charged. If left unchecked, Preston concluded, the situation would throttle western expansion. A royal commission agreed with Preston, and despite strong pressure from the shipping interests, the government passed legislation to control the rates.

Two years later Preston was again asked to investigate shipping rates, this time on the Atlantic. Once again he found that a combination of powerful interests was maintaining freight rates at an artificial level, and once again his conclusions were attacked by the companies concerned. When an agreement between the government and Sir William Petersen for a subsidized North Atlantic service was disclosed, the shipping companies were even more upset, and a special committee was appointed to investigate. Preston was once again at the centre of public attention.

Preston came to the Currie libel suit as an experienced litigator. In 1902 Preston brought the first of a series of libel actions against the Ottawa *Journal*. The *Journal* had published a letter written by Preston's cousin, William Rochester, who was annoyed by what he perceived to be an unfair attack made by Preston against his deceased father, John Rochester, a former member of Parliament. A newspaper is liable for misstatements in letters it publishes, and the *Journal* tried to settle the action part way through the trial when it realized that William Rochester's letter was not entirely accurate. But the paper refused to do more than apologize and pay the legal costs incurred to date. Preston insisted upon damages, and the case went to the jury. Despite a direction from the judge that was favourable to Preston, the jury returned a verdict for the *Journal*.[43]

Preston's second case against the *Journal*, in 1912, implicated Sir Charles Fitzpatrick, the chief justice of the Supreme Court of Canada. Preston publicly accused Sir Charles of making unfavourable comments about him to a Dutch financier through whom Preston was trying to form a syndicate to buy land in Canada. Sir Charles denied the charge, and Preston contemplated suing him.[44] The *Journal* learned of the squabble and published an editorial, which stated: 'The latest addition to Mr. W.T.R. Preston's Ananias club, which already has members all over the world, is the Chief Justice of the Dominion, Sir Charles Fitzpatrick.'[45] Preston contended that this amounted to an allegation that he was a liar, and he decided to sue. The trial judge, Mr Justice Middleton, interrupted Preston's spirited opening address to the jury to observe that the newspaper had not called him an Ananias, but rather had suggested that he was in the habit of stigmatizing those with whom he did not agree as people who did not tell the truth. The judge called a recess so that the parties could reconsider their positions. Philip D. Ross, the publisher of the *Journal*, said later that Preston agreed to withdraw the suit if the *Journal* would pay his costs. Preston apparently broke down in tears, pleading that he was in dire financial straits. Ross gave him one hundred dollars out of pity.[46] Preston's very different recollection of the event produced two more libel actions years later.[47]

At the time of the Currie action, Preston had a third suit pending against the *Journal*. This arose out of the publication of his book, *My Generation of Politics and Politicians*, in which Preston recounted his own version of the 'Ananias' case. According to Preston's account, Sir Wilfrid Laurier had corroborated his version of the dispute with the chief justice, and, at the suggestion of the trial judge, the *Journal* had settled the case with an apology. Shortly after the book appeared, the *Journal* refuted Preston's description of the case in a strongly worded article, which stated that his version was 'cut out of whole cloth,' and concluded: 'From the accuracy of Mr. Preston's version of this episode, the accuracy likely to pertain to the rest of the book can be gauged.' Preston issued a writ but did not proceed with the case, perhaps because he was preoccupied by his fight with Currie.

Preston was a small man who exuded energy and combativeness. He spoke quickly in a high-pitched, piercing voice. During the 1880s and 1890s, when he fought with all his energy as a speaker, organizer, and strategist, he 'became the best known and certainly the best abused of all the Liberal champions of that time.'[48] Even thirty years later, at the time of the Currie case, Preston was a well-known scrapper who could be counted on for a good fight.

5

To Sue or Not to Sue?

W.T.R. Preston insisted upon conducting his own defence; Frederick W. Wilson's lawyer, George Gordon, continued his efforts to settle the case. Gordon met George Montgomery, Currie's solicitor, in Montreal, and later renewed his suggestion that Montgomery should prepare a statement of facts which, if published by the Port Hope *Evening Guide*, would satisfy Currie that the record had been set straight: 'I would be pleased to urge Wilson to sign it. I have acted for him in other matters and I feel I could approach him and have considerable influence in inducing him to accept my view of matters.'[1]

At the same time, Currie was under constant pressure from his friends to drop the lawsuit. Just before he returned to the family home in Strathroy for Christmas, he seemed disposed to accept a full and complete retraction. He wrote to Montgomery, 'I sometimes think that the very fact that I entered action against the paper achieved a good deal of what I might hope to gain by prosecuting the matter to an end.'[2] In late December Currie's Toronto counsel, W. Norman Tilley, KC, learned that Mr Justice Hugh Rose had been assigned to the Cobourg sittings that were to commence 16 April 1928. Rose was an experienced trial judge with a sound reputation. Tilley wrote to Montgomery, 'I think he is the best judge you can have for this trial. I am writing so that you will have in mind the desirability of forcing the action to an issue before him at that date in case an amicable arrangement is not sooner made.'[3]

Montgomery agreed 'that Mr. Justice Rose should be as good a judge as we could get for this kind of trial.'[4] Gordon, however, continued to press for a settlement on Wilson's behalf, and even met with Currie to hear the general's explanation of what had happened at Mons. Montgomery cautioned Currie that even if he could come to terms with Wilson, Preston would not be willing to agree to anything short of a full-scale trial. 'We know that old Preston, if he has anything to say about [it], thrives on libel suits and would probably prefer to fight rather than settle so that nothing may come of Gordon's efforts.'[5]

Currie composed a retraction and sent it to Montgomery in mid-January. It was long, more than five typed pages.[6] Currie sensed that Wilson might find it too long, but he could not see how it could be shortened. He wanted a detailed statement of facts to be published and he felt that the *Guide* could hardly complain about the length of a retraction after what it had said about him. In the statement he set out all the allegations that had been made in the original article, and added:

It is only fair to ourselves to say that our comments were based on statements which had been made in the House of Commons at Ottawa by the late Sir Sam Hughes and also on statements made to us by ex-members of the Canadian Expeditionary Force ... We wish to say that we do not believe the statements made by the late Sir Sam Hughes with reference to Sir Arthur Currie's conduct of operations at Mons; neither do we believe the statements made to us by ex-members of the Canadian Expeditionary Force with reference to the same matter.

The draft went on to detail the points Currie would try to establish later in the trial, and concluded: 'We cannot say how sincerely we regret the publication of the article on June 13th last. There is no doubt that there has been much loose talk and unjustified comment about excessive casualties at Mons and our only satisfaction is that perhaps, after all, the publication of our unwarranted article has provided Sir Arthur Currie with the opportunity of placing the true facts before our readers and the people of Canada.'[7]

This went beyond asking the defendants to retract. They had to say that they positively believed the truth of Currie's version and that they repudiated things said not only by themselves but also by Hughes and others. Montgomery must have doubted that such a statement would be accepted, but he passed the document on to Tilley. Tilley quickly perceived the futility, not to mention the tactical risk, of giving such a document to the defendants. They were unlikely to accept it, and, as Tilley said, 'If they refuse I think we will rather weaken our position by putting the matter in such detail before them.' Tilley advised Montgomery that Currie should accept a shorter, simpler retraction in order to avoid the enormous risks of a trial; 'My own view is that libelous articles and retractions published in the Port Hope *Guide* are not of very great importance. On the other hand, a libel action of this character gets great publicity. If I were in Sir Arthur's place I would take almost any form of apology and let it go at that.'[8] Currie reluctantly composed a much shorter statement, which concluded: 'We do now withdraw, freely, voluntarily and without equivocation or mental reservation, any and all [of] the statements we made which in any way reflect upon the soldierly or humanitarian qualities of Sir Arthur Currie, and we now in the most sincere manner apologize to him for having so grossly wronged him.'[9]

In the end, the settlement attempts were unsuccessful. Even the shorter statement was unsatisfactory to Wilson and Preston. Although Gordon assured Montgomery that 'Preston would have nothing to say as to what Wilson would publish,'[10] it seems that Preston was able to persuade Wilson that they should fight it out and give the common soldier his day in court.

At this point Gordon bowed out, frustrated by his failure to bring about a compromise. Wilson retained the services of Thomas F. Hall, KC, who practised law in Cobourg, and Frank Regan, a forty-two-year-old Toronto counsel. Wilson could not afford to pay substantial legal fees, but Hall, whose roots in the Cobourg area went back four generations, was sympathetic. In 1921 Hall had been named King's Counsel at the unusually young age of forty. He carried on a general practice, but took a special interest in criminal law. After graduating from Queen's University at the age of nineteen, he tutored the children of a wealthy American family for three years to finance his legal education. Hall was a great friend and admirer of Frank Regan, and the two men loved to swap stories about the cases they had argued. It was probably Hall who got Regan to take on Wilson's defence.

Regan had grown up in Trenton, a town sixty kilometres east of Port Hope. He practised alone, doing mostly criminal defence work. Like Wilson, Preston, and Hall, he was a staunch Liberal, and he had counted himself a friend of Sir Wilfrid Laurier. Regan was a proud Irish Catholic. He did not serve in the forces during the war, but was said to have been 'a prominent worker in all patriotic movements' and to have assisted in Red Cross appeals and victory loan drives.[11]

In 1927 Regan was seen in the profession as a lawyer with a good future. Although at times he was erratic, undisciplined, and given to bouts of heavy drinking, he was a clever cross-examiner with good instincts for advocacy. The Currie case seemed to present him with a remarkable opportunity. The trial was bound to attract national attention, and Regan knew that his name would be on the front pages for days on end. The idea of taking the side of the underdog would have appealed to him. Sir Arthur Currie was a formidable foe, but for a lawyer of Regan's stripe that made the case even more attractive.

Regan knew that he would have to contend not only with Currie but with Tilley, a counsel of outstanding reputation. The contrast between the two lawyers could hardly have been greater. Regan was a scrappy fighter who did daily battle in the criminal courts, defending those whom society had not favoured. Tilley was more likely to be found in the corporate boardroom or pleading in the rarefied settings of the Supreme Court of Canada or the Judicial Committee of the Privy Council in London.

Tilley, like Currie, began his working life as a schoolteacher.[12] After working for two years at a school in Cainsville, Ontario, he entered Osgoode Hall Law School. His exceptional talents were soon recognized. When he was called to the bar in 1894 at the age of twenty-six, he received the gold medal as the leading student in his class. He quickly made a reputation as a superb litigation counsel able to deal with a wide variety of cases.

He first came to public notice in his early thirties, as counsel to the Manitoba government in a case concerning a scandal over the construction of the legislative building in Winnipeg. He was an expert in railway law, and he argued many cases for the Canadian Pacific Railway. He was a director of a number of important companies, including the CPR, the Bank of Montreal, Canada Life, and Royal Trust. He acted for the government of Canada and for the government of Newfoundland in the International Fisheries Arbitration at the Hague. During the war he acted for the government in the expropriation proceedings concerning the Ross rifle plant in Quebec.

Tilley was born in 1868 in the village of Tyrone, near Bowmanville, thirty kilometres west of Port Hope. He remained in touch with his roots, and despite his high-profile Toronto practice he would have felt quite at ease addressing a jury of Durham and Northumberland farmers. A large, stout man with a fine voice, Tilley devoted himself entirely to his work and was known for his thorough preparation and total command of the facts and law of any case he argued. He had an exceptionally quick mind and the gift of all great advocates, the ability to make his points forcefully and simply, so that his arguments seemed self-evident.

Tilley argued a remarkable number of cases in the Supreme Court of Canada and in the Judicial Committee of the Privy Council, Canada's court of last resort until 1949. Many of his cases are leading authorities to this day. Tilley argued many of the important constitutional decisions of the 1920s and 1930s. In 1927, the year Currie retained him, Tilley argued the *Tiny Township* case[13] on behalf of the attorney-general for Ontario in the Supreme Court of Canada. That case stood until 1987[14] as the leading authority on the rights of separate-school supporters, an issue that was as difficult and controversial then as it is today. Tilley argued the appeal in *Tiny Township* before the Judicial Committee of the Privy Council[15] in London for nine days in February and March 1928, and he returned to Canada little more than a week before the Currie trial began in April.

Although he was not particularly interested in politics, Tilley was considered for high public office more than once. In 1917, during the conscription crisis, Borden tried to entice Sir Lyman Duff, then a member of the Supreme Court of Canada and a close friend of Tilley's, to add strength and prestige to the Union government. Duff would oblige only if Tilley would join, but, despite Borden's plea, Tilley refused. Borden was bitterly disappointed. 'Duff and Tilley,' he wrote in his diary, 'lack the spirit which prompted our young men to cross the seas and go over the parapet.'[16] Tilley was later mentioned as a possible successor to Borden, but he could not be tempted away from the work he loved.

Unlike Regan, Tilley did not need the Currie case to make a name for himself. He tried to dissuade his client from going ahead with what he knew would be a bitter and costly fight. Currie continued to receive advice as to the wisdom of suing right up to the eve of the trial. Tilley was not the only one to tell him that the suit might be a mistake; many others agreed that the risks of a trial outweighed the possible benefits. Perhaps they were less certain than Currie seemed to be about the outcome. Certainly the trial would attract enormous publicity and provide Preston and others with a platform they could not otherwise hope for. Walter Gow, a prominent Toronto lawyer who had served as deputy minister of the overseas military forces in London and who had been in Mons on Armistice Day, wrote to Currie offering his assistance, but adding, 'I deplore the fact that you have felt it necessary to put

[Preston] in the limelight, which I am afraid is exactly what he desires. It is a pity to dignify a man of Preston's type by bringing an action against him, but I can only assume, as I do, that you were driven to it and no other course seemed feasible.'[17]

Currie was probably aware of and perhaps even influenced by other contemporary libel actions. A case similar in some respects to Currie's was brought by Sir Michael O'Dwyer in England in 1924.[18] The O'Dwyer affair was a cause célèbre which Currie probably followed with interest. O'Dwyer was the lieutenant-governor of the Punjab from 1913 to 1919. In his last year in office there had been serious disturbances in connection with the independence movement, and O'Dwyer had proclaimed martial law. There followed the infamous Amritsar incident in which British troops under the command of General Reginald Dyer opened fire on a huge crowd of unarmed civilians, killing hundreds. Three years later, Sir Sankaran Nair, formerly a member of the viceroy's executive council, wrote a book entitled *Gandhi and Anarchy*, an account highly critical of Gandhi and his followers but also hostile to O'Dwyer. Nair charged that O'Dwyer was responsible for acts of terrorism in the Punjab, and suggested that he bore personal responsibility for the atrocities at Amritsar and that he had employed brutal tactics to preserve his power. O'Dwyer sued for libel.

The trial lasted for over a month. General Dyer, whose conduct had been condemned by an inquiry established shortly after the Amritsar incident, was too ill to testify, but the court heard extensive evidence about that affair and many other bloody incidents. The trial became something of a public examination of contentious and controversial aspects of the British administrtion in India. Many highly placed officials regretted that O' Dwyer had brought the action in the first place, thereby inviting this unwelcome review of British practices. The trial ended dramatically. The jury announced that it was unable to agree on a verdict, and the parties agreed to accept a majority verdict. Eleven of the twelve jurors found for the plaintiff, and a judgment for £500 and costs was entered. In his summing up, Mr Justice McCardie took the unusual course of vindicating the conduct of General Dyer: 'Speaking with full deliberation and knowing the whole of the evidence given in this case I express my view that General Dyer, in the grave and exceptional circumstances, acted rightly, and in my opinion, he was wrongly punished by the Secretary of State for India.' The *Times* applauded Justice McCardie's pronouncement, and saw the verdict as 'a strong and a most useful declaration of the will of the British people to maintain their trust to protect India.'[19] The reaction in India was one of alarm. Justice McCardie had condoned acts of violence that had previously been condemned. Lord Oliver, secretary of state for India, quickly dissociated the government from Justice McCardie's remarks.[20] Although he was successful in the verdict, O'Dwyer had to endure a long and difficult trial, and it is questionable whether the net effect was the public vindication he wanted.

Another case that demonstrated the hazards of libel suits, and one that Currie, Tilley, and Preston probably followed, was the Gladstone libel action in 1927.[21] Captain Peter Wright, the plaintiff, had been a member of the British staff of the Supreme War Council; Currie might even have known him. Wright published a book entitled *Portraits and Criticism*, which stated that the late William Ewart Gladstone had been a hypocrite in his sexual conduct, and that what he did in private did not accord with what he professed in public. Lord Gladstone, the son of the former prime minister, was furious but frustrated by the legal rule that precludes a libel action on behalf of a dead person. His only recourse was to entice Wright into suing. Lord Gladstone wrote a letter to the Bath Club, of which Wright was a member, stating that Wright was a liar and a coward and adding, for good measure, 'he is a *foul* fellow.' The club expelled Wright, and he foolishly took the bait and sued Lord Gladstone for libel. The issue was the truth of Wright's slur on W.E. Gladstone. Although as defendant Lord Gladstone had to bear the burden of proving that Wright's statement was false, he succeeded in clearing his father's name. The case showed how dangerous a libel action can be for the plaintiff. There were also those who questioned Lord Gladstone's wisdom in provoking the suit, even though he had been successful. The *Times*, while applauding the verdict, asked 'whether the better course might not have been to treat [the author] and his book with silent contempt.' The libel was made in a single sentence of an unsuccessful book, and the trial had given it notoriety.[22] Might Currie's suit against the Port Hope *Evening Guide* not have a similar result?

Many confident plaintiffs have later regretted suing. The most dramatic example is an old case in which the plaintiff complained of a statement labelling him 'a highwayman.' He lost the case when the defendant succeeded in convincing the jury that the allegation was true. The plaintiff was immediately arrested, and shortly thereafter he was convicted of the crime and sentenced to death.[23]

Oscar Wilde's case in 1895 led to a similar though less drastic result.

Lord Queensbury described Wilde as 'posing as a sodomite,' and Wilde prosecuted him for criminal libel. Despite his quickness and wit, Wilde was devastated in cross-examination and Queensbury was acquitted. Wilde was immediately arrested, convicted of gross indecency, and sentenced to two years' imprisonment.[24]

There were several notable libel trials in Canada in 1927, none of which made the prospect of suing seem particularly attractive. An action against the Montreal *Star* brought by L'Union Co-opérative des Laitiers de Montréal was dismissed in February after a lengthy trial despite the fact that the newspaper had used some very strong language.[25] In the same month, the Toronto *Star* successfully defended an action by W.A. Boys, the member of Parliament for North Simcoe. The *Star* had printed a story which alleged that Boys had acted improperly on behalf of one of his constituents who had been charged with bribery. In March, Ernest V. Sterry, the editor of the *Christian Inquirer*, faced the unusual charge of blasphemous libel and was convicted by a Toronto jury. Sterry had written that in the Bible there are 'hundreds of passages relative to the Divine Being which any moral and honest man would be ashamed to have appended to his character,' and had described incidents from the Old Testament in an irreverent and facetious manner.[26] The prosecution case received world-wide attention and prompted an English member of Parliament to propose legislation limiting the scope of the offence in England. Describing the case as a Canadian version of the Scopes trial, the Toronto *Star* observed that the prosecution had only succeeded in giving Sterry's views wider coverage: 'Instead of hundreds hearing what this man has to say, hundreds of thousands in this city had his unimportant views thrust on them; and not here only, but wherever the English tongue is spoken and read ... It often happens when free speech is intefered with that one person is silenced and ten thousand set talking.'[27]

But not everyone urged caution on Currie. One old soldier wrote, 'It is about time you got after some of the dirt-throwers.'[28] Cy Peck, who at that time was a member of the legislative assembly of British Columbia, wrote to encourage Currie. Peck had defended Currie's name years before in the House of Commons against the charges made by Sam Hughes. Acknowledging that many thought the libel action a mistake and that Sir Arthur should pay no attention, Peck stated: 'Of course it isn't them that is being attacked. For myself I think there is a limit to this sort of thing – a time when one has got to give up taking everything lying down. This is a kind of supine philosophy nowadays which deprecates making a fight about anything or against anything. "Take no notice of it" they say, that be a damned motto for a full-blooded man.'[29]

A libel action is a costly and risky business, and Currie must have tired of being told that he was making a big mistake. But he remained determined. There was unquestionably something of the spirit of the old soldier eager to fight yet another battle and return to the days of comrades in arms. If he could win a war, surely he could win a lawsuit.

The Currie case arose at a time when views on the First World War were changing. Many people needed the perspective of ten years to begin to comprehend its meaning. The war was a cataclysmic event that had altered the economic, political, and spiritual outlook of the Western world.[30] Canada had never before known sacrifice on such a scale. The war had begun in a spirit of confident, romantic patriotism and the belief that the world could be made safe so that things would remain as they had always been. But the sense of permanence, stability, and optimism of those early days could not survive the cruelty and suffering engendered by a war in which the entire Western world seemed bent on destruction.

Currie's libel suit coincided with the beginning of a great flood of writing on the war that reflected this altered consciousness.[31] Until the late 1920s, writing on the war tended to be idealistic and romantic, depicting the front as a place where brave young men laid down their lives in noble sacrifice. Most people wanted to forget the evil and brutality of the war and to imagine that a new age was dawning. But ten years later the tone began to change. There was an outpouring of novels, reminiscences, autobiographies, and histories, and a resurgence of interest in the war and in the experience of the men at the front. Readers were exposed to accounts born of bitterness and disenchantment. Death, suffering, futility, and frustration replaced patriotism and idealism as the dominant themes. The German novelist Erich Maria Remarque's *All Quiet on the Western Front* appeared in translation the year after the Currie case, and made a great impact. Its poignant account of the doomed soldiers in the German trenches struck a responsive chord in some who had fought on the other side. That same year there appeared Richard Aldington's *Death of a Hero*, an imposing tale of the horror of war, and Robert Graves's autobiographical *Goodbye to All That*, which exposed the absurdities of the military. More and more the war was being described as a useless waste; the men on opposite sides of no-man's-land were seen to have more in common with each other than with the generals who put them there. Siegfried Sassoon's anti-war sentiments were the focal point of his autobiographical trilogy *The Complete Memoirs of George Sherston*, the first volume of which appeared in 1928. Henry Williamson's vehement tirade against politicians, generals, and profiteers, *The Wet Flanders Plain*, appeared in 1929, as did Frederick Manning's tragic *Her Privates We*, Hemingway's *A Farewell to Arms*, and Sheriff's *Journey's End*. Charles Yale Harrison's *Generals Die in Bed*, a Canadian novel as provocative as its title suggests, was published in the same year the Currie case took place. It describes, with brutal simplicity, the horrors of trench warfare. Although he seems not to have read the book until 1930, Currie's reaction to it is worth noting. He was so outraged that he complained to his book dealer: 'I am ashamed that you are offering such a book for sale. There is not a single line in it worth reading, nor a single incident worthy of record. I have never read, nor do I hope ever to read, a meaner, nastier and more foul book.'[32] The bookseller withdrew the novel immediately.[33] To an old comrade, Currie described the book as 'a mass of filth, lies ... [it] appeals to everything base, mean and nasty ... a more scurrilous thing was never published.'[34]

Currie thought that the country had not fully understood the role the Canadian Corps had played, and he saw his lawsuit as involving more than his own personal honour and reputation. It was as if he had a pre-war romantic notion of a noble and patriotic battle that had to be fought to vindicate his generation and restore meaning to the entire experience of the war.

Currie often expressed disappointment that the war had not brought a new era of peace, co-operation, and prosperity. There was still greed and dishonesty, and the tranquillity and stability of pre-war days seemed lost forever. He thought that if the 'old spirit' of the Canadian Corps 'could be revived once more in the men of this country, many problems now apparent would disappear.'[35] Currie saw the battle he would fight in the courtroom as a way to show Canada what the Corps had achieved and to reanimate the idealism of earlier days. Declining an invitation to a Vimy Ridge memorial dinner in Calgary shortly before the trial, Currie wrote: 'Please convey to my comrades my profound regret in disappointing them, but I am getting ready for another Corps battle to preserve sweet and clean the memory of Canada's final effort to see that moral forces should reign supreme in the world.'[36] As he said time and again in his suit against Wilson and Preston, he was fighting not only his own battle but also the battle of every officer and non-commissioned officer who had taken responsibility in leading the troops during the war.

Currie was aware that trial by jury posed special risks. How could he expect twelve Ontario farmers to have sympathy for a university principal and retired general taking on the local newspaper? At times he worried about what a jury would make of him and the military decisions he had made ten years earlier. He wrote to a friend that the defence would argue that the Canadians should not have advanced after 9 November because the armistice was coming. 'Of course, it is an untenable position, but one can never estimate the effect such an argument may have upon a jury.'[37] At other times he was more confident. 'Although many are sorry it is being tried by a jury largely composed of farmers, I am willing to trust to their good sense.'[38]

Tilley asked for a special jury. This institution, now abolished,[39] offered Currie the hope that the jury would be composed of men more sophisticated and wealthier than the average – as Tilley put it, men of a 'pretty good class.'[40] A special jury was selected from those on the current list for the grand jury. Grand jurors were chosen by the county selectors, who included the judge of the county court, the junior judge, the warden of the county, the treasurer of the county, and the sheriff. Grand jurors were to be individuals who, in the opinion of the selectors, were the most competent for jury service owing to their integrity and soundness of judgment.

The local sheriff, J.D. Nesbitt, chose a day early in March when the jury list would be stuck. No one could remember a special jury being requested in the United Counties of Northumberland and Durham, and the sheriff had to verify the procedure. Forty names were drawn by lot from the grand jury roll. Each party was entitled to strike off twelve names, leaving sixteen who would be summoned for the trial. As Tilley observed, the procedure 'affords an opportunity to object to persons who might be particularly friendly to the defendants.'[41] Currie wrote to Colonel L.T. McLaughlin, who lived in the area, for advice on jury selection. 'I have been warned by the defendants that it will be impossible to find a jury in which there are farmers of Durham and Northumberland who would give a verdict in favour of a soldier. This may be true, but I do not believe it. I feel that they are as fair, square and just as any men chosen from any other group.'[42] To narrow the list down to sixteen names, Tilley relied upon the judgment and local knowledge of the two local solicitors who were acting for Currie, Duncan Chisholm and Roy Willmott (who years later would serve as the first chief judge of Ontario's county and district courts). Regan and Hall were in attendance for the defence.

In the end, Chisholm and Willmott were rather disappointed with the final list of sixteen names, though they thought the majority were probably favourable. As Currie wrote to a supporter, 'My lawyers feel that luck did not favour them in the draw.'[43] Of the sixteen, seven were described as farmers, three as yeomen, and the others as gardener, agent, millhand, miller, and musician. Two were ex-servicemen.

6

Preparing for Trial

In March 1928, when the trial appeared to be a certainty, preparation began in earnest. Documents alone would not suffice; witnesses who had actual knowledge of the events of the last days of the war were needed. Preparing for a case of this complexity involves an extraordinary amount of work. Currie and his lawyers concentrated their efforts, but still did not know much about the case Wilson and Preston would present. It seems odd that neither side pressed for examination for discovery until shortly before the trial. This procedure, which is described more fully later in this chapter, permits each side to question the other on oath before trial about all the facts and details of the case. In modern practice it takes place months prior to the trial, and is an important element in pre-trial preparation.

The case began to take up much of Currie's time. He wrote personally to all senior officers who might be able to help him. They were scattered across the country, and Currie called upon them to rally to the cause he saw as being that of every officer: 'Will you help me to clear myself of this charge, which is not only a reflection upon me, but upon every officer and N.C.O. who led his men in the final days.'[1] Currie asked these officers for their own recollections, and he hoped they would help him collect information from others who had been involved. He met with many, and almost all were eager to help.

Tilley was not involved in the details of the preparation for trial. He was in England in the spring of 1928 arguing two cases before the Judicial Committee of the Privy Council. He did not return to Canada until 11 April, only a few days before the trial was to start. He immediately devoted himself to the case. It was arranged that Currie would go to Toronto to be close to Tilley. As Currie put it, '[Tilley and I] must spend every moment together.'[2]

In Cobourg, Chisholm took charge of local matters. As Currie's solicitor he was responsible for getting the case on the trial list, handling jury selection, and having subpoenas prepared for witnesses. He did the best he could to find out what the defendants were up to, and he relayed this information to Currie.

In Toronto, Tilley's partner, Reginald H. Parmenter, co-ordinated the gathering of documents and witnesses. Parmenter, then forty-eight years old, was an experienced counsel who had practised with Tilley's firm since shortly after his call to the bar in 1902. He was a keen sportsman who had played football for the Argonauts as a law student and had rowed at Henley in 1902. Parmenter was assisted by Cyril H.F. Carson, a junior lawyer who was very much in the background in the Currie case,[3] but who later would have a distinguished legal career. The two men prepared Tilley's trial brief and had the case fully organized by the time Tilley returned from England. Tilley could immediately start to absorb all of the details and plan the actual strategy for the trial.

In Montreal, Montgomery remained involved, although he played a less direct role than Colonel Wilfrid Bovey and Allan Magee, who spent days collecting information and the names and addresses of witnesses who could help Sir Arthur. Both men had served with Currie on headquarters staff in France during the war. Magee had become a successful Montreal lawyer. Bovey, a Cambridge-educated lawyer and author (he had already written one book on law and would later write books on French Canada) had followed Currie to McGill University. At the time of the trial, he was the director of extramural relations at McGill. Years later, he would be elected to the provincial legislative council.

All instructions and orders relating to the battle at Mons had to be assembled, and the date, time, place, and circumstances of every death had to be collected. Any information about the armistice or mention of a possible armistice had to be uncovered. Maps had to be prepared so that the significance of orders and events could be properly understood. A system had to be organized so that information about witnesses called at the trial by the defendants could be quickly obtained.

Magee and Bovey set up committees organized by city, division, regiment, and unit to collect and co-ordinate the information.

Despite the preparation and support he was getting, Currie remained deeply concerned. He was going to have to fight his case on unfamiliar ground, and he would not be in complete control. He repeatedly expressed the fear that Preston and Wilson would be allowed to widen the issue beyond the Mons incident, and for this he simply could not prepare. The possibility tormented him. It was difficult enough to assemble evidence that would meet the demanding standard of the law and that would prove his version of what happened at Mons. To do the same for the entire war was utterly impossible. Could the issue be confined to the Mons attack, where Currie felt he was on strong ground? The article had referred to Mons in comparative terms: 'There was much waste of life during the war, enormous loss of lives which should not have taken place. But it is doubtful whether in any case there was a more deliberate and useless waste of human life than in the so-called capture of Mons.' Would this not give Preston and Wilson an excuse to go over the entire war? Many aspects of Currie's character had been attacked in the article – his willingness to sacrifice life for his own glorification, his personal courage, and his ability as a military tactician. If he complained that his reputation had suffered, could not the defence try to show the truth of their insinuations by dragging up past incidents? Could one make a jury unschooled in military matters understand how decisions in the field were taken, and how loss of human life was necessarily only one of many factors to be considered?

An obvious source of information was the detailed records kept by the Department of National Defence. Here there were casualty lists complete with dates, times, and places, the diaries kept by each unit recording the nature of the operations they had undertaken, the orders issued and received, maps, and the names and addresses of those who had fought and who might be called as witnesses.

At first the department was co-operative, and provided Currie with the documents and maps he had shown Wilson when the two met in Montreal in November. As the trial approached, however, Regan and Preston also sought access to departmental records. Department officials were much less sympathetic to Regan and Preston than they had been to Currie.

The minister, Colonel James L. Ralston, was subjected to the conflicting pressures of politics and personal loyalty. Although he had been defeated in the 1926 general election, Prime Minister Mackenzie King made him minister of defence and found him a safe seat. Wilson and Preston were both faithful Liberals, and when they made it known that they were getting less help than Currie, Ralston felt the political heat. But Ralston had also served with distinction as an officer under Currie during the war. Once, without calling for volunteers, he crawled over the parapet into no-man's-land to rescue a wounded junior officer – not the sort of action thought appropriate for a commanding officer. Currie said that he should have been court-martialled, but shook Ralston's hand warmly as he spoke.[4] Ralston was severely wounded at Amiens and had received the Distinguished Service Order and Bar. (Years later, Ralston again was named minister of defence by King, but when the prime minister refused to implement conscription in 1944, Ralston resigned.)

Ralston admitted to Currie that he had 'already had extremely strong – indirect but very pressing, representations on behalf of the defendant in your case.'[5] From the department's point of view, the only solution was to be completely even-handed and to treat all requests for assistance, whether from Currie or from the defendants, on the same footing. In an apologetic handwritten note Colonel A. Fortescue Duguid, the man in charge of the departmental records who had also served under Currie, told his former commander, 'I am glad to know that you understand and appreciate the position ... as all requests for copies of documents have to be submitted to the Deputy Minister before action is taken, it would be well to write direct to him for any others you may require.'[6]

More formal letters explaining the procedure were sent to both Regan and Currie. Documents would be provided only if subpoenaed at trial, and the department reserved the right to refuse to produce certain documents for reasons of state. If the two sides could agree, the department would supply a copy of the list of documents asked for by subpoena, and would provide facilities whereby these documents could be inspected before the trial. Currie's request for certain orders was coldly refused by the deputy minister:

[Should the Department comply with your request] it would not be acting in the impartial manner which the circumstances of the case demand. Consequently, I must inform you that the Department cannot consistently do otherwise than maintain an impartial stand, and if the documents which you request are furnished this will only be done in the manner indicated above.[7]

You have asked for certain documents, but have not called for them by sub-poena, as will be necessary for you to do if you wish the Department to produce them at the trial.[8]

Neither side could compel the department to open its files for general inspection. The right to subpoena documents at trial does not include the right to inspect the files before the trial to find out what there is to subpoena. Although Currie must have been stunned when he learned that the government could not even provide him with this level of support, the situation was of even greater concern to Regan. The defendants had the burden of proving the truth of what they had published. As outsiders to the military establishment, they had far less access to information and personal recollections about orders and strat-egy than Currie. Without being able to search through the official rec-ords, war diaries, and casualty reports, their task would be even more difficult. They would have to exploit to the full their right to question Currie under oath on the pre-trial examination for discovery.

The purpose of a pre-trial examination for discovery is to permit the parties to a lawsuit to explore the opponent's case so that they go to trial fully prepared, knowing the case they will have to meet. Each side is entitled to ask the other any questions pertaining to the case. The questions and answers are recorded and can be used for certain pur-poses at the trial.

Early in March, Currie went to Cobourg to be examined. Parmenter went down to Cobourg to accompany and advise Currie. The first day of the discovery was set for Saturday, 10 March. Currie came by train from Montreal the night before and stayed at the Dunham Hotel, as he would during the trial. The hotel porter was reassuring. He was a former member of the Royal Canadian Regiment and was eager to dis-cuss the case with his old commander. He had been near Mons and could remember no casualties in his unit on the last day of the war.

Although discovery proceedings rarely attract media attention, the Currie case was different. Even though the trial was a month away, reporters were hungry for a story and wanted to know how the retired general would fare under oath. Parmenter was concerned about how Preston and Regan would behave. Currie's strategy was to confine the case to the narrow limits of the actual allegations made about the events of the last few hours of the war. The defendants wanted to broaden the issue to include other areas so that Currie's entire military career and his personal life could be explored. Parmenter hoped that the trial judge could be counted on to confine the issues. Discovery, however, is much less formal than trial, and it was to be expected that the defendants would be allowed considerable latitude. The situation could easily get out of control. Because the case had already attracted a great deal of publicity, Parmenter did not want members of the press present at the discovery to repeat matters raised by Preston or Regan that were, in a strict legal sense, irrelevant to the case. Parmenter asked J.T. Field, the local registrar of the Supreme Court, who also acted as special examiner (the officer who presides at the discovery), to rule that the proceedings should be held in camera. The registrar (who was Thomas Hall's uncle) agreed.

The reporters were annoyed at being shut out, and some immediately suspected that Currie was trying to conceal a weakness in his case. In the end, Parmenter's tactic was only partly successful. Eager for a story, but excluded from the discovery process, one paper resorted to publishing extensive extracts from Sam Hughes's speeches in the House of Commons attacking Currie.[9]

In response to Regan's questions, Currie explained the sequence of orders, starting with the one he received on 9 November 1918. Each document was carefully considered and explained. Currie said that he had not issued an order for an attack on Mons 'on the last day, almost the last hour and last minute.' He admitted that 'the fighting had been fairly severe from the time we began to approach Mons,'[10] but it was no worse than expected. It was true that veterans who had fought for four years had lost their lives on 10 November in the Mons vicinity, but Currie denied that this was an 'appalling loss of life.' He asserted that the town had been taken by 4:30 on the morning of 11 November, half an hour before the armistice was signed, and that there was no fighting thereafter.

Currie stated that his strategy was one he had been directed to follow by his superior officers. The Germans were in retreat, but pressure was kept up and contact maintained so that the enemy could not disengage and establish a new line of defence. He maintained that there really was no attack on Mons. Mons lay in the path of the objective set for the Canadian Corps. It was important to secure the town as part of the overall strategy of maintaining pressure on the enemy so that the war would end sooner, but Currie disclaimed any wish to take Mons because of its historical significance.

Currie provided Regan with a list of those killed in the vicinity of

Mons on 9 and 10 November comprising some thirty-five names, all but three of whom were killed in the operations leading up to and including the capture of Mons. 'We were not capturing Mons. We were capturing the high ground east and north-east of Mons as we had been told to do. Mons was in the intervening space.'

Currie's strategy became clear to Regan as the examination proceeded. The article had referred to the capture of Mons on the last day of the war, and Currie was going to try to confine the defence to that specific allegation. He would insist that the trial not develop into a more general inquiry about the last days of the war. The issue, as he saw it, was simply this: What happened at Mons on 11 November after the armistice had been signed?

Regan pressed Currie for details of the implications of each of the orders issued from the beginning of November. Was there not some discretion given to avoid loss of life at this late stage in the war? Currie described a meeting with Major-General Frederick Loomis, commanding officer of the Third Division, on the morning of 10 November when Loomis reported heavy machine-gun fire from all around Mons. He said that a similar meeting was held later that same day with Harry Burstall, commander of the Second Division. Currie instructed Loomis and Burstall to advance to Mons but to stay put if the firing remained heavy. 'What constituted heavy opposition would be left to the judgment of the man in charge of the company.'

To Regan, this was significant. Currie was agreeing that when an order was received, there was a certain element of discretion in carrying it out. Currie admitted, when pressed, 'If I felt that an order was wrong, that when it was issued the issuer of that order had not full knowledge of the situation, I would have a right to take it up with him, and it would be my duty to do so.' Regan tried to exploit this by suggesting that despite the orders he had received, Currie did have a choice about pushing forward against resistance at Mons. But though Currie admitted that everyone in receipt of an order had some discretion, he insisted that because any one person saw only a very narrow part of the front, that discretion was narrow and circumscribed. What appeared unreasonable to one person at one location might not be unreasonable when one had a grasp of the entire situation; therefore, orders were usually followed without hesitation.

But, Regan asked, could this discretion not apply when it was known that resistance would be met and, at the same time, that an armistice was imminent? What did Currie know about the armistice? Currie admitted that in early October he had heard that there was a reasonable hope that the war would end soon, and that he knew that the German envoys had actually crossed the Allied lines to discuss peace on the night of 8 and 9 November. He also admitted that he knew that Foch had given the Germans terms, with a forty-eight-hour deadline for acceptance, but he pointed out that pressure on the enemy was not to be relaxed during that period. He insisted that it was necessary to keep up the pressure and that by pushing the enemy in the vicinity of Mons the Canadians were only doing what was necessary to bring the war to an end. When Regan questioned the reasonableness of fighting on to the last minute, peace or no peace, Currie responded: 'If we had not continued pressing, I would have violated my orders. I would have acted unsoundly from a tactical point of view. I would have been traitorous to the troops on my right and left who were going on.'

Regan asked Currie to identify the specific points he took exception to in Preston's article. Currie was forthright and direct. 'I say generally the article is untrue, uncalled for, unfair and ungenerous. There is nothing to commend the article. There is no occasion for writing it ... It holds me up before the people of this country as a murderer – a man who didn't exercise due regard for the lives of the men under him. If that is true I do not deserve to be General of Reserve; I do not deserve to be Principal of McGill University. In fact I am charged with a crime which is punishable. But that article is not true.' Currie went on to repeat what he had said so often to his colleagues about the case. 'Not only is my own reputation, my own honour, my own integrity at stake, but also the reputation of every officer, and non-commissioned officer who commanded men in the Canadian Corps.'

Currie did make one startling admission. When asked whether he agreed with the statement 'There was much waste of life during the war, enormous loss of lives which should not have taken place,' he acknowledged the statement to be correct. He refused, however, to state where, in particular, there had been a waste of life: 'I am only admitting as a result of four years bitter experience that there was loss of life. Nobody regrets it more than I do.' But at Mons, he asserted, there was no waste of life – 'not a single Canadian killed on the last day of the war' – and even if Canadians had been killed, he contended, it could not be said that their deaths had been useless.

Regan examined Currie at length using war diary extracts, which, of course, did not minimize the amount of fighting that had taken place. He tried to get Currie to admit that an encircling movement would have saved lives and to agree that a push had been put on to capture Mons because of its symbolic value. Currie refused to concede that Mons had any particular significance, and maintained that it was nothing more than a place in the path of the objective set for the Corps. He did not deny that there had been fighting, but the fighting, he insisted, was less than bloody, and keeping up the pressure was well worth the price.

Regan read an extract from the records of the Third Division describing the capture of the village of Nimy on the northern outskirts of Mons 'in the face of heavy machine gun fire,' and another which stated that the advance on Mons 'met with stubborn resistance.' Currie did not know what casualties had been suffered, but he agreed that it was likely that there would have been some. He repeated that an advantage had been secured which justified casualties – namely, keeping up the pressure on the retreating army.

The examination could not be completed in one day, and had to be adjourned until the following Friday. In the meantime Regan announced that he would be bringing before the local judge, L.V. O'Connor, a motion that Currie be required to pay into court an amount that would provide security for the legal costs of the defence should Currie lose the case. This move was available to the defence under the rules of court because Currie was not an Ontario resident. The motion was well publicized. 'The action is putting us to no inconsiderable expense,' Regan told the press, 'and it is only prudent that we should take the measures the law allows to safeguard ourselves.'[11]

Preston was again in the news that week. The day before the continuation of Currie's examination, Preston addressed a Liberal association meeting in North Toronto in his old partisan style: 'You cannot make me believe that in a city of the wealth and intelligence of Toronto, the Liberals have no chance ever of a seat in one of the ridings.' To his usual political message Preston added some provocative remarks about the Currie case:

In the last few weeks I have been receiving so many letters from different parts of this country, from soldiers making statements, which, if published today, would, I think, shock this country to its very foundations ... I am not surprised the publicity about a certain legal action has brought letters to me in the last few weeks containing details of instances in the Great War by those who suffered, which I say in all seriousness that if they are proven no government can exist in this country that won't inquire into every phase of that war, no matter who is hurt. We may have to go to war again, not perhaps in my lifetime, but certainly in the lifetime of some who are here. But let us know what took place in this war. Let us know the facts, and let the facts be taken by us as a lesson to learn, and further, that no mushroom general be born, like Jonah's gourd, overnight, to send our men as they were sent in Flanders to their deaths.[12]

Currie's examination for discovery resumed on the evening of Friday, 16 March. The Toronto lawyers were late in arriving, and matters did not get underway until 9:00 PM. It was not until well past midnight that the examination was adjourned to the next day. Although the press was kept out again, one reporter somehow caught a glimpse of the proceedings and provided the following description:

On one side of the table sat Sir Arthur Currie, unperturbed smoking a briar, Colonel Wilfrid Bovey, his secretary, R.H. Parmenter, K.C. and D.H. Chisholm, K.C., his counsel. On the other side sat Frank Regan, pipe in mouth, T.F. Hall, K.C., F.W. Wilson, and W.T.R. Preston, the defendant. A lady stenographer sat at one end of the table facing a multicoloured map, measuring 10 feet by 5 feet, and showing the advances of the Canadian Corps from Arras to Mons and beyond. The features of this map were the main subjects of discussion during the four hours examination.

Mr Preston quietly rocked himself in a chair. Mr Wilson meandered up and down the room at times, puffing his pipe. The presiding officer now and again sought respite in an adjoining room, while Mr Regan and Sir Arthur Currie stood close to the map and with the stems of their pipes, pointed to the locations referred to in the questions and answers relative to the dates and kind of movements that were involved in the general advance on Mons ...

The battles ... were fought all over again, Sir Arthur explaining the various actions and movements in detail, and giving particulars as to casualties. Col. Bovey sat with his eyes glued to the map. He was a member of the Canadian headquarters staff during the whole of that period, and was keenly interested in the recounting of many well remembered incidents and details. There was little or no cross-firing between counsel, and the examination continued as quietly but with much less formality, as a class receiving instructions from a teacher on a blackboard. The tall figure of the principal of McGill University with the pedagogical horn-rimmed glasses was the instructor and Mr Regan the pupil, whose thirst for geographical knowledge and historical facts of the part the Canadians played in the war seemed to be insatiable, and who wanted that knowledge at first hand.[13]

The discovery continued the next day. Proceedings were delayed in the morning when Parmenter thought someone had stolen his brief-case, which contained many important documents pertaining to the case. To his embarrassment and to the amusement of the others, it was found in his hotel room, where he had absent-mindedly used it to prop open a window. The discovery resumed, and was interrupted in mid-afternoon so that Regan's motion for security for costs could be heard. The motion should have been a routine matter (and indeed, in the end, Judge O'Connor prevailed upon counsel to agree on the amount – $2,000 – that Currie should have to post). But the press was allowed to observe the proceedings, and Regan did not waste his opportunity. He proclaimed that as a result of what he had learned in the discovery process he was now convinced that the official records had been fal-sified. 'If it were not for the unfortunate fact that the records were made up to mislead and not to present the true state of affairs the mat-ter would be simple. We say the records have been deliberately falsified, and we propose to bring men here to say so, men from every unit en-gaged at the Battle of Mons.'[14]

Between seventy-five and one hundred witnesses, Regan contended, would have to be called to establish what had really happened. Regan 'proposed to put men in the box who would say their comrades were killed at quarter to eleven in the forenoon of November 11, 1918 and their bodies were seen lying in the gutters.'[15] Chisholm represented Currie on the motion and protested that Regan was merely playing to the press, but Judge O'Connor seemed unwilling or unable to control Regan. (O'Connor had been appointed to the bench only three months earlier; before that he had practiced law in Sam Hughes's town of Lindsay, and Currie's lawyers thought that he favoured the defendants.)

The charge that the records had been falsified and that as many as a hundred witnesses were going to be called must have been very un-settling for Currie. But even more unnerving were some of the ques-tions posed by Regan when the discovery resumed. The first day of Regan's examination a week earlier had gone more or less as expected. But Regan was not content to leave matters there. As Currie said later, 'He sought by his questions ... to fight the whole war all over again.'[16] Regan taxed Currie on his conduct at Passchendaele and at many other battles. This was just what Currie had feared. Despite Parmenter's ob-jections, the special examiner permitted Regan to ask many of these questions, and Currie was forced to answer.

Currie was shaken by Regan's attempt to probe into two very embar-rassing areas which, so far as Currie was concerned, had nothing to do with the case. Regan sought to explore what came to be known as the St Julien incident, a matter that had been referred to by Sir Sam Hughes in his House of Commons attack on Currie. It involved charges that Currie had left his post at a crucial point during the first gas attack. Currie insisted that he had acted properly; he had faced a very difficult situation and had had to leave his post to get reinforcements. Hughes had implied that Currie was a coward.

Even more worrying for Currie were Regan's attempts to pry into certain details of his pre-war business dealings. Regan's questions suggested that he had information showing that Currie had misappropiated regimental funds just before the war broke out. Currie was not ready for this, nor, it seems, had Parmenter previously heard Currie's version of these matters. Parmenter realized immediately how sensitive the issue was, and he strenuously objected to the questions. He counselled Currie not to answer.

Regan threatened to ask the court for an order to compel Currie to answer his questions. Parmenter feared that the motion would be brought before Judge O'Connor at Cobourg, 'the idea being that he is perhaps somewhat lax in his rulings.' The judge's conduct of the application for security for costs had not been reassuring. Parmenter feared that on the discovery motion Regan would be allowed 'to broadcast for the benefit of the press all sorts of irresponsible and irrelevant statements,' thus making the case as unpleasant as possible for Currie in the hope that he might back down and withdraw the libel suit.[17]

Parmenter planned to request that the motion to compel answers be heard in camera, something he acknowledged to be 'a very unusual course.' He recognized that Regan could mount a superficially attractive argument to justify requiring that the questions be answered. If Currie was claiming money to compensate him for damage to his reputation, should not the defendant be able to raise matters to show that his reputation was worth less than he suggested? Case law, however, had established that the defendant in a libel action can offer evidence of general bad character or reputation in order to reduce damages, but cannot give evidence of particular acts of misconduct. Moreover, the evidence adduced must be confined to the particular trait in the plaintiff's character attacked by the defaming statement. This rule is designed to prevent a libel trial from becoming an unrestricted witch-hunt into all aspects of the plaintiff's past. Even if there was evidence of financial misconduct on Currie's part, Parmenter argued, that was evidence only of a particular act of misconduct unrelated to the aspect of Currie's reputation attacked by the article.

To understand the impact of all of this upon Currie, some background is needed.[18] Currie's financial difficulties in 1914 have already been mentioned. When he assumed command of the Fiftieth Highland Regiment shortly before the outbreak of war, he did so with the assurance that the funds necessary to make the regiment a success would be provided, in part, through a government grant. The first instalment was to be used to pay a firm of Glasgow merchants for regimental uniforms. When the money arrived, however, Currie deposited it in his own account. Four days before Canada declared war, another cheque came from the Militia Department. It too was deposited in Currie's personal account. Currie was attempting to put his financial affairs in order before assuming the command he had been offered, and in the end he used over $10,000 of government money, which he was holding in trust for the regiment, to cover his personal debts and obligations. Major Cecil Roberts, who succeeded Currie as commanding officer of the Fiftieth Regiment, immediately became aware of the shortage in the regimental accounts and demanded repayment. The matter festered for three years, but Currie was in no position to repay the money.

The defalcation came to the attention of the Militia Council and the overseas minister, Sir George Perley, shortly after Currie's appointment as Corps commander. It caused considerable consternation. Because of Currie's high rank, the situation was politically sensitive. The Militia Council was advised bluntly that 'Sir Arthur Currie, instead of using the last advance of $10,883.34 for the purpose of paying the clothing bills, deposited this money in the bank to his own credit, and used it to pay his personal obligations.'[19] Perley wired the prime minister that it 'would be disastrous from every point of view if the matter became public.'[20] Perley, himself a wealthy man, offered to put up half the money if his cabinet colleague Edward Kemp would do the same. Kemp replied that the Militia Department would pay the Glasgow firm and recover from Currie after the war. A draft order in council was prepared to authorize this irregular expenditure, but it was never passed. In the end, Currie paid up when two friends serving with him in France, Victor Odlum and David Watson, lent him the money. Currie repaid his comrades in regular instalments over the next two years.

Although the debt had been discharged, the fear that the matter would become public haunted Currie for years. When it was raised by Regan during the examination for discovery, Currie was particularly upset. Could it be that this episode, which he thought had been successfully concealed and long forgotten, would stand in the way of his attempt to clear his reputation once and for all?

Currie explained the incident in a letter written to Parmenter after the examination for discovery:

When war broke out I was the officer commanding the 50th Regiment Gordon Highlanders of Canada. As Officer Commanding I was responsible to the Regiment and to Government for the funds of the Regiment. I left Victoria in August, 1914 with the responsibility of accounting for some $8,300. I arranged with two of my friends – Mr. Sam Matson of the Victoria Colonist and Mr. Arthur Lineham, a prominent financial agent – to put up this amount should it be called for by the Regiment or by the Government. I left Victoria knowing that the matter would be cared for, if any demand was made. As a matter of fact no demand was made by the Regiment or by the Government, and in June, 1917, as soon as I was personally financially able, I handed over the money to the then Treasurer of the regimental funds. This was a civil responsibility long since discharged and should not be made an issue in this trial.[21]

Currie may have been correct in saying that the incident had little to do with the trial, but his version of the affair was misleading. Currie seems to have been concerned about what the records in Victoria would show. He made a discreet inquiry and was advised by telegram: 'Fire seventeen destroyed all records. Accountant – Aud. General Ottawa might be able to supply.'[22] There is nothing in his papers to indicate that he pursued the matter; no doubt he wished to avoid arousing any further interest in the incident.

Another aspect of Currie's pre-war business dealings was raised by Regan. He had had a serious falling out with his partner, R.A. Power, in 1914 over responsibility for partnership debts. After Currie left for Valcartier, Power became convinced that he had been cheated. Currie wrote to Parmenter, 'There was nothing too bad for [Power] to say about me during the war. It became an obsession with him. I treated him most generously and far beyond any legal responsibility. Surely my business relations with Mr. Power have no bearing upon a case in which I am suing the Port Hope *Guide* for writing a libelous article about Mons.'[23]

Currie was confident that he could meet any challenge from Power, but he would need to produce an agreement the two had signed just after the war to show that Power's claim had been fully paid. A friend, Todd Aikman, had kept Currie's copy of the document in Victoria during the war so that he could 'use it if Power still continued his slanderous statements.'[24] Aikman had since died, however, and no one in Victoria could find the agreement.

Currie was unnerved by the discovery. His worst fear was that his foes would use the trial to launch a general attack against his record and reputation, and it now seemed clear that Regan and Preston were prepared to do just that. 'I think the purpose of the whole thing is to go muck-raking, to injure me personally as much as possible, and incidentally to throw discredit on all who are at all proud of their records in the Corps.'[25]

Currie became convinced that Power and Garnet Hughes were plotting against him, prompting the defendants from behind the scenes. The 'smear campaign' of the defence 'only goes to show how active one's enemies are.'[26] If mud was to be thrown at him, he would have some to hurl back. Garnet Hughes, he recalled, had been arrested for drunk driving in England a few years after the war, and he asked Colonel Ross Hayter in London to get details.[27] Hayter replied that Hughes had been convicted in June 1922, and had been fined two pounds. How Currie expected to use this information is not clear. Perhaps he thought that Hughes would come to the trial to testify against him.

Some days he regretted having brought the action at all. At times his reaction to the experience of being examined bordered on paranoia. In a letter to Parmenter, Currie wrote: 'The thought comes continually to me that there is something more behind this than I know of. They knew I was touchy about Mons so they registered on that sore spot. Because I have been hurt so much in the past over the repetition of these lies I took this action, and there is no doubt that there are people who are going to make it the occasion of fastening upon me as much mud as they can.'[28] To an old military comrade he confided: 'This libel suit of mine ... I do not mind admitting ... is giving me a great deal of worry ... I sometimes think this article about Mons was simply an excuse. They knew I was very tender on that spot and so they goaded me into taking an action and now they are going to try to bring in everything that they can which can injure whatever reputation I have got.'[29]

An old friend mentioned to Currie that he had seen Garnet Hughes, who 'seemed to be engaged on some mysterious mission.' Currie was certain that Hughes was behind some of the mud that was being thrown. 'I think I can guess what Garnet's main activity is at the present time. The threat he made to me in London when I refused to take him as GOC 1st Division is being carried out at the present time.'[30]

Currie was so confident of his own version of what had happened on the last day of the war that he could see no ground on which the defendants could stand. Why were they willing to let the matter go to trial? 'The fact that they are makes me believe that there may be more behind this thing than appears on the surface. It may be that Preston is but firing the balls that others have made. In my examination for discovery he sought by his questions not only to fight the whole war all over again, but to bring in everything he ever knew or heard which might in any way reflect on me. Someone had taken the trouble to coach him very well.'[31]

Parmenter tried to reassure Currie. The defendants were entitled to give evidence of bad character or reputation in mitigation of damages, but such evidence had to relate to the particular trait attacked by the libel. A plaintiff suing in defamation need not show uniform propriety of conduct throughout his entire life. If Regan tried to pry further into Currie's financial dealings by asking the court to order Currie to answer questions to which objections had been taken, Parmenter was confident he would be unsuccessful.

Currie was determined to go ahead with the trial despite the risks, which seemed to be ever-increasing. The defendants threatened to bring in 'the mothers of boys who were killed on Sunday, November 10th to give evidence,'[32] and Regan claimed he had a hundred disgruntled soldiers ready to testify to the slaughter at Mons. Currie saw these tactics as blackmail, and refused to be intimidated.

Preston's examination for discovery took place on 5 April, the day after the case was formally entered for trial at the spring assizes. Currie's Cobourg solicitors, Duncan Chisholm and Roy Willmott, conducted the examination. It seems surprising that Parmenter did not go to Cobourg to take the measure of Preston. Tilley, of course, was still in England. No transcript of the examination has been traced, and it was not mentioned at the trial. The press was kept out, but it appears that the examination took less than half a day. Preston was in a confident mood; he joked with reporters as he entered, and showed them a review of his recently published book. He carried under his arm a copy of a book on the war which he had just received from England.

Chisholm was instructed by Parmenter to question Preston in four areas. First, he was to explore the defendants' reliance upon the records of the House of Commons and information from ex-soldiers. Preston was to be asked to specify the particular debates in the House of Commons that he relied upon, as well as any information from ex-soldiers that would be used to support the defence of justification. Second, Chisholm was to ask for details about the numbers and names of soldiers alleged to have been killed or wounded on 11 November. Third, he was to find out when the defendants had acquired the information on which their article was based. Fourth, he was to ask for disclosure of the contents of letters alleged to have been received from ex-soldiers.

Parmenter realized that he was telling Chisholm to find out more than the plaintiff was legally entitled to ask. In the case of a libel published in a newspaper, the plaintiff is not entitled to obtain the newspaper's sources of information; but Chisholm was to try anyway.[33]

Although Preston had boasted of the availability of hundreds of witnesses before the discovery, it seems that at the discovery itself he could name only two men, Arthur Fisher and William Woodlock, as his sources of information. Both were residents of Port Hope and both were officials of the local branch of the Canadian Legion. Preston refused to be pinned down when he was asked whether the words 'commander-in-chief' had been intended to refer to Currie; he replied that the words referred to the person who had issued the order for the attack on Mons, whoever he might be.

Frederick Wilson, the owner and publisher of the Port Hope *Evening Guide,* was not examined until Thursday, 12 April, the eve of the trial. Chisholm conducted the examination, though Parmenter was in attendance, as were Regan, Campbell, and Hall, who represented the defendants. Wilson was nervous and evasive. He admitted that Preston had written the article, but he himself had suggested it when he read about the commemoration of Mons. Like Preston, he refused to admit that the article had been aimed at Currie or even that a reader of the article would assume that Currie was its target. He was unable to name any source other than Arthur Fisher, the secretary of the Veterans' Association in Port Hope, and he said that he had made no special inquiries into the Mons incident. He relied upon casual conversations with returned men and upon the Hansard report of Sir Sam Hughes's remarks in the House of Commons. The examination could not have taken more than two hours in total.

Little had been learned of the defendants' case from the examination for discovery, but Currie and his advisers had compiled a list of possible witnesses, including those subpoenaed by the defence. Inquiries were made to former officers living in the Cobourg area about these men and about others who might testify.

A few days before the trial was to begin, Regan decided that he would try to force Currie to answer the questions he had asked about his prewar financial dealings and about the allegation that he had abandoned his post at a crucial time during the first gas attack at St Julien, near Ypres.[34] He filed a formal notice with the court requesting an order that would compel Currie to answer his questions. The specifics of Regan's questions became publicly known as soon as he filed his motion.[35]

Currie suspected that Regan was more interested in publicity than in getting an answer. The motion was argued on 12 April, the day of Wilson's examination. Judge L.V. O'Connor again presided. Parmenter represented Currie. The proceedings were closely watched by reporters, who were eager for a story and frustrated by the fact that the examination for discovery was held in camera. Regan saw to it that they were not disappointed. He read at length from the transcript, and when Parmenter objected that he was simply playing to the press, Regan chided: 'Don't be afraid of publicity. You will get plenty of it at the trial.' Regan also read Hughes's House of Commons speeches and referred to other parts of the examination where Currie had been advised not to answer. He implied that Currie had something to hide, and wondered aloud whether he would even testify at the trial. Parmenter exclaimed angrily that the suggestion was ludicrous. Regan's legal argument was that the questions he sought answers to would shed light on the true nature of Currie's reputation and character. 'When a man is suing for damages to character and reputation, the jury have a right to know what was this character that is claimed to have been damaged.'

Parmenter was worried about how Judge O'Connor might rule, particularly as the judge seemed unwilling to control Regan's antics. Parmenter suggested that if His Honour had any doubts as to the merits of the motion, he might consider leaving the matter to be resolved by the trial judge, Mr Justice Hugh Rose. Parmenter went on to argue that Regan's questions were not proper. The defence was entitled to give evidence of general reputation, but could not go into specific instances not covered by the alleged libel. He contended that Regan was merely trying to embarrass and inconvenience General Currie, since the questions bore no relation to the crux of the article – that Currie had sent men to the slaughter on the last day of the war for no reason but self-glorification.

Judge O'Connor gave his ruling immediately, and, as Parmenter had feared, it was in Regan's favour. In the judge's view, the questions were relevant to Currie's promotion to Corps commander, a fact specifically pleaded in the statement of claim. The judge also found that the questions might shed light on Currie's reputation and were therefore relevant to the amount of damages he might recover. In addition, the article referred to unnecessary waste of life throughout the war and to the government's failure to recognize Currie's contribution after the war; it was possible, the judge said, that the questions were relevant to these matters as well.

These were not very convincing reasons, but to appeal Judge O'Connor's ruling would only delay matters and perhaps draw more attention to the very aspect of the case that Currie wanted to avoid. On Saturday, 14 April, Currie duly attended before the local registrar. Regan was entitled to ask questions related to the two specific ones Currie had been ordered to answer, and the examination lasted almost the whole afternoon. Unfortunately, we do not know how Currie dealt with these awkward questions. Part of the discovery transcript was introduced into evidence at trial, and the description of the examination given here is based upon those extracts. However, no copy of the full transcript of the examination has been found. It is likely that all copies of the transcript have been lost or destroyed. Regan and Preston would have had copies, but these have not been traced. The court file would have contained one, but with a disappointing disregard for history, all of the court records in Cobourg were destroyed in the late 1940s. We can surmise, however, that Regan scored some points. After Currie's death, when his records and papers were being assembled for his biographer, Parmenter suggested that all copies of the examination transcript be destroyed.[36] Allan Magee agreed that 'the examination for discovery might prove a dangerous document in the future,'[37] and that Parmenter's recommendation should be carried out. It seems likely that this is what happened.

In any case, discovery was extremely unsettling for Currie. He began to realize that he was in for a long, tough fight, and that the battle was one he might well lose.

7

The Trial Begins

Mr Justice Hugh Rose was assigned to the Cobourg assizes in the spring of 1928.[1] Rose was almost exactly the same age as Tilley, and the two knew each other well. Both had been called to the bar in 1894. Rose, the son of a High Court judge, had practised in Toronto with the firm of Beatty, Blackstock, Fasken and Chadwick, and had been appointed to the High Court division of the Supreme Court of Ontario in 1916. He was a careful and diligent judge, well liked by the bar and by his fellow judges. Although on occasion he seemed austere and aloof, Rose was known for his polite and gracious courtroom manner and for the interest he took in the younger lawyers who appeared before him.

Hugh Rose never married, but lived with two maiden sisters. When he went on circuit, his sisters always packed his bags and made sure he took along a tin of their home-made cookies. The sheriff was instructed to serve two cookies each afternoon with his lordship's tea. (The cookies must have run out during the Currie trial, which went on much longer than expected.) Rose loved golf and was a long-time member of the Toronto Golf Club. He was interested in the affairs of the University of Toronto and served for several years on its board of governors.

Justice Rose refused to read the papers the lawyers had filed for a case before he heard arguments: he wished to come to the issues with a completely open mind. When an authority was cited, he often asked to have the volume handed to him so that he could read the case then and there. The meticulous attention he gave to his work was particularly evident in his oral judgments. He was known to pause for several minutes at a stretch, formulating his thoughts and striving to find the phrase most apt for the occasion. Perhaps his best-remembered judgment is the one he gave in the *Tiny Township* case[2] on the constitutional aspects of separate school funding. Tilley had argued the case, and many others, before Rose; Frank Regan had seldom appeared before him. Rose was not well known to the public, and he refused to grant an interview shortly before the trial: 'I don't believe in publicity and that sort of stuff.'[3]

The spring assizes for Northumberland and Durham were to begin on Monday, 16 April 1928, in the afternoon.[4] The weather in Cobourg was unusually warm. The case was tried in Victoria Hall, the town's architectural jewel, which had been completed in the 1860s when Cobourg rivalled York as a port and commercial centre. Victoria Hall still houses a council chamber, a concert hall, and a splendid courtroom modelled after the Old Bailey.

The town was invaded by journalists and soldiers. Currie and his former comrades stayed at the Dunham Hotel, where many a war story would be told. Frank Regan stayed at the home of his friend and co-counsel, Thomas F. Hall, KC, throughout the trial. (Mrs Hall, a teetotaller, was displeased by Regan's drinking.)

After lunch the courtroom was filled to capacity. Journalists and prospective jurors occupied most of the space, and many Cobourg residents who had hoped to get a seat were disappointed. Currie, impassive, wearing a dark blue suit and a starched blue shirt and collar, entered the courtroom a few minutes before two o'clock with Tilley, Parmenter, and Chisholm. Preston came in alone, carrying a heavy load of books. He had announced that morning that while he did not intend to cross-examine all of the witnesses, he would question some 'just to let them know that I am there.' Wilson and Regan entered a few minutes later. Wilson's two Cobourg lawyers, Hall and W.A.F. Campbell, joined Regan at the defence counsel table.

That morning, the newspapers reported the victory of the New York Rangers over the Montreal Maroons in the fifth and deciding game of the Stanley Cup final. The sports pages also described the early phase of the major league baseball season, and as the trial unfolded over the next two weeks there was speculation that if Babe Ruth continued to hit home runs at his current pace, he would exceed his record of sixty set the year before. For its first week, the Currie case had to compete on the front pages with accounts of the first east-west flight across the Atlantic by a heavier-than-air machine. The feat was accomplished by a German crew and plane, the *Bremen*, which had not quite made it to New York but had landed on desolate Greenely Island in the Strait of Belle Isle between Newfoundland and Labrador.

Special arrangements had been made to accommodate the reporters who invaded Cobourg to cover the trial. On the upper floor of the courthouse specially installed telegraph equipment began to clatter as soon as the proceedings started, and for the next three weeks sent out detailed accounts of the trial to newspapers in Canada, the United States, and elsewhere. Most of the journalists were themselves ex-servicemen. The court reporter, Robert Dickson, transcribed every word of the proceedings with special interest. He had served as a sapper with the Eighth Battalion, Canadian Engineers, and had finished the war just outside Mons.[5]

The opening of assizes was always an occasion in Ontario county towns, and this time the whole country was watching. Sheriff J.D. Nesbitt, in cocked hat and carrying an unsheathed sword, supervised the seating arrangements. Shortly before two o'clock, still with sword in hand, he ushered Justice Rose to the bench. The crier called the proceedings to order. Sheriff Nesbitt followed the custom of presenting His Lordship with white gloves to signify that there were no criminal cases to be tried.

Two cases had precedence over Currie's on the civil list. In the first, a routine motor vehicle case, Currie's two solicitors, Chisholm and Willmott, acted for the plaintiff and the defendant respectively. But that case was put over, and the other had been settled on the courthouse steps. The case of *Currie* v. *Preston and Wilson* was called at 2:30 PM.

The first task was to select the jury. The special jury list contained sixteen names. Tilley had to remind Justice Rose of the procedure for selecting the twelve jurors who would try the case.[6] From the original list of forty names selected by lot from the grand jury roll, each party had been entitled to strike twelve. Sixteen remained, and from them twelve were drawn by lot at the trial, with no right of challenge. The last man selected, Ernest Cyer, a farmer from Clark Township, asked to be excused because of his wife's illness. A thirteenth was chosen and the jury was sworn. The final selection included five farmers, two

'yeomen,' a miller, a millhand, an 'agent,' a gardener, and a 'gentleman.'
Two members of the jury were veterans.

Tilley opened his case. He was entitled to make an opening statement, and before calling his evidence he explained to the jury how the
case would proceed. It was admitted that the offending article had been
published; the plaintiff had only to establish that it was defamatory.
The defendants had pleaded justification and it was for them to prove
the truth of what they had written. Tilley then read the entire article
aloud without interruption. There could be no doubt, Tilley contended,
that the defendants had stated that Currie himself gave the order to
attack, intending to glorify himself at the cost of needless human
slaughter. It was a serious charge, one made worse by the refusal of
the defendants to retract.

Tilley's address was brief, but he made clear the two points that were
to be the foundation of his case. First, he urged the jury to remember
that the defendants had to establish the truth of the precise allegation
made against Currie – that he had personally ordered an attack with
disregard for the lives of his men in order to glorify himself after he
knew that the armistice was about to take effect. Second, Tilley asked
the jury to remember that the Canadian Corps and its commander
were but part of a vast plan of allied operations, a cog in a great
machine, and that Currie himself had orders to follow: 'These operations are not carried out at random, [they] are not carried out by individual decisions. These decisions are all embodied in a plan of operation that is designed and set out by those having supreme control, and
it is for others to see that those orders are carried out. The Canadian
Corps that was in France in 1918 was not over there on a jaunt of its
own or acting on its own initiative.'

The plaintiff's evidence was then called. It was presented in less than
two hours, and much of that time was occupied by Regan's cross-
examination. Tilley's strategy was simple. At this stage of the trial he
needed to prove only that the words used by the defendants were defamatory of Currie. On the crucial issue of the truth of Wilson and
Preston's account of the Mons attack, it was to Currie's advantage to
reserve his case until he heard his opponents' evidence and knew
exactly what points he had to meet. At this point, Tilley had to prove
only the bare essentials of Currie's case. The more contentious parts
of the plaintiff's evidence could be left for reply.

Tilley introduced the newspaper article as an exhibit and called as
a witness Ralph Hodgson, the registrar of deeds for the east riding of
the County of Durham. Hodgson had been a sergeant-major during the

war; he was one of the few non-commissioned officers who would testify on Currie's behalf. The article did not name Currie directly, and
Hodgson was called to prove that the ordinary reader would infer that
its sting was directed at Currie. Hodgson swore that when he read the
article, he took 'commander-in-chief' and 'headquarters staff' to mean
General Currie and none other.

In cross-examination, Regan tried to turn Hodgson to his own advantage. Hodgson admitted that Currie was known as 'Corps commander'
rather than 'commander-in-chief,' but he refused to admit that this
left any doubt that Currie was the target of the article. Despite Regan's
persistent barrage of questions, Hodgson would not budge. The line of
questioning was surely a hopeless ploy on Regan's part, and Hodgson
stepped down from the witness stand smiling. There could be no serious doubt that the article was directed at Currie: everyone knew that
the defendants had come to the trial to prove that Currie had mis-
behaved.

The plaintiff's case was completed by reading into evidence extracts
from the examination for discovery of each of the defendants to establish their identity and their relationship to the newspaper and the article
in question. Included was a portion of the discovery in which Preston
himself actually used the phrase 'commander-in-chief of the Canadian
army' in reference to General Currie.

Tilley then announced that the plaintiff's case was closed. Regan
immediately rose from his chair to move for a nonsuit – a determination by the judge that the plaintiff had failed to establish even those
basic points necessary to require an answer from the defence. Hodgson
had been asked whether he believed what the article said of Currie,
and he had replied that he did not. Regan contended that his client
was entitled to judgment then and there: '[The plaintiff's] own witness
said that his opinion was not altered ... by reading it.' To have the judge
rule at this stage, however, Regan would have had to agree not to call
any evidence of his own, a very risky ploy, and one he did not seriously
contemplate. After being advised that evidence would certainly be
called by the defence, Justice Rose reserved his ruling until the end of
the case.

Regan called to the stand Lamont Hagey, the librarian of the Toronto
Globe, and attempted to introduce a copy of the *Globe* article of 13
June 1927, which described the unveiling of the commemorative
plaque at Mons. This was the article that had prompted Wilson and

Preston to write their own piece. Tilley questioned the admissibility of the *Globe* article. Regan contended that the Port Hope *Evening Guide* article mentioned cable dispatches describing the ceremony. He wanted to prove that these dispatches had actually been sent and received. 'I don't want to be caught. I thought I would prove our case up to the hilt if we could.' Ostensibly, his purpose was to prove the truth of one fact in the *Guide* article. But the *Globe* article mentioned more than the existence of a Canadian Press cable; it referred to 'the men of the Canadian Corps who fell in the fighting for the town' and emphasized Canadian valour and the cost in lives. There can be little doubt that Regan's real purpose was to bring before the jury the *Globe* description of the taking of Mons. But that description was a second- or third-hand account, and was inadmissible hearsay. Tilley finessed Regan by withdrawing any objection to the witness's stating that a cable actually had been received. 'The contents of the paper I quite object to. I do not want to block my friend, but the whole point [he is trying to prove] is that cable dispatches were received that morning.' This clever strategy allowed Tilley to keep potentially harmful material from the jury and at the same time appear to be making a generous concession by yielding on a point of evidence. The *Globe*'s account of the ceremony at Mons was, for the time being at least, excluded.

The first veteran to be called by the defence was Harold Fox, a Port Hope resident who had served with the Canadian Corps as a signaller in the Twenty-first Batallion, Fourth Canadian Brigade, Second Division. He began his story by describing how he had recovered from wounds sustained at Amiens, a crucial battle in the great offensive of the last hundred days of the war. On 9 November 1918 Fox had rejoined his unit about ten miles from Mons. As Fox told his story, the centre of attention began to shift away from the lawyers and the dry legal bones of the case. Here was the first ordinary soldier who would describe in the formal, unfamiliar, and often uncomfortable forum of the courtroom days of suffering, death, and valour. The audience listened intently.

Fox's unit had advanced to within a mile of Mons on 10 November 1918. One man, a Private L. Sullivan, was killed, and some others were wounded. Fox's unit dug in, and the advance was carried forward by another unit, the Fifth Brigade. A message regarding the armistice came at about 7:30 on the morning of 11 November. Regan continued his questioning:

Q Did you see any dead in Mons or on your way into Mons?
A We passed – Oh, I should say, half a dozen or more Third Division men.
Q Well, what were they, alive or –
A Dead.
Q And where were they?
A Well, just where they fell, where they had been killed the night before.
Q Near what place?
A Well, some of them were on the outskirts of Mons, some of them were prac-
tically right in Mons.

Regan noted that General Currie had sworn on discovery that, so far
as he knew, no Canadians had been killed on the last day of the war.

Q Do you differ with Sir Arthur Currie?
A Well, these men would not be brought into Mons and left lying there. If they
were taken into Mons they would be buried [on] the day.
Q What do you mean by that?
A Well, if they were killed on the 10th they would not be taken into Mons
and left lying on the ground where I saw them.

Tilley pressed this point in cross-examination:

Q Will you tell me why you suggest that these men could not have been killed
before 10 o'clock on the night of the 10th?
A Germany occupied that territory.
Q How do you know?
A Well, we could see the flashes of the shells coming.
Q From Mons?
A From Mons ... From the outskirts of the city facing our lines.

According to Fox, both sides fired until eleven o'clock on 11
November. There were even several shots fired after the armistice: 'Just
a question of who was going to have the last word.'

Tilley tried to minimize what Fox knew about the fighting on 11
November: 'At any rate, you stopped on the 10th and took no more
part in it?' Fox had to admit that was the case.

Edwin Joyce was called next. He was a local farmer, a frail, elderly man
who spoke in a shaky voice. Regan began his examination:

Q You had a boy at the front?

A Yes, I had. He got killed.

Q Have you got his picture here? May I see it? [Joyce handed Regan a photo-graph.] You say that is the picture of your son?

A That is my son, yes.

Q What is his name?

A Frederick.

Q Any initial?

A Frederick we called him; that is his name. We always call him Fred.

The photograph was poignant but irrelevant, and it was undoubtedly with these two factors in mind that Tilley objected. Regan left the photograph and continued his questioning. 'When was he killed?' 'He was killed at 11:30 on the 11th of the month,' Joyce replied. Again Tilley objected. The witness had no firsthand knowledge of the time of his son's death, and his evidence would be hearsay.

Regan again returned to the photograph. 'I thought perhaps the jury might care to look at the picture of one man that we were endeavouring to prove was killed.' Justice Rose did not allow the photograph to be shown to the jury. Regan then produced the letter Joyce had received from a chaplain advising him of his son's death. Again, such evidence was inadmissible, but in front of the jury Tilley's position was delicate. 'Would you let me see it? he asked. The letter, one of hundreds like it written by the chaplain delivering the heartbreaking news to the fathers and mothers of those who fell, was simple and eloquent:

Dear Mr. Joyce,

It is my very sad duty to write you of the death of your son, Cplr. F.J. Joyce, no. 58985, 20th Canadian Battalion. He was severely wounded in the chest and jaw, and brought to this casualty clearing station yesterday and died shortly after he was brought in, and was buried by me today at 2:30 p.m. in the Auberchichort British Cemetery, grave 8, plot 1, row c.

Should you want a picture of the grave, write to the Director of the Graves Registration and Enquiries, War Office, Winchester House, St. James Square, London, sw.

A plate with his name, rank, battalion and number on it will be placed at the head of his grave on a cross.

His personal effects will be sent to the base and thence to you.

I feel most keenly for you in your affliction. It was so sad that he was killed the last day of the fighting. He was quite conscious when he was brought in and I talked and prayed with him. Of course, it was with difficulty that he spoke as he was wounded in the jaw. However, I could understand perfectly.

He was a noble fellow and I trust also a devout Christian. I believe you will meet him in heaven when this strange life is over.

With deepest sympathy to you and all his relatives, I am,

Most sincerely yours,

(signed) Andrew D. Reid
Pres. Canadian
Chaplain.

Tilley certainly did not want the jury to see the letter: better to admit the cold fact. 'I do not see that the letter adds a thing. I do not want to embarrass my learned friend, and particularly I do not want to embarrass the young man's father about giving evidence as to his death ... It says just as the father says, that he was killed on the last day ... I am willing to accept the father's statement on that, but this does not add a thing to it.'

Tilley had made a slip, however. Although Currie had said all along that not a single Canadian was killed on the last day of the war, he and Tilley had discovered shortly before the trial that a man named Price had been killed on 11 November 1918. Tilley had confused 'Joyce' and 'Price' and thought that the witness's son was the man Currie was now prepared to admit had been killed. He should not have made the admission. Colonel Bovey, sitting at the counsel table with Currie and Parmenter, leaned forward to correct him. 'Just a minute, please,' Tilley said. 'I am told that I am confusing the name with another name.' Still further consultation at the counsel table produced a generous concession. 'I want to facilitate my friend as much as I can about it, particularly as I spoke without proper instructions before. In this case I am quite willing that my friend should put in the letter.' The letter was read and entered as an exhibit.

The task of cross-examining the father about the loss of his son was a delicate one. Tilley handled it gently but effectively. 'You have to rely, of course, on information from others as to when your son died?' 'Well, sure,' Joyce answered. 'Then you do not know how far back the receiving station that is referred to in this letter ... was from Mons at all.' 'No. He was shot by the Germans, that is all I know,' came the reply.

Further details of Joyce's death were provided by the next witness, Corporal Joseph Smith, who had enisted with Joyce at Toronto. Smith had seen his friend alive and well 'on the right of Mons, at 3:30 or 4:00 AM. on the 11th.' Smith and Joyce were both carrying rations to the front. 'There were lots of machine gun bullets flying around that morning. I know that, because we was all ducking for them.' He next saw Joyce between 10:00 and 11:00 AM on 11 November at the dressing-station, but he could not say exactly where it was or where he and Joyce had been. 'When you are advancing like that, day in and day out you haven't got any idea how far you are from any place; you simply go, and that is all. I just can't tell you the distance.'

Once again Regan sought to put before the jury the stark horror of the war.

Q Could you give us any description of the injuries sustained by Joyce, how he was wounded?
A Well, he had ... it was thirteen machine gun bullets Joyce had in him.

Tilley objected, but only mildly. 'I submit this is not material, unless it is going to show how he was hurt.' Justice Rose came to Regan's rescue: 'Unless it bears upon the question as to how long he may have lived after being wounded.' Regan accepted: 'That is the point I had in mind.' He then asked for further description.

Q How many machine gun bullets did you say?
A Thirteen.
Q Thirteen machine gun bullets?
A He was hit in the face and mostly from the stomach up, the chest.
Q Did you speak with him?
A Yes, I asked him how he was feeling. He said 'No good,' he was dying.
Q What condition was he in, did you say?
A He was dying then; the man was sinking fast, you might say.

The hearsay evidence rule confounded the defence throughout the trial. The truth of an assertion must be established by firsthand evidence. A witness is permitted to testify only about what he or she actually saw or heard, and cannot relate to the court the observations or perceptions of others. Much of the information that Wilson, Preston, and Regan had been able to gather was second-hand.

One witness described the funeral held at Mons on 13 November 1918, and produced a photograph showing several coffins and an impressive assembly of civic and Canadian military officials. 'Can you tell us when these men were killed who were being buried in that picture?' Regan asked. 'Well, only just from what I heard from the officers and the rest of the troops,' the witness replied.

Tilley objected to such obvious hearsay. Regan fought back; it was unlikely that Justice Rose would admit the evidence, but perhaps the jury would sympathize and accept the facts implied by his question. 'My Lord, we are in this position: as fighting goes on, and part of a unit ... may be engaged in the fighting, the other part might remain outside of Mons. A part will go in and ... one or two men will be killed, and when it rejoins the other part of the company the men will talk about what has happened during the fighting, and they will be told so and so was killed ... at a certain place.' But Justice Rose was not interested in learning about Regan's difficulties: 'Tender your questions and I can rule on them.'

The next question produced a ruling that was hardly unexpected. 'What was the common talk among the soldiers and the officers and the population of Mons with reference to the time these men were killed who were in the funeral?' In disgust, Justice Rose replied, 'Oh, no, no, no!'

Regan could not resist adding, for the jury's benefit, 'Well, I was under the impression that when a thing was notorious, as that would be over there, that I might be able to give evidence of it. However, I won't press that.'

It was difficult for most non-lawyers to understand why this sort of evidence should be rejected. The Toronto *Telegram*'s headline read '"COMMON TALK" NOT EVIDENCE IN LIBEL CASE.'[7] If something was 'common talk,' could it be wrong for a newspaper to publish it? The Toronto *Globe* received letters to the editor (which it did not publish for fear of being cited for contempt) complaining that the defendants were being unfairly hampered in the presentation of their case.[8] As a matter of law, however, the ruling excluding the evidence was undoubtedly correct.

Regan asked another witness what he had learned from an acquaintance from another unit about casualties during the night of 10–11 November. Tilley jumped in quickly: the witness could testify as to what he had done but not as to what he had heard. Regan pressed for an answer, and before Justice Rose had ruled, the witness said: 'I heard then that "A" Company had suffered casualties.' Ignoring Tilley's objection, Regan persisted: 'What do you mean by casualties?' 'Dead, killed,' came the answer. 'How many?' 'As far as I know, six,' the witness said. Tilley repeated his objection, and Justice Rose ruled that the evidence was improper.

Regan attempted to extricate himself, again perhaps with less hope of persuading the judge than explaining to the jury the difficulties posed by the rule against hearsay. 'We must just as well face the difficulty first as last. I would like to make the position of the defendants clear on this. If you will notice the article, you will see that it is based upon what the defendants heard – "it was common talk among the soldiers that while the staff were congratulating themselves" – and so on.' Regan argued that the defendants had to rely on statements made in the House of Commons and elsewhere. 'They, relying, I say, upon these facts that they heard, and upon others as well, write this article. Now, I submit that they are entitled to produce in evidence what they heard.'

Tilley ridiculed Regan's position. 'What my friend seems to think he is entitled to do is this: say in his newspaper that he is repeating gossip, and then produce the gossip as proof of the fact. Now, that, I submit, cannot be done.'

Justice Rose agreed that the evidence was not acceptable proof that there had been casualties. Was it not, however, admissible and relevant to the issue of damages? Even if the defendants could not be entirely excused because the article merely repeated gossip, should they not be treated more leniently if the libel was current?

Tilley was ready for this point. The defendants, he observed, had been given prior notice of Currie's action, and they could have published a retraction. The Libel and Slander Act provided that if the newspaper retracted, damages would be reduced. Wilson and Preston had refused to retract; instead, they came to trial pleading that they had told the truth. Tilley argued that they should not be allowed to introduce questionable evidence under the guise of mitigating the damages, since they had refused to retract. 'One of the gravest things a newspaper can do, is to publish all the hearsay without verifying it and knowing that it is true. It would open the door to every sort of abuse ... In fact, I submit it would aggravate the damages if it had any effect at all ...'

Regan tried to rephrase his question. 'What did you learn about the losses of "A" Company?' Justice Rose would not allow the witness to answer until he explained how he had learned of the losses. 'In the ordinary way that all losses were heard of,' the witness said, 'just casually, that so many had been killed.' That statement showed that the evidence was obvious hearsay and could not be admitted. Still, would it not affect the jury? There could be little doubt about what the witness had to say from the wrangling that had gone on.

Several times Regan attempted to elicit evidence that he must have known was inadmissible, hoping that the jury would take it into account despite its formal rejection by Mr Justice Rose. It is considered improper for counsel to present information to the jury when the supporting evidence is inadmissible. Regan clearly thought that it was his duty to help his client in any way that he could. He refused throughout the trial to allow the technical rules of evidence to stand in the way of the fullest possible defence, particularly since his client's modest means may have limited the pre-trial preparation. But a lawyer must observe the rules of the game, and there is little doubt that by telling the jury about evidence he knew to be inadmissible Regan was violating a basic rule of legal ethics.[9]

Regan questioned George Wass, who had walked into Mons on the evening of 11 November 1918. 'Did you see any poster there?' Regan asked, pulling out a copy of the burgomaster's proclamation that had been hastily issued on the morning of 11 November after the liberation of the city. It stated, in bold letters, 'The 3rd Canadian Division, at the cost of heavy sacrifices, penetrated the city at 3:00 o'clock this morning, thus avenging, with brilliant success, the retreat of 1914.'

Tilley quickly objected: 'I don't know what this proclamation is or how it is evidence in the case.' Regan replied, 'I cannot bring the Burgomaster.' The proclamation was excluded, but Justice Rose saw Regan hand it to a journalist. The document was not evidence, he warned, and if published could lead to a charge of contempt.

Regan's parade of defence witnesses continued for three days. Ordinary soldiers all, they were carefully surveyed by their former commander as they made their way to the witness-box. Some were in the stand for only a few minutes. Some seemed eager to testify. Others were hesitant. Many added little of substance to the evidence, but Regan hoped that their presence would show that men from the ranks supported the defence case.

To win the case, Regan had to prove that Canadian soldiers were killed at Mons on 11 November. Many of the witnesses he called swore that they had seen dead Canadian soldiers on that day. William Smith, an engineer with the Third Division, saw a dead Canadian pulled from the canal on the morning of 11 November. John McKay, a signaller with a machine-gun battalion, walked into Mons with two friends on the day following the armistice. 'Going through Mons, an old Belgian called to the three of us. We goes over, and he shows us in a shed – it was a kind of store shed, built of stone. I saw three Canadians and two dead Germans ready for burial in white wooden boxes.' Albert Mason, a company sergeant-major with the Twentieth Battalion, went into Mons at about one o'clock on 11 November.

Q On your way into Mons did you see any dead Canadians?
A Three, Sir.
Q Did you recognize any of them?
A One of them, Sir.
Q What unit did he belong to?
A I believe he belonged to the Princess Pats.
Q Did you notice anything peculiar in connection with these bodies?
A They were lying on stretchers, some of them – I am not sure whether the three of them had flowers on them or not. Some of them had flowers on them, evidently placed there by the civilian population.
Q Can you say whether they were in Mons itself or outside?
A Absolutely sure they were in Mons.

Not all of the defence witnesses could be so certain. One man was sure he had seen two dead Canadians as he entered the city just after 11 AM on 11 November, but he could not say precisely where. Another witness, John Overend, added a grisly detail: 'Two hundred yards from the city square I saw two dead Canadians lying practically in the gutter ... I saw one German about 20 yards away, and as we passed that German there was a lady ... stepped off the sidewalk and gave this German a kick.' A Port Hope veteran, Joseph Golding, swore that he saw 'between half a dozen or a dozen' dead Canadians, but most of the defence witnesses said they had seen only one or two. Some were nervous and reluctant to testify; perhaps they were not eager to help the defence. Others, however, clearly sided with Wilson and Preston.

Robert Hill, another Port Hope veteran, described Mons on Armistice Day as follows: 'When we came to Mons at daybreak [on 11 November] there were some Belgian women; these dead were laying there – I think they were 3rd Division men – and they had flowers on them, and they called us over and showed us the dead. I went over to see if I knew any of them, you see, and they couldn't understand why

we didn't show some emotion on account of these men being dead.'
There was, Hill said, a feeling of joyfulness on hearing that the armistice was coming into effect. Regan asked, 'How did you regard any
further fighting after you learned that the armistice had been signed?'
'Well, I will have to leave that to your imagination ... After fighting
two or three years, you know the war is over, and you have to continue
it – I have to leave that to your imagination.' Regan asked Hill to elaborate. 'Well, if you expect me to analyse my feeings, a fellow that has
been in the war a couple of years, he don't have any feelings.' 'You
don't have any?' 'No.'

Morley Drake came from Stratford to testify. His unit, the Eighteenth
Battalion, had come up to the position of another, the Nineteenth, on
the night of 10 November. The Nineteenth had been held up just outside Mons at Cipley by a German machine-gun post. An artillery battery of eighteen-pounders was brought up to attack the enemy
emplacement at about 9:30 PM.

Q What happened after the battery went into action?
A Well, we could see the shells lighting among the Germans and see stuff
   flying when they exploded, and then they quit firing and the 19th went right
   over the German position.
Q You mean by that they captured the German position?
A Yes, they captured it.
Q And where did they go?
A Well, they went over the hill out of our sight. We never seen any more of
   them ... They advanced right ahead ... in the direction of Mons.

Drake then described what he had seen on the afternoon of 11
November.

A I got a little curious to see what happened up at the German machine gun
   post, and took a walk up there ... I didn't start out with anybody, but I met
   a fellow going that way ... and walked along with him.
Q What did you see?
A We seen three dead Canadians laying there, about fifty yards from the post.
Q Three Canadian dead of which battalion?
A Well, the 19th, I should judge.
Q Could you see Mons from this point?
A Not till after you got over the hill, on top of the hill.

In cross-examination Tilley tried to establish more precisely where this skirmish had taken place: 'Can you say which direction they were from Mons?' Drake gave the only honest answer an ordinary soldier could give. 'No, I can't say which direction. I never had nothing to do with direction. We always followed what we were told.'

Cecil Belk had ended the war as a lieutenant in the First Brigade, Canadian Field Artillery. At the time of the trial he was still in the reserves. Belk had walked into Mons on the night of 11 November.

Q Did you see any dead soldiers?

A I saw two or three dead soldiers.

Q In Mons?

A Just on the outskirts, just before we actually got into the walled section of the town, I saw two or three dead soldiers – Allied soldiers.

Q Where were they lying?

A On the sidewalk.

Regan's next question amounted to a speech.

Now, this war had been going on for practically four years. Sir Arthur Currie was Commander of the Canadian Corps ... He knew two days previous to November 11th that the German envoys had come over to Marshal Foch to ask for terms of peace: he knew that Marshal Foch had given the German envoys the terms of peace, and had given them so many hours, he tells us forty-eight hours, in which to sign; and he knew that the German army was incapable of giving or receiving battle ... He also knew that the armistice had actually been signed at five o'clock in the morning. Now ... was any further offensive fighting ... which resulted in the loss of life ... on the part of the Canadian Corps justified, after the knowledge had reached Sir Arthur Currie that the armistice had been signed? Would you say that was justified or not?

Justice Rose asked Tilley whether he had any objection to the question. Tilley said no, and, as it turned out, wisely so. To Regan's disappointment and Tilley's amusement, Belk answered: 'Well, it is not a question on which I would care to pass any opinion, Mr. Regan. Sir Arthur Currie commanded the Corps. Whatever he did must have been quite O.K., O.K. as far as the battery was concerned.'

Tilley chuckled, and Regan protested: 'This may be a laughing matter to you, Mr. Tilley, about these men being killed over there. It is not a laughing matter to us, or to their dependants.' Tilley suddenly became serious. 'No, it is not a laughing matter. It is far from a laughing matter. When we are through with these addresses to the jury, I might just remark that I think this witness has gone far enough with opinion evidence. He says he can't put himself in the place of General Currie, because he never was in that position, and he doesn't want to say what he would have done if he had been in that position.'

Belk was obviously uncomfortable. 'I am very anxious, Sir, not to say anything which is other than real evidence. I just want to state what I know.' Regan pressed him for his views, however, and the witness answered reluctantly: 'Well, I will say this, that if a man knew for certain – and we knew nothing for certain during the war – if a man knew for certain that armistice had been signed at 5 o'clock in the morning, it is very obvious that no further hostilities are necessary. I don't know whether General Currie knew that or not.'

William Teddiman, a sergeant in the Fifty-second Battalion, Ninth Brigade, Third Division, went into Mons after 4:00 PM on the afternoon of 11 November. He testified in a confident manner.

Q Now then, on your entry into Mons did you see any dead Canadian soldiers?
A I did.
Q How many would you say that you saw?
A Three or four ... They were lying on the paved way ... either on the road or on the adjacent embankment. We couldn't help but notice them.
Q What Battalion would you say they were?
A 42nd Canadian Highlanders.

Teddiman's unit had been at a town called Wasmuel, nine or ten kilometres southeast of Mons, on the evening of 10 November. The enemy fire was particularly intense. During the previous two weeks, as the Germans were pushed back, artillery fire had been light; but that evening things changed. 'The impression was ... that the enemy had more or less dug in for a final stand to.'

Shortly before 9:00 AM on the morning of 11 November, Teddiman's commanding officer ordered him to draw equipment for the men from battle stores; the company had been ordered to go into Mons, relieve another unit, and engage the enemy. 'When I had the company up on parade, checked over, I went to company headquarters and reported the company was ready for inspection. The O.C. Company then informed me that he had received word that hostilities would cease at 11:00.'

Tilley, sensing a point helpful to Currie, interjected, 'I didn't hear what time he said that was.' Teddiman replied, 'At 10:15, approximately.' He continued, 'I did not pay very much attention to the mere fact that the armistice was signed. We had heard so many previous rumours.' 'Then what was done?' Regan asked. 'The men were then dismissed with the order to stand by their billets.' If anything, this evidence helped Currie's case, for it suggested that the pressure was relaxed once the armistice message came.

Regan returned to the subject of the Canadian bodies seen by the witness. Teddiman explained the procedure for clearing the dead and wounded. He had no definite proof that the men he saw had been killed on 11 November, but he could not imagine that they would have been left there for more than a few hours. 'It was a sort of triumphal procession all the way through. I could not conceive of any members of the Canadian Expeditionary Force being allowed to lay out on the street by the populace that was showing an exuberance of spirits at being relieved from the Germans.'

This reasoning could readily be turned around to cast doubt upon the witness's own story that there were bodies on the roadway, and the chance was not missed by Tilley. Emphasizing that the witness had not come into Mons until late on the afternoon of 11 November, Tilley asked him: 'How many men would there be went past these three dead bodies that you speak of?' 'Well, I think a conservative figure would give approximately five or six hundred.' Tilley suggested that it would have been unusual for five to six hundred men to march by without tending to the bodies. The war, after all, was over.

The witness began to realize that he had put himself in a difficult spot, and he became uncertain. Perhaps civilians were looking after the bodies, he suggested. Tilley asked whether there were inhabitants in the vicinity. Teddiman could not remember. Tilley pressed him:

Q I thought, from what you said, that probably five hundred men would pass them because they would expect the inhabitants there to take them up, and now we have it that you don't know that there were any inhabitants.

A No, pardon me ... the impression that I conveyed was not that if the five hundred men of my battalion didn't pick them up, the civilian inhabitants should. I am only giving that as my reasoning.

Q Oh, quite. And the jury will take it for just what they think it is worth – but that is your reasoning?

A That is my reasoning.

There was one Canadian fatality at Mons on 11 November about which there was no doubt. 'I have the record of a man named Price,' explained Colonel Logie Armstrong, a representative from the Department of National Defence who sat patiently through the trial providing official records as they were requested by counsel. 'This is a "circumstance of death" report. The unit is the 28th battalion. The name is Private G.L. Price, regimental number: 256265; rank: Private; date of death: November 11, 1918; cause of death: killed in action. Private Price was killed by an enemy sniper near the canal at 3 minutes to 11. He was shot through the right breast and died shortly after being hit, although every attention possible was given him. He was buried at the Communal Cemetery in the Town of Havre.'

In 1968, fifty years to the day from his death, several of Price's comrades returned to the canal just outside Mons where he was killed and erected a memorial plaque on a house nearby to honour 'the last Canadian soldier to die on the Western Front in the First World War.' The account of his death given beside his photograph in the Mons City Museum states that he was fired upon by the enemy as he approached the bridge that crossed the canal. He took shelter in the house just beside the canal, and the occupant told him to be careful. 'Despite this advice, Price went out to attack the enemy with his Lewis machine gun, but he was mortally wounded by a bullet in the region of the heart.'

8

Another Currie

On the second day of the trial, very much to the alarm of Sir Arthur Currie, Regan called a witness who also bore the surname Currie. John Allister (Jack) Currie, who was sixty-six years old at the time of the trial, had had a varied career as a businessman, journalist, and politician. He sat in the House of Commons from 1902 to 1921 as the Conservative member for North Simcoe, and represented the Toronto riding of St Patrick's in the provincial legislature from 1922 to 1930. In Parliament and in the legislature he was partisan and scrappy, and he certainly did not lack self-confidence. Jack Currie's turbulent career was on the wane by 1928, but he remained a well-known and controversial figure.

To understand the significance of this other Currie at the trial, some background information is needed. In 1892 Jack Currie had helped to organize the Forty-eighth Highlanders as a militia unit. During the war the regiment formed part of the First Canadian Division as the Fifteenth Battalion, sometimes known as the 'Red Watch.' Currie's own account of the battalion's achievements was contained in a book published in 1916, entitled *Red Watch: With the First Canadian Division in Flanders.*

Jack Currie was the commanding officer of the Red Watch at Neuve Chapelle and at the second battle of Ypres at 1915. He returned to Canada in August 1915 under something of a cloud. It was said that at

Ypres, near St Julien, he had been found behind the lines rather than with his men during the first German gas attack. This came to be known as 'the dugout incident.' When he returned to his seat in the House of Commons in 1916, Jack Currie made a lengthy speech describing conditions at the front and focusing in particular on conditions encountered at Ypres.[1] Currie concluded his account, which included many details of gallant deeds, by acknowledging that there had been some gossip about his personal conduct. He was not one to underestimate his own accomplishments. 'The men in my regiment and my officers know that when a battle takes place and I am there with them it is my duty to be there to lead them, rifle in hand; and after the battle is over I am the man who knows whether they comported themselves with bravery and dignity or not.'[2]

Currie then read a letter he had received from General Richard Turner recommending Currie for 'mention in dispatches' for services rendered at St Julien. Currie concluded: 'If anything has been said or done since to my injury there are only two men who stand between me and my decorations that might have come to me, or any "mention in despatches," and these were General Alderson and the Minister of Militia [Sir Sam Hughes] here. One was six miles back of the line all through the fight, and the other was attending to his duty in Canada, several thousand miles away. I choose to take the verdict of the man who stood over me in the trenches and the men who fought along side of me.'[3]

Jack Currie's speech was fully reported in the press. Sam Hughes, who had not been in the House when Currie spoke, decided that he had to respond to Currie's charge that a decoration had been earned but withheld. Rising in the Commons the next day on a point of privilege, Hughes disclaimed any responsibility for Currie's not having been decorated. Hughes explained that he had investigated the dugout incident. There had been a rumour, the minister told the House, that during the St Julien battle Jack Currie was found in a dugout to the rear of a British Division some considerable distance from his regiment. The fact was, Hughes said, that the man in the dugout was not Jack Currie but Arthur Currie, 'who had a perfect right to be there, was there looking for reinforcements from the British division to help in the fight. General Currie had a perfect right to be there, because it was his duty to look for reinforcements.'[4]

A friend sent a press clipping reporting Hughes's comments to Arthur Currie in France. Although Hughes had allowed that he had

'had a perfect right to be' in the dugout, Arthur Currie denied that he had been behind the lines, and thought that any possible confusion between his own actions and those of Jack Currie was damaging. He was upset by what he read, and immediately wrote to Hughes:

Let me say that I will not be mixed up in any way with rumours concerning Colonel J.A. Currie. I have nothing whatever to say of his actions at Ypres or at any other place.

In the second place, I know you are a man who loves truth and fair dealing. You want a fair deal yourself and you are inclined to give the other fellow always a little better than a fair deal. At least, you will not do him an injustice. I think it is fair to you to ask if you ever made the statements in the paragraphs attached [from the newspaper report]. If so, it is fair to me to tell you that you have been misinformed.[5]

Arthur Currie explained that he had never been 'behind Ypres,' but that he had visited the British divisional headquarters very briefly during the fight to get reinforcements.

Hughes attempted to set the record straight. On 30 March 1916 the prime minister, Sir Robert Borden, rose in the House to read a telegram sent to him by Hughes: 'In reply to Colonel John Currie in the House, I made the statement that General Currie during the St. Julien fight had been behind Ypres. General Currie assures me that this is erroneous, and at no period of the battle was he back at Ypres; he was in the lines of the British divison, but as I said before for a perfectly legitimate reason. Will you be good enough to correct this before the House.'[6]

But in 1919, when he decided to go after Arthur Currie on other matters, Hughes changed his tune on the dugout incident. On 29 September 1919, in one of his rambling speeches about the war, Hughes told the House of Commons that Jack Currie, still a member of Parliament, had been the victim of false rumour and that he had suffered for years because of it. Hughes read from Arthur Currie's letter of 1916 and stated that it proved his point. Arthur Currie admitted having gone to the British dugout to request reinforcements. In his telegram to Borden in 1916, Hughes had said that Arthur Currie had a right to be in the dugout, but now he thought differently. In 1916 he had been told that Arthur Currie had been sent back by General Richard Turner to ask the British officer, General Thomas Snow, for reinforcements. However, Hughes now insisted that no orders directing Currie to go back to Snow's headquarters could be found. This meant that Currie had broken the basic maxim that an officer in command of a brigade must stand to his post and use other methods of communicating with the rear. Hughes charged Currie with having left his brigade in the command of an inexperienced officer when he should have used his telephone or sent the staff officer.[7]

On 16 June 1920 Hughes again attacked Sir Arthur Currie on the dugout incident. The House was debating the militia and defence estimates, and other members had spoken in praise of Currie. Hughes, however, condemned him:

There has been no officer, military or otherwise who has received more commendation by way of propaganda than General Sir Arthur Currie, except maybe the President of the Privy Council (Mr. Rowell) and the ex-Minister of Finance (Sir Thomas White). I have no objection to anything that may be said about General Sir Arthur Currie, except that the Minister of Militia and Defence or anybody connected with the Militia Department of this Country must know that scores of men – I will not say one or two or three or a dozen – are regarded throughout the length and breadth of this country in military circles as infinitely superior to General Sir Arthur Currie as a general or as a gentleman.[8]

According to Hughes, Currie had 'allowed another officer, Colonel Jack Currie, to remain under the odium of being a coward, of running away and hiding in a British dugout and being kicked out by a British General.' Hughes claimed that Arthur Currie had been promoted before the facts were known, and he added: 'Had I remained in office six weeks longer, not only General Currie, but several other officers would have been asked to hand in their resignations. I was confusing the two Curries ... '[9]

It may well be that Jack Currie had been dealt with unfairly, but there seems to be no serious question of any impropriety on the part of Arthur Currie at St Julien. He had acted responsibly in a difficult and confusing situation when a mistake could have been disastrous. His section of the line was threatened and he badly needed reinforcements from an adjacent British unit being held in reserve. When a British officer had refused to help, he decided to go back himself and lead the men forward. But the rumour had created suspicion in the minds of many, and Frank Regan thought he could use the incident to discredit the reputation of his opponent.

There was more than a touch of bravado in Jack Currie's evidence at the trial. Sir Arthur thought he was drunk.[10]

'About the 12th of August, 1914,' Jack Currie said, 'I volunteered the battalion, and it was accepted by General Hughes, and then went to Valcartier and then overseas with the Canadian contingent.' 'You went to France in command?' Regan asked.

A Yes sir; I wouldn't take a staff appointment. I preferred to go with my own battalion.
Q You were offered a staff appointment?
A Yes, sir.
Q And you preferred to go with your own battalion?
A Yes, sir. I thought I would get to the trenches then. I wouldn't perhaps if I were on staff. I might be left in London.

It quickly became evident that Jack Currie's testimony was going to be contentious. Regan began to ask him about the second battle of Ypres, and in particular about the incident at St Julien. All of these incidents had occurred in 1915, and Justice Rose, prompted by Tilley's objection, asked Regan how the early battle could be relevant to what happened on Armistice Day. Regan's answer revealed that the strategy of the defence was to escape the confines of the specific charges made in the article. The evidence was being tendered, he said, 'to show that enormous loss of lives occurred at that particular time through the conduct of the plaintiff that should not have taken place, and which the [Evening Guide] article alleges.' He then referred to the passage from the article which stated that there had been 'much waste of human life during the war, an enormous loss of lives which should not have taken place.' Tilley quickly pointed out that the specific allegation in the article was that the loss of life at Mons had been deliberate and useless. There was no suggestion that the plaintiff had been responsible in any way for other loss of life.

Regan, however, had a second point. 'I am also pressing it for this reason, that at this battle I hope to be able to establish the fact that the conduct of the plaintiff was such that would not reflect any credit or honour upon him, that his character is called into question at this particular battle, because it was at this battle that the story got out.' The jury, of course, still had no idea what 'the story' was. Whether or not Justice Rose knew, he astutely interjected to stop Regan before either he or Jack Currie could blurt out anything. But Regan insisted that evidence of the dugout incident, still a mystery to the jury and perhaps to the judge, should be examined for the light it would shed upon Sir Arthur Currie's character and reputation, matters clearly put in issue by the action itself.

Tilley, perhaps sensing that Regan's argument was becoming more appealing, made a concession which, though startling to the jury, made Regan's task in having the evidence admitted a good deal harder. Tilley pointed out that Sir Arthur had said that 'there always is ... waste of life ... in every war' and that he had never denied that there had been a waste of life in the First World War.

The legal argument went back and forth inconclusively, and Jack Currie, still in the witness stand, could not restrain himself. 'It is very painful for me to be here after so many years, and not be allowed to say a word on my own behalf.' Justice Rose observed, 'Well, you are not being tried, as far as I know.' Jack Currie retorted, 'Oh, I have been tried for 13 years.'

The judge decided that he could not reject the evidence in the abstract without knowing the specific questions Regan wanted to ask. He allowed the witness to explain the tactical disposition of troops on the occasion of the first German gas attack at Ypres in April 1915. As Regan got to the crucial point, Rose instructed Currie not to answer until a ruling had been made. Regan put the question: 'Did you see any loss of life that should not have taken place in respect to the battle?' Without waiting for the ruling, Jack Currie quickly said, 'Yes.' His Lordship was annoyed. 'I told you not to answer.' But Currie added, 'Lots of it.'

To Sir Arthur Currie, the trial seemed to be getting out of hand. The defendants were slinging mud that was quite unrelated to Mons, and it would be impossible for him to defend his conduct in every battle of the war. Tilley pleaded with Justice Rose to confine Regan. He repeated his earlier point: the plaintiff, he said, conceded that there had been great loss of life during the war that should not have taken place 'in the sense that that takes place in every war, because officers are not always omniscient, and it must always happen ... What my friend seems to think here is that so long as he can bring evidence that reflects on character ... and ... reputation ... that that is sufficient.'

Justice Rose, perhaps fearful that any other ruling would lead to a prolonged examination of the entire war, said that he would 'not allow an inquiry as to whether due skill was shown by the plaintiff at the battle of which the witness speaks.' Regan refused to give up. Returning to the still mysterious incident, he said, 'There is another phase to this event, know as the Second Battle of Ypres, that affects the issues between the parties, and that is known as the dugout incident.'

By now the jury must have been both intrigued and bewildered. The judge disclaimed any knowledge of the dugout incident. Jack Currie was itching to say something. 'I am not represented by counsel, my Lord; I will have to depend on you.' Regan pulled out one of Sam Hughes's House of Commons speeches. Tilley objected that any reading from Hansard would be hearsay. Justice Rose agreed that Hansard could not be read, and Jack Currie became more impatient. 'I suppose I can't make a statement, my Lord?' 'No,' the judge replied. But Jack Currie would not be silenced: 'I was not in the dugout that day.' Justice Rose firmly interrupted: 'You may not make any statement except in answer to questions.' He ruled that the story of the incident, whatever it was, could not assist the jury in deciding what had happened at Mons three and a half years later.

Regan still would not give up. 'Will you allow this witness to state anything about the character of the plaintiff?' After much argument, Regan was allowed to put the following question. 'Do you know what reputation as a military commander and as an officer the plaintiff possessed prior to the publication of this article?' Jack Currie answered, 'My knowledge is based on a statement made by Sir Sam Hughes in the House of Commons.'

Justice Rose was extremely annoyed by Jack Currie's flagrant disregard for the previous ruling: 'Witness, in a moment you will be committed for contempt of court. You have heard that question ruled out.' Jack Currie interrupted, trying to say someting else about Sir Sam Hughes. The judge, unaccustomed to disrespect, became even more annoyed. 'I am very much inclined to commit you at this moment to prison for contempt of court in disobedience of an order. Now, one more act will probably bring about that result. If you have any regard for the safety of your witness you had better be careful of the type of question you ask him, Mr. Regan.' But despite the warning, Currie again tried to say something about the reputation that Arthur Currie's 'commanding officer gave him,' meaning Sir Sam Hughes. Justice Rose emphasized that the witness must state only whether he knew what reputation, if any, Sir Arthur had. Jack Currie replied ironically, 'He had none – like politicians, like myself, we have no reputation.'

After warning the witness not to answer until he judge had ruled, Regan asked: 'Were you in any dugout – ' Justice Rose interjected: 'Oh, you needn't ask him that sort of thing. That is all.' But Jack Currie could not restrain himself. 'I have been charged with that again and again, Your Honour.' The only answer he got from the bench was an order to get out before he was held in contempt. Currie laughed defiantly. The judge was white-faced with anger. The spectators were startled by the abruptness of his remarks and astonished to see a member of the legislature come within an ace of being held in contempt of court, a reaction echoed by the Toronto *Globe*'s headline next morning: '"GET OUT OF THAT WITNESS BOX OR I'LL HAVE SHERIFF REMOVE YOU" JUDGE TELLS COL. JOHN A. CURRIE.'[11] Sir Arthur Currie was relieved to see his namesake ejected from the courtroom; not surprisingly, the defence seemed a bit deflated by this setback.

Regan tried to recall Jack Currie to the stand the next day, stating that he had another question to ask. Tilley objected. Jack Currie, sitting in the body of the courtroom, again could not restrain himself. 'My Lord, just before I am called –' Justice Rose: 'Wait a moment, please.' Jack Currie, rosy-cheeked and smiling, rose from his chair and sauntered toward the box. He got within ten feet of the witness-box and removed his coat as if preparing for a fight. He moved closer to the witness-box, then halted at the end of the counsel table: 'Well, my Lord, I want to make a statement – '

This time there was no warning. The judge leaned forward and said sharply, 'You will make nothing.' Then, twisting in his chair, he snapped an order. 'Mr. Sheriff, will you please remove him from the court until he is sent for.' Sheriff Nesbitt rose to take Currie from the courtroom. No one made a sound. The sheriff called to the chief of police, standing at the rear of the court, to come and get Currie. Currie went out with the suggestion of a smirk on his face, and was asked to accompany the chief to his office. After this ignominious departure, he was not heard from again during the trial.

Although the daily papers provided detailed coverage of the trial, journalists were careful not to express their own views about who should win. A few days after the Jack Currie incident, the Toronto *Star* did publish an editorial entitled 'The Place of Dugouts in War': 'Until the Currie Preston litigation has come to an end it might be sub judice to discuss the activities of the Canadian expeditionary forces on armistice day at Mons. But the question of the use of dugouts in war having been ruled out of the case at Cobourg with special reference to individuals during the second battle of Ypres, thirteen years ago, its consideration does not involve anyone in contempt of court.' The editorial writer asserted that some people had an 'unmilitary conception of dugouts' and regarded them as places of refuge for would-be soldiers. However, the fact was that for the superior command 'the place of duty during conflict was the dugout ... [the] centre of intelligence in the nerve centre that controleld all effective warfare.' Regan saw this as a thinly veiled defence of Arthur Currie's conduct, and asked the judge to cite the newspaper for contempt. Rose declined to consider the matter unless it was raised in the proper form by way of a formal motion. At another point during the trial, Regan complained about a resolution passed at a reunion of the Fourth Battalion at Hamilton commending Currie for his 'splendid service' and adding that 'at no time did we feel that in any way you failed to carry out the interests of the men under you.'[12]

Although neither incident gave rise to a finding of contempt, all of the lawyers involved, including the judge, were obviously concerned about public statements or expressions of opinion on the case that might influence the jury. The result was that although the trial was well reported in the press, the editorial writers carefully avoided commenting or speculating as to the likely outcome. The reader was left to form his or her own opinion without the benefit – or hindrance – of editorial comment.

Regan wanted the jury to know that Currie was unpopular with the men in the ranks, but again he was confounded by the rules of evidence. He asked Albert Mason, one of the men who was prepared to testify against Currie, 'Mr. Mason, can you give the jury some idea what was General Currie's reputation among his men? How was he regarded?'

Tilley did not want Mason to answer. He quickly objected that evidence of Currie's reputation during the war, rather than at the date of the libel, was not relevant. Justice Rose pressed Regan for clarification. 'You are speaking now at the time of the war?' Regan equivocated: 'I am speaking now of what General Currie is asking $50,000 for.' But, when further pressed, Regan had to admit that his question related to the time of the war rather than to the date of the article.

Currie was unwilling to rely upon this technical legal point, however, and he leaned over to instruct Tilley to withdraw the objection. Tilley obliged: 'General Currie suggests to me that I should withdraw my objection to this question if this witness wants to express an opinion on that.'

This made Regan suspicious. 'I would like to get this settled now ... I have a number of witnesses, and I don't want to be putting them into the box and taking up the time of the court.' But the judge insisted that he could only deal with each question as it was asked. Regan was asked to put his question again, but this time he rephrased it. 'What do you say about his popularity – ' Tilley jumped up and insisted that the court reporter read back the question that had been asked the first time. The reporter quickly flipped through his notes, and then read: 'What was General Currie's reputation among his men? How was he regarded?' The witness answered: 'That is pretty hard. Reputation or popularity may be different ... I could not answer for reputation.'

Although he knew that the question was bound to provoke an objection, Regan could not resist asking, 'Well, was he popular among his men?' Despite the attempts of both Tilley and Justice Rose to stop him, the witness answered: 'He was not as popular as the others.' Regan pretended not to have heard. 'What was your answer? I didn't catch it ... I heard him say something about "not as popular as" and I didn't catch it.' 'As the others, he said,' replied the judge, apparently resigned to the fact that the disputed evidence was not going to be kept out. But he ruled out of order any comparison of commanding officers when Regan asked, 'What do you mean by the others?' Regan observed sarcastically: 'Well, at least I would have assumed that Sir Arthur would have been willing to have had his position with his men compared with other officers.'

Tilley dealt with the situation cleverly. He adopted a lofty tone: 'I do not propose to ask for comparisons in popularity between General Currie and other generals, be they those that are dead or those that are alive. Such a thing would be very improper.' Tilley stated that he would not be drawn into invidious comparisons. To explain what the jury must know by now – that Currie was less popular than the others – Tilley added, 'possibly his popularity and his efficiency might go in an inverse way.'

Regan continued to fence, insisting that his question was proper. 'He may be a very skilful commander, and at the same time he may be a man, as we say, who would order his men into battle up until one of them was killed at 3 minutes to 11 o'clock. That is two different things – head and heart, if I may put it in a blunt way ... I am dealing with his humanity, how he felt towards the private soldier.' The judge was unmoved, and refused to allow Regan to continue on this tack.

A few minutes later, Regan tried again with another witness, Robert

Marshall: 'How was General Currie liked among his men, Mr. Marshall?' It was immediately pointed out that the same question had already been ruled out of order, and Regan rephrased it: 'What was his reputation among the men?' But the witness decided to answer the first question anyway: 'He was not very popular.'

Justice Rose thought that Regan could have avoided this reponse, and a heated exchange ensued. Although his argument was ostensibly directed to the judge, Regan was ever-conscious that the jurymen were listening, and his comments were intended for their ears. 'I want the jury to get the benefit of this evidence – ' Rose interrupted: 'The jury will get the benefit of every bit of evidence which you tender and which seems to me to be relevant.' 'Well,' responded Regan, 'I don't like to see any evidence left out because of my inexperience on the one hand and my friend's vast experience on the other, and your Lordship's attitude to strictly enforce the rules of evidence. That is the point I am trying to make ... Now, if I don't know just how to put it so as to bring it within some particular rule that will satisfy your Lordship, I regret it, of course. But you understand why I am trying to get this evidence out. I want to get it out for the purpose of showing that Sir Arthur Currie was at times indifferent to the comfort and safety and welfare of his men.' If the rules of evidence would not allow a witness to say it, Regan, it seemed, would say it himself.

Regan then asked Albert Mason for his views on the propriety of what had happened on 11 November.

Q What would you say about any further offensive fighting on the part of the Canadian Corps after its commander knew that the armistice had actually been signed and that hostilities would cease at 11 o'clock?
A Well, if I received orders at 5:30 on that morning that the war would cease at 11 o'clock, I certainly would not have ordered an offensive.
Q You say that because you were one of the men that had to do the actual fighting?
A I was in the war and I knew what war was, knew what the losses were.
Q And knew what fighting was in the front line trench?
A Yes, Sir.

'Not back in a headquarters chateau, a mile behind the line,' added Regan.

'What did you say your position was, Mr. Mason? Tilley asked in cross-examination. 'Company sergeant major,' the witness answered.

Q And your view is that if the word went out that the Germans were to be carrying on the war until 11 o'clock, it was advisable that the Canadians should stop? Is that it?

A No, Sir.

Q Well, isn't that what you have said?

A No, Sir, I did not imply that.

Q You understand that the Germans were to carry on the war until 11 o'clock?

A They were not attacking. It was us that were attacking.

The witness had to admit, however, that the Germans were setting up rear-guard actions in retreat, and improving their position by retiring.

Q Would it be your view that the Canadians should stop and not take the position that they were told to take, though the Americans, the French and the British were taking the advanced position?

A I should take the view that an extra few miles or few kilometers was not necessary.

Q Do you know that the position that they were taking up in the front involved a line of miles?

A Yes, Sir.

Q Is it your opinion, then, that they should not have done that ... and that General Currie should have refused?

A He couldn't very well refuse, I suppose.

Q I am not asking you whether he could. Is it your opinion that he should have done so? ... Is that your opinion?

A Yes, Sir.

Q That he should say to whoever was responsible for directing what was to be done up till 11 o'clock that day, 'I refuse to carry it out and support the British and French, even though you tell me to do so,' is that your opinion?

A Yes, Sir.

Regan recalled another witness, William Teddiman, to give his opinion on the need for further fighting on 11 November. 'Tell me whether any further fighting at all in the Canadian Corps was justified after Sir Arthur Currie learned that the armistice had been signed?' 'I would say no,' the witness answered. Teddiman, anxious to display his knowledge of military matters, went on to explain the tactics of retreat and pursuit. The final point he made provided a nice opening for Tilley's cross-examination. Regan asked what a reasonable commander would have done upon hearing of the armistice. Teddiman replied that 'orders could be conveyed to the main line, the front line, or the units that were in touch with the enemy, to desist from further offensive, but to just keep in touch with the retiring army.' Tilley then asked:

Q When you say 'keep in touch', what do you mean?
A By throwing out patrols.
Q Being in positions of danger. You mean that?
A Yes.
Q You don't mean getting out of the danger line?
A No, no, absolutely not.
Q You mean to keep in positions of danger where casualties may occur?
A It was probable they would occur, yes.
Q So that you would not expect to stop casualties, would you?
A I grant you, no.
Q Is it your view that what you have said applies, although by the terms of the armistice it was not to be effective until 11:00?
A I grant you.
Q That is to say, the armistice should be acted on before it would become effective as between Germany and the Allied armies, is that right?
A Correct.
Q How long in your opinion – because you are a man competent, you think, to give opinions – how long would it take for the news that the armistice was signed ... to reach all necessary parties in the Canadian army?
A Anywhere from one hour to three hours.
Q Is it a matter of surprise to you to find that some did not hear of it until half past ten?
A No, it is not.
Q Was each one to sort of drop tools and stand, irrespective of what his comrades were doing ... they not knowing that there was any armistice at all?
A Oh, absolutely not.
Q Therefore, it was essential that they all should stop at the same time?
A Absolutely, yes.
Q Otherwise, their comrades might be in serious difficulty?
A Possibly so, yes.
Q If some were pushing on without knowledge that others of their comrades had stopped, that would not be quite what you would recommend, would it?
A No.
Q Then wouldn't it be desirable to fix a time after the armistice was signed up to which the operations were to be carried on ... and have them stop at the end of that time?
A It was perfectly logical to expect that, yes.

Q And wouldn't a fair time to fix be 11 o'clock?
A For the cessation of hostilities, yes, absolutely.

Tilley had managed to turn the witness around completely. Regan tried to rescue him in re-examination, but to no avail. Teddiman could only splutter, 'I am in a difficult position.'

William Dodd, a Toronto *Star* reporter who had been with the Fourth Division at Valenciennes, brought to the stand a book published in January 1919 containing details about the personnel of every unit in the British army, including the Canadian Corps. Regan questioned him:

Q Is Sir Arthur Currie's name mentioned in there?
A Yes, his name is mentioned.
Q What does it say about Sir Arthur Currie there?
A It says he was a commander, gives his title, dignities.
Q What else?
A It also gives him three aides-de-camp on his staff.
Q Three aides-de-camp. Does any other corps commander have that many?
A No, not three. Two usually, sometimes one.
Q How many Army Commanders have three aides-de-camp?
A I don't think there are any.

Justice Rose became impatient. 'This is very interesting, but has it anything to do with the present case?' Regan replied, 'At the very time that Sir Arthur Currie was calling for reinforcements, that the country was being told we were short of men – ' He was cut short by Tilley, who observed that the information in the book probably related to the date of its publication, 1919, rather than to the end of the war.

Regan attempted further justification. 'There is suggestion in the article ... that for the purpose of vain glory this attack was made on Mons. Now I think the jury might like to know just the precise type of man that Sir Arthur Currie was ... I submit that it is relevant in this way, that where a man is so vainglorious and consumed with the idea of his own importance that he goes to work and has three aides-de-camp, when his Army Commander over him has only one – ' Justice Rose interjected, 'Oh, nonsense!' But Regan went on: '– that it helps the jury to appreciate the type of man whose case they have to try.'

9

Defensive Strategies

On the morning of the third day of the trial, Frank Regan adopted a highly dubious strategy. The defendants' evidence conflicted on most points with Arthur Currie's version of the Mons attack. Regan was confident that the ordinary soldiers he was calling as witnesses were making a good impression, and he wanted the jury to know right from the start that Currie denied virtually everything they said. The problem, as Regan saw it, was that Currie's evidence would come in reply after all the defence witnesses had testified. This gave Currie the last word and made it impossible for Regan to present his case in the way he would have preferred – in response to Currie's testimony. Regan decided that somehow he had to get Currie's version before the jury first so that he could contradict Currie on specific points as he led his evidence. To accomplish this, he read to the jury almost everything Currie had said on his examination for discovery.

Regan's ploy was certainly permitted by the rules of court, but the more conventional tactic is to read only specific extracts containing favourable admissions. Indeed, there was little to be gained and much to be lost by reading the entire examination. It would merely serve to put Currie's case before the jury twice, once through Regan and then again when the general himself entered the witness-box. More important, there was a substantial risk that the jury would be less receptive to the defendants' witnesses if it was known from the start that Currie would contradict them on every significant point.[1]

The reading began. Regan, spelled by his co-counsel Thomas Hall, read page after page of the transcript, a ploy as monotonous as it was futile. Regan may have thought that the tactic would allow him to put before the jury the answers Currie had been compelled to give concerning his pre-war financial transgressions. If so, he was sadly mistaken: Justice Rose refused to admit any of that information into the trial record, and ruled it irrelevant to the issues raised by the libel action. A defendant in a libel action is entitled to show that the plaintiff does not have a good reputation by calling witnesses who can say how the plaintiff is regarded in the community, but a defendant is not permitted to offer evidence of specific instances of misconduct not covered by the libel. The purpose of the rule is to prevent the defendant from turning a libel trial into a mud-slinging free-for-all.

At one point, as Regan put it, 'so that the monotony of reading the examination might be broken,' he called a witness to contradict something Currie had sworn to on discovery. The question Regan asked, however, was ruled out of order because it called for an expression of opinion, and Regan had by then exhausted the statutory limit on the number of opinion witnesses he was entitled to call.[2] Regan did not hide his annoyance and frustration: 'Then do I take it that no matter what Sir Arthur has said in his examination for discovery, I am not to be allowed to call witnesses to contradict it?'

That, of course, was not the ruling, and the judge decided to put his foot down: 'Mr. Regan, what is the use of putting these absurd propositions to me? There has been no such ruling ... The ruling is that you have had more than the statutory number of witnesses expressing opinions.'

Regan then thought of something else. 'How about this point, my Lord? There are two defendants. Are each of them entitled to three experts?' But Regan was only acting for Wilson, and Preston refused to co-operate: 'I think I will ask my learned friend Mr. Regan not to represent me in this matter.'

This rebuff from his ally did not knock Regan off stride. He simply persisted in attempting to have the witness answer. When he was stopped yet again by the judge he exclaimed, 'Well, I might just as well throw away this examination for discovery if I am not going to be allowed to contradict Sir Arthur ... I can't do it after he goes in reply. I am through.'

Justice Rose was annoyed: 'Mr. Regan, I do not know whether the purpose of such remarks is to endeavour to get the jury to believe that you are being unduly oppressed in your presentation of your case ... You have spoken in a very offensive way ... If you attempt to follow unauthorized practice, I have no option but to prevent the success of your attempt.'

The third day of the trial ended after several more hours of reading from Currie's examination for discovery. After the session, Regan approached the bench. He was concerned about the comments the judge had made, and feared that press reports would state that the judge had rebuked him for saying something offensive. The judge agreed to review what he had said with the court reporter.

At the opening of proceedings the next day, Justice Rose generously gave Regan the benefit of any doubt. Addressing Regan in open court, he said, 'I thought that the phrasing of your statement of your position as to the admissibility of certain evidence was unfortunate ... I think that the statement made by me really went no further than that. Lest the impression may have got abroad that I thought that you were intending to say something that ought not to have been said, I make this statement now, so that if there is such an impression, it may be corrected as far as possible.'

Regan thanked the judge, and added, 'Sometimes my choice of language may not be a happy one, but I may assure your Lordship that it is only the tongue that offends.'

Although the Department of National Defence records were an important source of information on many issues, the Minister had decided before the trial that neither Currie nor Wilson and Preston would be afforded open access to them. But the diaries and casualty reports locked away in the ministry files could hardly be ignored, and Regan had subpoenaed virtually everything that could shed any light upon the capture of Mons. Colonel A. Fortescue Duguid, the director of the Historical Section of the Department of National Defence, and his associate, Logie Armstrong, had brought crates of documents down from Ottawa to Cobourg for the trial. They were joined by a lawyer, Judge Advocate-General Colonel Reginald Orde.

Regan, of course, did not know what was to be found in the department's records, and had little time to rummage through them to see if there was any ammunition he could use in defence of his client. To facilitate matters, Duguid and Armstrong met with Regan and spent several hours explaining to him the nature and contents of the records.

Armstrong produced for the trial a list of the number of men killed in the entire Canadian Corps from 1 November to 11 November, which he had prepared after laboriously sifting through the various diaries and reports.

KILLED

		OFFICERS	OTHER RANKS
NOV.	1	3	127
	2	3	28
	3	2	13
	4	2	33
	5	3	33
	6	4	72
	7	1	36
	8	0	17
	9	1	10
	10	8	49
	11	0	1
TOTALS		27	219

In addition, 100 officers and 1,594 soldiers of other ranks were shown as having been wounded between 1 November and 11 November.

However, in the case of some units involved in the Mons attack, the diaries gave the total number of casualties for the last three days of the war, 9, 10, and 11 November, with no separate indication of the casualties for 11 November. With apparent justification, Regan questioned the figures Armstrong had given. The Field Service Regulations required that daily entries be made showing the name and rank of any casualties, and department officials had to admit that this had not been done. Regan pressed for a better account. By the fifth day of the trial, a list was produced based on individual casualty reports, showing that on 10 November 34 had been killed in action, 25 had been wounded and subsequently died, and 199 had been wounded. But Duguid and his associates still insisted that only one man had been killed on 11 November.

Regan decided that he could not ignore the department's casualty figures, and that if they did not help his case he had to explain why. His assertion startled the entire courtroom. 'We say that these records which deal with the publication of the casualties to the world were deliberately falsified for the purpose of keeping from the world the knowledge of the loss of life – ' Justice Rose, astonished by what he heard, interjected: 'Were deliberately falsified by [or] under the direction of the plaintiff?' Regan stood his ground. 'Yes, I am prepared to go this far, and say that these records were deliberately falsified by, under, or with the knowledge and consent of the one man most responsible for the suppression from the world of the knowledge of these casualties.'

Rose immediately made it clear that he would force Regan either to substantiate his charge or to make a humiliating retreat. Tilley stiffened and prepared himself to respond to the challenge Regan had thrown. 'My Lord, my position is this. I did not suspect that the article ... either expressly or by implication [alleged] that there was a falsification of the records made by, or with the concurrence or at the request of Sir Arthur Currie; but if that charge is involved in the article, I want the defendants to say so, and if they do say so, I welcome any evidence with regard to it ... I am prepared to meet it.'

It was a bold statement on Tilley's part, but tactically sound. It indicated to the jury that Currie felt that he had nothing to hide. More important, if the defendants could be driven to taking extreme positions, the more dubious their whole case would seem, and the jury might be more generous in their award of damages.

Immediately, Regan found himself in trouble. Preston took exception to Tilley's suggestion that the falsification charge was advanced by both defendants. Tilley pressed for an explanation. 'Is Mr. Preston taking the position that the evidence that is now being put in is not for his benefit?' Tilley's ploy was intended not so much to probe the legal niceties of Preston's position, but to drive a wedge between the two defendants.

So far, Preston had hardly been heard from. He rose to explain his position. 'I will take advantage of any evidence which is brought in ... to avoid my bringing it in and making a long double case.' However, he insisted, he was 'absolutely alone' in his own defence. Tilley could not resist ridiculing Preston's stance. 'Now he says on the one hand he is with us all, and he is taking my evidence and Mr. Wilson's evidence, and the next minute he is alone and taking no person's evidence.' Preston protested, 'I am not answerable to Mr. Tilley.' Tilley quickly agreed: 'I am not suggesting that you are. I am glad I am not responsible.'

Regan was now in a doubly embarrassing position. The jury knew that Preston was the real source of and inspiration for the article, yet he was distancing himself from Regan's suggestion that Currie had falsified the records. At the same time, Regan knew that he had gone too far in making the charge, and as both Tilley and the judge pushed him for clarification it gradually became apparent that he would have to make an embarrassing retraction.

Was it his position that the words of the article implied the falsification charge, asked Justice Rose. Regan was evasive. Rose paused to explain the dispute to the jury, and as he did so Regan turned to say something to a journalist. The judge noticed his movement and warned, 'Mr. Regan, this is rather important. I should deem it courteous if you would listen to me instead of talking to the reporter behind you.' Regan, embarrassed, replied, 'I just for half a second thought I heard somebody saying something in my ear, and I just turned for the casual part of a second. I was listening intently.' 'It would help me if I thought I had your attention,' said the judge, and continued his pursuit. 'Didn't you say to me that concealment was at the instigation or with the knowledge or with the concurrence of the plaintiff, and that [it] was implied either in the newspaper article or in the pleadings?'

Regan's retreat was an awkward one. 'Oh, no, no, I did not. Oh, no, my Lord. At least, I may have said words that conveyed that meaning to your Lordship ... That is not the meaning that I desired to convey to you, because the article says nothing about war records or about the concealment of the facts.' He then added, rather feebly, 'I don't know whether it is fair, to an inexperienced counsel as I am –' But Rose would not let him get away with that. 'I assume that counsel undertaking to conduct the case is satisfied and that his clients are satisfied of his qualifications for the task which he has undertaken ... and that I am not to make differences between counsel and allow latitude to one because he is inexperienced and refuse it to another because he is experienced ... Remarks as to inexperience are utterly misplaced to me.'

Both Tilley and the judge were determined to settle the question of the falsification of records once and for all. Tilley explained, 'I cannot, in the interests of my client, allow these suggestions to be made and persisted in with evasive ... answers, quibbling on words ... I want my friend to take his stand.'

Preston again rose from his chair. 'Mr. Tilley has asked the question about the defendants. I desire to state that neither in the article nor in the pleading was there any thought [that] Sir Arthur Currie ... had anything whatever to do [with], or suggested, any falsification of the records. If I can make it any plainer, I am quite disposed to do it.'

Justice Rose, feeling that he was finally getting somewhere, persisted: 'That is very definite as to one defendant.' Regan quickly added, 'I thought I had been equally definite,' and then made it clear that he accepted what Preston had said. Although he was relieved, Rose could not resist saying, 'Well, I must have been very dense, because I had not grasped the fact until now.' As if to demonstrate that he could not be humiliated, Regan returned to a forbidden topic: 'Well, that is what I say, perhaps my choice of language, owing to my inexperience, has misled your Lordship.'

This laid to rest the suggestion that the war records had been falsified. Much of the morning had been taken up trying to have Regan either stand behind or withdraw his startling and apparently ill-advised statement. He could hardly have risen in the jury's esteem. Had the case for the defence been harmed? The jury might well think that allegations made in the article were equally ill-considered. By clearly distancing himself from Regan, however, Preston had perhaps gained credibility.

The defendants had called Orde, Armstrong, and Duguid to the stand, and Tilley was entitled to cross-examine each of them. He used the opportunity to make points in Currie's favour. When Tilley questioned Duguid, it became immediately apparent that the witness had a familiarity with the events of November 1918 that went well beyond the records of which he was the custodian. 'At 6:40 AM,' Duguid testified, 'on 11th November, 1918, I was staff officer on duty at Headquarters, 3rd Canadian Division at Jemappes. At that hour I received a verbal message over the telephone fromm Col. A.A. Magee, who was staff officer on duty at Canadian Corps.' This was the armistice order, received by Duguid himself on behalf of the Third Division.

Tilley was anxious to develop an explanation for Currie's erroneous statement on discovery' that no Canadians had been killed on 11 November. Colonel Orde explained that the department had supplied Currie with a list of those lost during the last days of the war which failed to show the death of Corporal Price on 11 November. A more careful subsequent search had revealed records indicating that Price had been killed as described earlier by other witnesses, minutes before the armistice took effect, just a few miles northeast of Mons. But Orde insisted that so far as the records showed, he was now certain that there were no other deaths recorded for 11 November.

Although the allegation that the records had been falsified had been put to rest in a formal sense, the jury might have had lingering doubts, and Tilley got Orde to give a brief but clear explanation of how the diaries were compiled. A war diary was kept by each battalion or battery. The duty of writing the diary usually fell upon a junior officer, often a man who was in combat and who had little time to accomplish the task. Information regarding casualties would come from other men or from daily casualty records that were sent in. The date for which a casualty was recorded depended upon when the officer got the information; in the circumstances, this was not necessarily the same day the casualty occurred.

Orde explained that official casualty records were made at field ambulance posts, and that if a man went to a casualty clearing station behind the line a similar record was completed there. All of this information was collated and summarized at a base in Rouen and then sent to the main records office in London. Orde explained that a complete check of all these records had been made to enable him to prepare the list he had produced for Regan.

Tilley then asked Orde for details regarding the positions of the various units said by the defence witnesses to have lost men in the final hours of fighting. At one point, Tilley could not recall exactly what the evidence had been. Justice Rose came to his rescue, demonstrating the care with which he took notes: 'Here you are, Mr. Tilley, in your cross-examination, you wouldn't have a note of this.' The judge then read a verbatim record of the relevant passage from the evidence.

A total of fifty-seven men from the Canadian Corps had been killed on 10 November. Tilley pressed Orde for any details available in the records as to where these men had been killed. While the reports were sketchy, no one was actually shown as having been killed in Mons itself on 10 November. Tilley was determined to convince the jury that even if men had been lost in the last hours of the war, they had not died within the limits of the city of Mons.

How much had been known about the possibility of an armistice before 11 November? This was a crucial issue, but here again Regan would struggle with the problem posed by the hearsay evidence rule, as well as with the very specific allegation that had been made in the Port Hope *Evening Guide* article.

Reports from the London *Times* showed the steady progress of peace talks from early October. Regan tried to introduce these newspaper accounts to show 'that on November 9th, when Sir Arthur Currie issued the order that resulted in the attack and capture of Mons, he knew or ought to have known that fighting would cease within a few hours. I am producing the London *Times*, which contains references to the peace negotiations and their progress, which was available to Sir Arthur, to substantiate the statement of the defence in that respect.'

Tilley objected that those writing for the *Times* 'certainly were not in charge of giving directions for the conduct of the war.' The judge asked whether the reports might not be admissible simply to show that there was available to Currie information from which it would have been reasonable to conclude that there was no need to continue operations.

Tilley politely derided the suggestion that a general in command of his forces should decide 'what should be done in the field by reading the London press.' It was clear that by referring to a date earlier than 11 November, Regan was trying to escape the very specific statement his clients had made in the *Guide*. 'The point of this article is that between the signing of the armistice and its coming into effect at 11 o'clock, after it was known that there was to be an armistice ... there was this mad order given that sacrificed Canadian lives.'

Regan suggested that Tilley was being far too technical and that the issue really was whether there had been any unnecessary loss of life in the push towards Mons once it became clear that an armistice was imminent and that the war could not last much longer. 'I am unable to follow his argument, his remarks about the last day, the last hour and the last minute. Now, a thing cannot be ridiculous and have any weight. It is ridiculous to argue that any order issued on the last minute would be the order that we have referred to here.' Just as Currie had feared, Regan was trying to broaden the issue.

Justice Rose would not let Regan off so easily, however. 'It is what you say in the newspaper ... It is a statement of fact, that a mad idea was conceived after the armistice had been signed and before it became effective.' Tilley added emphatically, 'Signed by both sides.'

The tiresome argument went back and forth. The judge excused the jurors until the point was settled, and after the twelve men had trudged out of the courtroom, Regan complained: 'Your Lordship I don't think appreciates the difficulty the defence has had to get evidence.' Rose replied, 'I don't think I am concerned with difficulty at all. I am concerned with the legality of a course pursued.' The newspaper reports of the imminent armistice were excluded.

Regan asked one of his witnesses, a man from the ranks, 'When did you hear about the armistice?' Tilley interjected, again determined to confine the case to the specific factual issues pleaded: 'The question is when the commanding officer heard of the armistice.' Regan retorted, 'I assume that these private soldiers had some interest in the armistice. There were others beside officers.' Even if it was beside the point legally, Regan's plea for sympathy for the common soldier was effective. But he wanted to go further. Had the witness 'heard of any talk about the armistice before he learned about it officially?' Again, it became clear that the defendants were trying to shift ground to a charge less specific than the one they had made in the article.

'What we say,' explained Regan, 'is that the plaintiff knew for weeks that there was going to be an armistice, that according to the summary of the First Army, all ranks knew for a week before that there was going to be an armistice almost any day.' General Haig himself had stated that the Germans had taken such a drubbing that they could neither give nor refuse battle. Regan read the crucial passage from the report of the First Army; 'It was known by the 10th of November throughout the Army that an armistice concluding hostilities might be signed within the next day or two.'

The witness was allowed to explain that it was 'common gossip' that the German envoys had been through the Allied lines to obtain terms, and that the men were eager for the armistice to come quickly.

William Nickle, the son of a former Ontario attorney-general, had enlisted as a private and had been wounded in action three times. He rose to the rank of major, and received the Military Cross. During the later stages of the war, Nickle served as private secretary to General Richard Turner, the chief of general staff in London. Nickle became a lawyer after the war, and would later follow his father into politics, serving in the Ontario cabinet under Leslie Frost in the 1950s and John Robarts in the 1960s. As a politician, Nickle took an interest in the law of defamation, and twice proposed (unsuccessfully) amendments to the Libel and Slander Act that would have protected reporters who refused to disclose their sources of information.[3]

Nickle was one of the few officers Regan called to the stand. His evidence related to the receipt of early word of the end of hostilities. On the morning of 9 November he had received a telephone call from Canadian Corps headquarters in France, and was told to advise Turner that it was expected that an armistice would be signed at any time. This meant that no further troops were to be dispatched to the front. Regan asked whether Currie would not have been in possession of this same information. Nickle made it clear that he was uncomfortable with the question: 'He can answer that. He knows whether he was phoned. I don't mind telling you that I am here under subpoena, and it is not any wish of my own to come up from Kingston today.' But when pressed, Nickle did say, 'My best opinion would be that Sir Arthur Currie would know as much as we knew, because he usually knew where he was going.'

'You are friendly to Sir Arthur? You have nothing against him?' Regan asked. 'No,' replied Nickle with a chuckle, 'except perhaps he might have promoted me but didn't.'

A Port Hope resident, Frederick Lingard, had been a wireless operator with the Fourth Canadian Division, and had been on duty the night of 10 November 1918. 'Did you receive any messages after you went on duty?' Regan asked. 'Yes, Sir, a message saying that the armistice –' 'A message from whom?' interjected Justice Rose. 'The 4th Division Headquarters,' Lingard responded. 'When did you receive that message?' Regan continued. 'Between 10 and 11.' 'Between the hours of 10 and 11 on November 10th?' 'Yes, Sir.'

Tilley became concerned. Apparently, the witness was going to swear that he had received an official message about the armistice several hours earlier than Currie had thought possible. Tilley quickly objected that unless the message itself were produced, the evidence could not be admitted. Regan replied, 'This is the man that took the message. That ought to be the best evidence.' Tilley refused to give way: 'His recollection of the message ought not to be as good as the message itself.'

The judge knew straightaway that there was really no basis upon which Lingard's evidence could be excluded. He had taken the wireless message himself. Regan was allowed to continue: 'What did the message say?' 'That the armistice was to be signed on November 11th at 11 o'clock,' said Lingard.

Tilley did not cross-examine the witness at length. Although Lingard had been on the stand only a few minutes, his evidence of such early official word of the armistice was extremely significant. Currie had assumed all along that there would be no challenge to his recollection that no word had come before the morning of the eleventh.

On this point, and several others, Regan recalled Colonel Orde to have him explain what could be found in the ministry records. By continually recalling Orde, Duguid, and Armstrong to the stand in the hope of gleaning further information from the records, the defence was, as Tilley acidly observed, conducting a discovery within the trial. Although Regan had had limited access to this material, he did have to admit that the ministry officials had been helpful to him since the trial began. Still, he persisted in conducting tiresome searches through various documents in front of the jury. Not only did this indicate that the defendants were less certain of their facts than they should have been, it also risked discrediting the evidence the defence had led.

No trace could be found of the early armistice message Lingard had sworn to. Regan realized that this could discredit Lingard's assertion that there had been such a message. In his questioning of Orde, he tried to salvage something by casting doubt on the records themselves:

Q If that order that Lingard said he received was in fact received by him, it should appear in this war diary.
A Not necessarily at all.
Q Where would it appear?
A It would not appear. It has probably been destroyed or lost while they were marching along. You couldn't carry several crates of messages and reports ... When the necessity for keeping a message like that had ceased ... it was naturally destroyed or burned up or used as kindling.

Rather than accept that answer, which at least made Lingard's evidence consistent with the fruitless search, Regan suggested that if Lingard's version was not in the war diary, the war diary must be wrong.

Tilley pointed out the flaw in Regan's logic with a rhetorical interjection. 'If there was such a message.' When Regan continued to assert that the message should have been recorded in the diary, Tilley pushed the point further. 'Supposing I admit that if such a message was sent it ought to be in the diary, and it is not in the diary, and it likely was not sent, would that satisfy my friend?'

At the opening of the fourth day of the trial, Regan drew to the court's attention a photograph of a copy of the armistice message which had appeared in the Toronto *Daily Star*. It had been received at 6:05 AM, forty minutes earlier than Currie would admit Corps headquarters had received word of the armistice. The jury still had not been allowed to see the newspaper photograph, and Regan, again confronted by rigorous rules of evidence, could not expect to persuade the judge to admit it into evidence. A photograph of this kind could be admitted only if

the original document could not be found and the origin of the photograph could be fully explained. The rule is designed to protect against
the admission of fabricated or altered documents. Regan still managed
to contrive a way to tell the jury what the message said. He recalled
Duguid to the stand to ask whether the original was to be found any-
were in the government's files. Regan explained that to enable Duguid
to accomplish his search he would have to describe the document as
accurately as possible, a ploy designed to enable him to tell the jury
what the document said before its admissibility had been established.
This provoked a lengthy wrangle, which had just the result Regan expected. The newspaper photograph was excluded, but he had succeeded
in making the time of its receipt known to the jury.

Regan then called to the witness stand Eyton Warburton, a reporter
from Kingston, who had seen the original order and knew who had it
at present. Warburton would say only that the document was in the
possession of an ex-member of the Second Brigade, Canadian Garrison
Artillery, who did not want to be identified since he was still a member
of the armed forces and it was illegal from him to have kept the document. Warburton refused to disclose the man's name. To do so would
be to breach a confidential source, a matter as sensitive to a reporter
in 1928 as it is today. Regan threatened to take steps to compel disclosure, but the judge seemed unsympathetic.

Regan made sure that the jury would have no doubt about the contents of the document. He insisted upon making a speech, under the
guise of legal argument, intended solely for the jury: 'It seems to me
that the jury ought to have before it all documents that are pertinent
to this issue. Here are documents which deliberately contradict the
plaintiff with respect to the hour at which notice of the armistice was
received by himself. He says he got notice at 6:45. The document there
is 6:05 – a difference of 40 minutes.'

On Currie's side, a decision was quickly made not to attempt to keep
the document from the jury at this stage. Colonel Reginald Orde leaned
forward from the body of the courtroom, over the backs of the reporters,
to inform Tilley that he would undertake that the informant would
not be prosecuted if his name were disclosed.

Regan was given the name of the man the newspapers described as
the 'mystery witness,'[4] and arrangements were made to have him come
to Cobourg to testify. Tilley then also provided Regan with the name
of the man who had actually received and signed this version of the
armistice message. With a flourish, Tilley announced: 'Here is the

gentleman's name, his business address, his house, his telephone number at his office and at his house. I don't think I can do anything more to hunt up witnesses than that.' 'Your efforts are appreciated,' Regan replied sarcastically.

The 'mystery witness' duly appeared the next day, shortly after lunch. He was Alfred Cruchley, who had served as a sergeant-major, and he had two messages which he had brought back from overseas as souvenirs of the war. The first document was a signaller's message sent to the Second Brigade, Canadian Garrison Artillery, at 11:00 PM, 10 November, marked 'Operational Priority.' It indicated that the Canadian Corps continued the attack with the objective of capturing Mons and the high ground in the vicinity, and that the artillery would continue to operate in liaison with the attacking brigades.

The second document was of greater interest to Regan. It was the armistice message received by the signallers and then repeated to the batteries in the brigade. Regan confidently asked Cruchley to give the hour the message had been received; very much to Regan's annoyance, the witness said he could not tell. How could that be, Regan fumed. Cruchley had given the hour of the previous message. But the witness adamantly refused to say what the notation '6:05' meant.

Tilley, no doubt amused by his opponent's lack of success with Cruchley, knew that he still had to clear the matter up in cross-examination. He established that messages were received by a signaller by telephone and then written down, with a notation made of the time. The copy Cruchley possessed did contain the notation '6:05' in its text, but another notation seemed to indicate that it had actually been received at 9:00 AM.

'Anything on this document that records any hour before that time [9:00 AM] would be something he would put on from some other source, not anything to do with what he [the signaller receiving the message] did himself?' Tilley asked. 'Exactly,' the witness replied. 'And if the inference is that 6:05 is the time of the original message given to him over the telephone, it would depend upon the accuracy of the transmission as to whether that would be the exact hour or not?' 'Yes, Sir.'

The message was hardly convincing proof that anyone had known of the armistice at 6:05. That time could easily have crept in as an error in transcription as the message was relayed from signaller to signaller. Regan was undaunted, however, and tried to make his point in re-examination. He got nowhere. Tilley objected that his questions were improper re-examination. The judge was exasperated: 'The trouble about ruling promptly and sharply on your questions is that I do not want to create any misunderstanding. I do not want to create the impression that evidence that ought to get in is being excluded, and I fear that I may create such an impression if I rule the way really I ought to rule. Yet because you do not follow the regular practice, the proceedings are prolonged.'

Regan's own frustration surfaced. 'If your Lordship will permit me, I think it is my duty to make this observation. I think you should know that we have had great difficulty in getting witnesses.' Tilley observed acidly, 'If you haven't got a good case, you are bound to have.'

The story of the message Cruchley had kept as a souvenir was completed by the next witness, William Caldow, the man who had received it on behalf of his battery. Caldow, by 1928 a Toronto stockbroker, had served as a lieutenant with the First Heavy Battery, and had been fifteen to twenty miles west of Mons on 11 November.

Regan asked him when he had received the message. 'As I recollect it, it was fairly early in the morning, but I couldn't specify the time.' Caldow remembered that he was the only officer out of bed when the message came, and agreed with Regan that on the basis of what was recorded on the message it seemed likely that it was sent out at 6:05. But he also agreed with Tilley that he had nothing to do with writing the time '6:05.'

Q You were not the one who was issuing the message?
A No, I received it.
Q And therefore 6:05 has nothing to do with anything you did?
A No.
Q Your real connection with the message is your acknowledgement on the back of it that you had been notified of the contents of that message.
A Yes, Sir.

On Friday afternoon, toward the end of the first week of the trial, Colonel Orde was recalled to the stand by Regan and put through a lengthy rehash of the casualty figures he had previously given. It was a repetitive exercise, and Orde was not the most patient of witnesses. He was weary from having gone through it all with Regan the night before. 'Well, we gave you the whole thing up till 2:00 o'clock last night, Mr. Regan,' Orde replied to one question.

Regan made little headway, and seemed to be groping. He continued on until the afternoon break at 4:20. When the jury returned, it was announced that the court would sit on Saturday morning, adjourn for the rest of the weekend, and reconvene on Monday afternoon. To get home for Sunday, some jurors would have to catch trains on Saturday. Tilley suggested that an evening session be held. One member of the jury displayed his anxiety over the amount of time the trial was taking: 'I think we should try to get this through some time, because we are farmers and it will soon be time to start work.'

No one had thought the trial would take more than a week. Justice Rose had a matter on his list for the next week that had to be re-assigned to another judge. Tilley complained, 'I have very important work next week, and I don't know what I am going to do about it.' A Toronto *Telegram* headline read, 'MONS CAPTURED IN THREE DAYS; LEGAL BATTLE ENTERS SECOND WEEK.'[5]

Regan, however, was the one who would have to carry the burden of an evening session. 'I want to hurry this as fast as I can, but I really am not able physically to go on at night. I was not at all well yesterday. I almost collapsed ... We had been going from half past nine till 6:00 which, as your Lordship knows, is an hour and a half longer than what is usually expected.' When the judge observed that those were his usual hours, Regan added, 'Well I have not had the pleasure of practicing before your Lordship as often as I would like to have.'

Rose repeated Tilley's suggestion that an evening session be held, and one juror showed his frustration by remarking, 'Make it an all night session.' Regan replied, 'It is a lot easier for a person sitting down than it is being up here on your feet and trying to figure this thing out.' The juror answered, 'I don't believe it is!' and the courtroom rocked with laughter.

The end of the day finally came when Regan sank heavily to his chair with an audible sign of relief at 7:00 PM. He had made few points with Orde, and had succeeded only in testing the patience of judge and jury alike.

The case for the defence was drawing to a close on Saturday morning. Regan called Wilson himself to the stand. The trial had been an enormous strain for Wilson, as it had been for Currie, and Wilson was less able than Currie to cover his nervousness. When he testified he spoke in a low voice, so low that the jury had trouble hearing him. The judge had to ask him to speak up and turn to face the jury.

'How did you come to publish the article? Did you discuss the article with anyone before it was published?' Regan asked. Wilson mentioned his discussion with Preston. 'Now, tell us how that discussion came to take place?' 'Through reading a dispatch, a cable dispatch, in the Toronto *Globe* of June 13th, 1927,' Wilson answered. Regan held a copy of that issue of the *Globe* in his hand. 'This is the paper you read?' 'Yes, Sir.' 'Now, will you read to the jury the article that is contained in the *Globe*?'

The *Globe* article had been ruled inadmissible on the first day of the trial, and Tilley quickly objected. Regan argued that the article was relevant to show that Wilson had some basis for believing in the truth of the Mons article, and that even if found liable he was entitled to have this considered when damages were assessed. Tilley sensed that Justice Rose was attracted by Regan's argument, and withdrew his objection. So much had already been admitted that might have been stopped. Perhaps the best strategy at this point was simply to let the jury see whatever Regan tendered so that there could be no lingering feeling that Currie had covered something up. The article, which spoke of the blood of brave Canadians spilled in the battle for the town, was read in its entirety.[6]

Having succeeded on this point, Regan pressed his luck on a more contentious issue. He asked Wilson if he had relied on anything else in his decision to publish the *Guide* article. 'Well, I have read in Hansard –' Regan picked up a book from the counsel table. It was the volume of Hansard containing the report of Sir Sam Hughes's attack on Currie in 1919. This time Tilley objected vigorously. Hughes's statements were direct and explicit. If the jury knew how closely the *Guide* article followed what Hughes had said, it might well conclude that it was unfair to blame Wilson and Preston for merely repeating the words of a former minister. Tilley contended that Hughes's statements were nothing more than hearsay and therefore inadmissible.

The judge was not so sure. Regan argued that in order to determine the damages, the jury should be allowed to see what had been the basis for the article. He hoped, of course, that the jury would take Hughes's remarks into account on the issue of liability as well, and excuse his client altogether. Counsel were unable to cite any supporting cases. Tilley argued that since the defendants had not retracted, but were defending on the ground of truth, the evidence should not be allowed in mitigation of damages. He conceded that by pleading the defence of fair comment the defendants had technically put their state of mind in issue, and that Wilson could therefore testify as to his own state of mind, but it would be an impossible and endless task to examine everything that had produced that state of mind. Justice Rose was uncertain of the point, but then put his finger on a passage from a textbook he was consulting which tended in the plaintiff's direction. He decided to exclude the Hansard extract.

While evidence showing that the plaintiff does not have a good reputation may be offered in mitigation of damages, a defendant is not allowed, under the guise of mitigation, to lead evidence of second-hand statements supporting the truth of the very libel that is the subject of the lawsuit. If it were otherwise, the basic rule requiring that the truth of what the defendant has written must be established by firsthand evidence would be seriously undermined.[7] It would be difficult, if not impossible, for the jury to take rumour and suspicion into account on the issue of damages, but to ignore them when deciding the issue of liability.

Regan was taken aback by the ruling. He asked for time to consider his position and research the point further. Rose became impatient. 'Oh, Mr. Regan, time, time, time! You must have contemplated how you were going to present your case when you began to present it.' Tilley tried to rush Regan on. It was nearing the end of the day and the end of the week, and it was to Regan's advantage to delay closing his case so that he could use anything that came to light over the weekend. Regan returned to the ruling. Justice Rose insisted that he go on and not just try to run out the clock. The wrangling went on until Regan pointed out that the appointed adjournment hour had come: the judge had promised to stop just before one o'clock so that one of the jurors could catch a train home for the weekend. 'Is there a later one that would do you nearly as well?' the judge asked. One of the jurors answered, 'I was the one that spoke, but I can get away later. I will stay a while longer.'

Rose decided to sit for another half hour. Regan protested, but the judge insisted that he proceed. There was a long silence. 'Please proceed, Mr. Regan. We have been waiting. Time is limited, and we have been waiting now several minutes for the next question.'

For once, Regan was at a loss for words. He could think of nothing else to ask Wilson, but he did not want to close his case. He brought up the meeting Wilson had had with Currie in November. Wilson's letter suggesting the meeting had been headed 'without prejudice.' If the discussions were 'without prejudice,' evidence of what had transpired could not now be given, but Regan was unable to find another topic to explore.

Tilley was indignant: 'One very seldom has to explain these things in a courtroom.' But Wilson responded, 'Well, I didn't know there was anything at all private or without prejudice in our interview.' Tilley protested that it was improper to permit Wilson to testify about the meeting, but, having made the point that Wilson was being devious, he did not press his objection.

Wilson explained that Currie had referred him to the maps and orders displayed in his office and had insisted that the article was untrue in every respect. Currie had asked where Wilson had gotten his facts. 'I said that it was through what I had read in Hansard and through reading that report in the *Globe*, and also in talking with returned men.'

Regan continued: 'Now, what was your motive, Mr. Wilson, in writing this article?' 'I thought there had been so many rumours afloat about this particular phase of the war that it would be a good thing to have it settled,' Wilson answered. 'Was there any malice on your part towards Sir Arthur?' 'None whatever. I did not know Sir Arthur, never had met him, never had heard a speech from him ... never even heard him by radio, and I had no personal malice in the matter.' Wilson's voice faltered. The strain was becoming unbearable. He felt faint and had to sit down. Regan handed him a glass of water. The examination struggled on for fifteen or twenty painful minutes, until, much to the relief of Regan and Wilson, and perhaps of the jury, the first week of the trial came to a close at half past one.

The second week of the trial began on Monday, 23 April, at 2:00 PM. Those on the jury who were farmers had risen at 5:00 AM to catch trains for Cobourg. Sir Arthur Currie had gone home to Montreal for the weekend, and had not yet arrived when the session began.

Wilson entered the witness-box, and Regan returned to the pre-trial meeting with Currie. Tilley rose, with Wilson's 'without prejudice' letter in his hand. Tilley's strategy was subtle. This was all very confusing to the jury, he said. Any lawyer would know that 'without prejudice' discussions were not admissible at trial. But because of his desire to get on with the trial and to permit the defendants to say anything they wanted, he would waive the objection and allow Regan to proceed.

Regan, however, had covered most of what had been said between Wilson and Currie on Saturday, and had little else to ask. Having appeared to make a generous concession regarding the admissibility of the interview, Tilley would now use the situation to discredit Wilson in cross-examination:

Q Were you aware that you had put 'without prejudice' on your letter?
A Oh, yes.
Q Were you aware of that when you were giving your evidence on Saturday?
A Oh, yes ... Without prejudice to my standing.
Q Listen. You were down there to try to get something from Sir Arthur that you could use against him and he couldn't get anything from you to use against you. Was that the point?
A I went to Montreal at my own expense, with an open mind ... to be convinced that I was wrong in the article.
Q Will you please stop talking and answer the question? Did you, when you planned the interview, did you think you had it arranged so that you could use whatever was said against Sir Arthur but he couldn't use anything that was said against you? Was that your plan?
A Oh, I wouldn't agree to that, Sir.

Wilson's denial that he had had the help of a lawyer in drafting the letter, even though the statement of defence had been filed a few days before the letter was sent, sounded unconvincing. Tilley returned to the interview and to what Currie had said to Wilson.

Q Did he tell you that he thought your article was a very unfair article?
A He certainly did.
Q And did he tell you to withdraw it?
A After talking with me, he said, 'Now, Mr. Wilson, what are you going to do about it?' And my reply was, 'Sir Arthur, I am going to do just what I think is right.'

Wilson said little else. As he stepped down from the witness stand, he seemed a fragile, almost pathetic figure, barely able to withstand the pressures he had brought upon himself by defending the suit. Would the jurymen find fault with his behaviour, or would they have sympathy for their local journalist, and perhaps even admire his determination to stand by what he had printed?

10

General Currie's Reply

The first witness called on Currie's behalf was Colonel Allan Magee, the Montreal lawyer who had done so much to help Currie prepare his case. Magee went overseas with a battalion he helped to organize and train, the 148th, which was officially affiliated with McGill University. The 148th had to be broken up to reinforce other units, and Magee joined Currie's staff. He worked closely with Currie right up to the end. (He would serve again in the Second World War, training hundreds of McGill graduates as officers, and then move to Ottawa as the executive assistant to the minister of defence, Colonel James L. Ralston.) Tilley began his questioning:

Q Your name has appeared on some of the copies of the order with regard to the armistice that came through on the morning of the 11th. Did you receive that message?

A I received a message from First Army ... at 6:30 ... which I took down over the telephone.

Q It came in by telephone?

A [The armistice message was read out yet another time, and Magee continued.] Now, on receipt of that message I telephoned it to the divisions. To the 3rd Division I am certain, as I spoke to Col. Duguid at that time. I could not say definitely that I telephoned to the 2nd Division, but immediately upon telephoning, I then sent a signal message. Now, a signal message means that I wrote out the order similar to this, handed it to the signallers for dispatch to the 2nd and 3rd Divisions and other troops concerned. First it was telephoned in order to expedite matters ... as to the 2nd Division I cannot say, but a signal message was sent to both divisions at 6:45.

Magee explained the mechanics of transmitting such messages to the units.

Q Now, what is the number of the message as you sent it out?
A G.121.
Q [Tilley directed Magee's attention to the message the defendants relied upon as having been received at 6:05 AM by the artillery brigade.] Now then, do you see a message there with the same number on, G.121?
A Yes.
Q Can you explain 6:05 on this photographic copy?
A I cannot explain why that is 6:05. It may be for 6:45 ... The message would never go over from Canadian Corps to the 2nd Brigade C.G.A. ... because the 2nd Brigade C.G.A. would be under the command of the Canadian Corps Heavy Artillery ... so that the Corps H.Q. would not ordinarily under any circumstances send a message direct to that brigade. So that there must have been some error in connection with that message.

'Should not some exception have been made,' asked Regan in cross-examination, 'for this very unusual message, in order to get it out more quickly?' 'The quickest way to get it out to all concerned would be through the proper channels,' Magee answered.

Regan had noticed that different pencils had been used to make notations on the armistice message Magee had written, and that the hour of the message was written over the original. He asked Magee to examine the original notation he had made of the message from the First Army when he had received it over the telephone.

Q Did you use different lead pencils in writing the message?
A I couldn't tell you whether I used different pencils or not. [Magee admitted that the message bore the marks of different pencils.]
Q Now then, do you notice the figures 6:30?
A Yes.
Q What is significant about the figure '6'?
A It is plain enough; it is written over some figure but –

Q There is a figure beneath the figure '6'?

A Yes.

Q What was the figure beneath the figure '6'?

A I can't tell you.

Q Does it look like the figure '5'?

A I couldn't tell you.

Q Well, you had better look and explain this to the jury why there is some confusion of figures there.

A I can't explain why there is any confusion of figures. It is overwritten with the 6:30.

Q It looks to me like the figure '5' was going to be made there.

A Well, it may have been a '2'.

Q It may have been a '2'. How could it possibly have been a '2' if it was at 6:30 that it came in?

A Well, as I say ... 6:30 is the correct time.

Q When did you write this note at the top? There is a note, and following the word 'note' are the words, 'This is written down by me as received by phone from First Army, A.A.M.' When did you write that?

A That was written down some three or four months ago.

Q Some three for four months ago? After the [legal] action started?

A Yes.

Q How did you come to write it?

A With a pencil and my hand. That document I regarded as a valuable document. I had it put away with other war records, and I made that notation on top just as a means of indicating what the document was and what significance it bore.

Regan then attempted to resurrect Lingard's evidence that a radio message of the armistice had been received much earlier than 6:30 AM.

Q Was there any message sent out by wireless?

A None.

Q None whatever?

A None from the Corps.

Q Did you receive any by wireless?

A We received one I think at 9:30 in the morning from the Army.

That answer hardly helped. Regan had been fishing for something that would make the jury suspect that Magee had altered the message to cover up its early receipt, but he got nowhere. He decided to turn to another area.

Q You were back at Valenciennes?

A Yes.

Q About 19 miles back at Mons. Where was Sir Arthur at the time?

A He was in Valenciennes.

Q And what time did you take the message to him?

A It went over by a runner, by a messenger, I imagine.

Q When did you send it to him?

A Almost immediately I had written it out.

Q He would get it by what time?

A I would say – I can't say what time.

Q He says he got it at 6:45?

A Well, I imagine that would be about right – it was just across the street.

Q I understand that Sir Arthur was taking a bath when he got the news, and he continued with his bathing before taking any action on the matter?

A Well, you say so, but I don't know anything about it at all.

Q I suppose when you got the message, Col. Magee, that morning, that you were not at all surprised?

A How do you mean surprised, Mr. Regan?

Q Oh, you know what I mean.

A I was surprised. It was the first intimation that I had of the armistice.

Q Never dreamed of the armistice going to be signed?

A I knew of the envoys being over, but insofar as the armistice coming through at that particular time, it was a surprise.

In re-examination, Tilley touched on the potentially damaging implication that Magee had tampered with the armistice message. Holding the message up, he adopted a mocking tone, trying to ridicule Regan's contention that it had been improperly altered. Regan was annoyed. 'My Lord, I would like to object to this. It may be amusing to Mr. Tilley, but it certainly was not amusing to the men fighting in Mons at that particular hour, about the time that they got out, and I don't think that this is quite proper in reply. He should have brought all that out when he had him in chief.'

William Grafftey, the commander of 'D' Company, Forty-second Battalion, was one of the first Canadians to reach Mons on 11 November 1918. He spoke crisply and directly. His testimony was dramatic and significant. Everyone in the courtroom listened intently as he explained the advance his company had made. The company, which was billeted in Jemappes, received orders to advance on 10 November. On the road from Jemappes to Mons they came under intermittent shell and machine-gun fire. By 11:00 PM the company had established a post beyond the Mons railway yard and within the boulevard that forms the perimeter of Mons. By midnight the whole company had advanced to this point. The city was quiet, no shots were being fired, and there was no movement by civilians. Between midnight and one o'clock Grafftey and his sergeant had gone at least halfway into the Grand'Place without encountering the enemy. They concluded that the city had been evacuated.

At 1:30 AM four German prisoners were captured at a machine-gun post near the station and brought to company headquarters. By 4:30 AM it was reported that all platoons were in the city at Place de Flandres. At dawn, between 6:30 and 7:00 in the morning, Grafftey proceeded through the centre of the city; he was met by civic officials and taken to the Hôtel de Ville, where he later met his commanding officer, Colonel Royal Ewing.

At about 7:45 AM the armistice message was received by the company signal officer, and Grafftey notified his men. 'We took to billets and our company show was over.'

But Grafftey's company had lost twelve men, two of whom were killed in action and ten wounded. Some of those wounds proved fatal days later. The two killed in action died at the western outskirts of Mons between 2:00 and 4:30 on the afternoon of the tenth. Tilley asked:

Q There were no casualties after 4:00 or 4:30?
A I did not see any casualties after 4:30, and I know the company did not receive any casualties after 4:30.
Q And then from that time on you were not under fire, and you found Mons, when you got inside it, you found it evacuated?
A Easy going.

Regan was quick to contrast Grafftey's account with the version of the advance given in the Forty-second Battalion war diary. He read: '"As the majority of the machine guns were located on the right flank and the heaviest opposition was coming from this quarter, it was decided to force an entrance to the extreme left along the southern edge of the Conde-Mons Canal to work through the city and cut off the machine guns operating on the southern canal bank.''' Grafftey agreed that at five o'clock he had seen a machine-gun that was not firing but preventing an advance.

Q It was manned?

A Yes.

Q So that there was machine gun opposition directly in front of you after 5:00 o'clock?

A Absolutely.

Q Then why did you tell this jury here a few minutes ago that from 5:00 o'clock until midnight of the 10th–11th you experienced no heavy machine gun resistance in front of you? Will you explain that?

A Heavy machine gun [fire] – not resistance.

Q Oh, I see; you distinguish between fire and resistance?

A You asked me if I heard any fire after 4:30.

Regan read on, trying to establish that Grafftey's version of an easy advance contradicted the story told in the battalion war diary. '''At 2200 hours Capt. W.A. Grafftey and Lt. D.M. Handy with No. 16 platoon left the post ... and under cover of two Lewis guns which engaged the enemy on the right passed through the Mons railway yard and entered the city at a point near the station at 2300 hours. The enemy machine guns were still covering the approaches to the city. "A" Company worked its way under very heavy machine gun fire to the bridgeheads in Q.13.B. and Q.14. Both of these bridges were destroyed and the canal could not be crossed.'''

Grafftey admitted that he had heard some machine-gun fire to the south after midnight. Could it have been from part of the city south of the boulevard, an area not occupied by Grafftey's company, where one of Regan's witnesses swore he had seen dead Canadians the next day? 'It might have.'

The Toronto *Globe* gave more prominence to its report of Graffety's evidence the next morning than to the now notorious decision of the Supreme Court of Canada, handed down that same day, holding that women could not sit in the Senate because they were not 'persons' within the meaning of the constitutional provision relating to appointments to the Upper House.[1] The headline read 'WAR'S LAST DAYS RETOLD IN CALM ONTARIO TOWN BY VETERANS OF MONS.' The story opened: 'Complacent Cobourg heard today a war story it won't soon forget. It was almost ten years old. But it was stamped with all the spontaneity and appeal of the best-seller, and it had the crowd in the court-room in the Currie libel trial open-mouthed with astonishment.'[2]

There were many senior officers in the courtroom, waiting their turn to testify on behalf of Currie. But before they were heard from, several ordinary soldiers and junior officers were called by Tilley. He feared that if he led with the senior officers, he might give the jury the impression that the case was nothing more than a contest between the officers on Currie's side and the troops on the side of the defendants.

Joseph Freeman, now a private chauffeur, had been a transport corporal attached to the Forty-second Battalion. He told of four men killed by a shell at Jemappes. On the morning of the tenth, at about 6:00 AM, the men got up as usual to breakfast and feed the horses. By 9:30 the Germans were shelling the town. 'We were standing in this farmyard. There was eight of us, our farrier was shoeing a horse, and there was an aeroplane came over and he dropped a signal to his artillery, and the first thing we knew we were all – four was wounded and one killed outright and three died of wounds.' 'One killed outright?' Tilley asked. 'One killed outright and three died of wounds and four wounded.' 'What happened to you?' 'I had my foot blown off.' Nothing Freeman said helped Currie, but at least he was a man from the ranks prepared to stand up for his commander.

James Page, the regimental sergeant-major of the Forty-second Battalion, took part in two parades on 11 November, the first at 11:00 AM and the second in the afternoon when Currie was there. He had seen a dead Canadian on his way into Mons early on the morning of 11 November, but this had not dampened his enthusiasm for the celebration. Tilley was anxious to meet Preston's charge that the men had had their rifles turned on Currie. 'After the parade we gave three cheers for General Currie in the usual manner, which they generally done on all parades, and we gave it with good heart.'

Paul Hutchison, another Montreal lawyer, had been with 'A' Company, Forty-second Battalion, as a junior officer. From Jemappes on the morning of 10 November, his unit proceeded towards Mons with orders 'to take care and go easily, and if we had any difficulties not to incur casualties, so far as possible.' Along the way there was some shelling. In the afternoon the company commander with the platoon ahead sent back a message that as a result of machine-gun fire from across the canal, two men, Daigle and Brigden, had been killed, and Hutchison was asked to get his men into the houses at the side of the road and await further instructions. The machine-gun was guarding the road from Cuesmes at the point where it reached Mons, on the other side of the road. The firing stopped at about midnight. At about two o'clock Hutchison received word that Captain Grafftey's company was in the city and that he was to bring his platoon up. The Germans had blown the bridge, but a makeshift affair allowed the company to cross. It appeared that the Germans had left. By five o'clock on the morning of the eleventh, they were on the boulevard being greeted by civilians. Tilley questioned Hutchison:

Q Now, will you compare that method or that procedure on the part of your unit about the 10th and 11th with methods that prevailed some times before, when you were in other active operations?
A Well, previous to Valenciennes, two or three weeks previous, there would be a set plan of attack.
Q Did you have anything of that kind in connection with your operations about Mons?
A No, Sir.

Regan cross-examined at some length, but to little avail. He read Hutchison an extract from the First Army report.

Q 'These machine gunners continued throughout the night to fire heavily on all troops of the 3rd Canadian Division to cross the Canal.' Do you agree with that statement?
A We certainly got in during the dark and there was no firing on us.
Q Well, will you say that statement is not correct?
A No, I won't say it is not correct. I was only in one particular spot on the front ... and on that particular spot, to the best of my recollection there was no firing after midnight.

At times Regan's questions were unnecessarily argumentative and nit-picking:

Q Now, you have used the word 'dawn.' The use of the word 'dawn' is one of the words that you are told not to use by the Field Service Regulations, is it not?
A I don't know Field Service Regulations off by heart, Mr. Regan – two large volumes.
Q Well, I don't ask you to know them off by heart; but where words are forbidden to be used, such as 'dawn' or 'dusk,' you would naturally remember them, wouldn't you – a barrister?

A I might, yes.
Q And the word 'dawn' is one of the words that the Field Service Regulations forbids you to use?
A I don't remember that ... I used 'dawn' in the witness box, Mr. Regan. I don't even say that I would use it in a report.
Q You would not use it in a report?
A No, I would not.
Q Then why are you using something in the witness box that you would not use in a report? Why? Don't you think the jury are entitled to the same accuracy from you as the men who get a report from you?
A I would try to give my evidence in clear language here, and to avoid military terms.
Q The word 'dawn' is not a military term, is it?
A No, exactly, that is why it would not be used in a military report.

Tilley was able to poke fun at Regan's dislike of unmilitary language and at the same time support his case: 'It is astonishing how many careless soldiers there are. I see in a report of the First Army, which I understand is a British document, it speaks of "dawn." It says: "by dawn the town was cleared of the enemy, and the advance guard of the Division enthusiastically welcomed by the inhabitants." '

In his cross-examination of Eric Findley, the commanding officer of 'C' Company, Forty-second Battalion, Regan stumbled onto the fact that the witness had seen dead Germans in Mons.

Q You did not see any dead in Mons at all, I suppose?
A Two Germans.
Q Two Germans; where were they, what part?
A They were on this boulevard here.
Q That is on the eastern outskirts of the city. When did you see them?
A I saw these men after my company had established itself up at this post.
Q At what hour?
A It must have been about 7:30 in the morning.
Q Would it be possible that these two dead Germans that you saw were among the men referred to in the First Army Report, as follows: 'the crews of which' – that is, the machine gun post – 'were all either killed or captured?'
A I cannot speak of that.

Regan read again from the First Army Report: '"There was no pause during the night of the 10th-11th."' Regan speculated that this must refer to a period 'from dusk till dawn following,' but he was corrected by Findley. 'Those are expressions we are not going to use in this court.' Chastened, Regan continued. '"There was no pause during the night of the 10th–11th November. All ranks felt the impulse to drive the enemy as far as possible before the armistice was signed. The Canadians had the additional incentive of recapturing Mons before the close of hostilities."'

Findley agreed that everyone was eager to get into Mons, but he disputed the additional-incentive point: 'Mons was in the path of the ground that we wanted to occupy, and therefore we occupied it, we passed through it.' Regan then suggested that Mons did have special significance. Findley had to agree: 'Yes; we knew what had happened at Mons in 1914.' 'And you were anxious to take it back before the war ended?' 'We would far sooner find ourselves in Mons than find ourselves out in the fields,' Findley answered.

Regan returned to the report. '"The capture by the 2nd Canadian Division of the low hills south and south east of Mons during the previous afternoon had rendered the enemy's hold on Mons precarious and his line of retreat from it still more seriously threatened by a further advance during the night by this Division towards St. Symphorien and the high ground between it and Mons. The enemy's main forces evacuated the town, but numerous machine gun posts were left in with orders to hold out as long as possible. These machine gunners continued throughout the night to fire heavily on all attempts of the 3rd Canadian Division to cross the canals. At 4:30 two companies following the patrols entered the outskirts of the town and quietly disposed of the machine gun posts, the crews of which were all either killed or captured."' But Findley insisted that regardless of what had happened elsewhere in the line, he had seen no fighting after midnight.

Details of the action taken by Princess Patricia's Canadian Light Infantry were given by Captain Kenneth Burness. His company had advanced on the afternoon of 9 November toward the south of Mons. He arrived with an advance guard at about 5:00 PM on the ninth on a main road leading north into Mons, Faubourg de Bertimient. He saw a couple of Germans, who ran away. A patrol continued to advance into Mons to make reconnaissance. A German patrol was met coming from the opposite direction, and the Germans were all killed. Shortly after, two more Germans were encountered and killed.

Burness realized that there also were Germans on his left and his

right, and that he was out of touch with his own troops. He decided
to settle in, hoping the enemy would retire as they had on the two
previous evenings. But between 8:00 PM and midnight the Germans
made three attacks, and each time were repulsed. 'Shortly after midnight Corporal Carleton took the relief for the Lewis gun post, which
was established at the corner. As his relief was passing this hedge some
Germans – how many I don't know – jumped through the hedge,
which was quite thin, and he was shot with a revolver and was killed.
That was between midnight on the 9th and 1:00 o'clock on the morning of the 10th. The men who were with him attacked the Germans;
they, I believe, killed one and captured a machine gun which the Germans had brought up with them. Again, before 2:00 o'clock in the
morning, the Germans made a fifth attack, which was also repulsed,
and I had no further casualties.'
     'What instructions, if any, had you, Mr. Burness, about casualties?'
Tilley asked. 'No definite instructions about casualties. We were to
keep in touch with the Germans, and as I was very weak, I could not
press them very hard, and therefore I would not risk having many
casualties.'
     Burness's company was relieved by the Royal Canadian Regiment at
about six o'clock. On the next day, the eleventh, they moved toward
Mons through Cuesmes, and as they were marching up the Faubourg
they saw between six and ten dead Germans, presumably the Germans
who had attacked the night before. 'Did you see any Canadians?' Tilley
asked. 'Saw no Canadians there at all,' Burness replied.
     In cross-examination Burness said that he did not know how many
attacking Germans had been killed: 'I have no idea at all, it was dark,
and we could not see them.'
     Regan tried again to get the burgomaster's proclamation before the
jury. 'Did you see this proclamation that the mayor issued, the Burgomaster of Mons?' he asked. 'I did see one pasted on the walls at
Mons,' said Burness. 'Is this the one you saw?' Regan asked.
     At this point Reginald Parmenter objected that the document had
already been excluded. Regan replied that now he was using the document for cross-examination – 'If for no other ground, on the ground of
credibility.' But he intended to use it for more than credibility, if credibility was the point at all. 'What I mean is this,' Regan explained. 'If
the jury saw this they might prefer to believe what the proclamation
of the Burgomaster said rather than the witness.' The description of
the capture of Mons in the proclamation was hearsay and could not

be used in the manner intended by Regan. The judge refused to reconsider his earlier, and undoubtedly correct, ruling excluding documents of this kind.

Regan would not be put off his familiar technique of reading other accounts of the taking of Mons in cross-examination and then asking the witness to agree or disagree. He read an account written by a journalist, Livesay: '"The first shot fired at Mons in 1914 was by the 5th Lancers, now attached to the Canadian Corps, and an officer who fought here then was killed an hour and a half before the armistice. The Canadians, with an inspired sense of historic fitness, had sworn to be in Mons while the war lasted."' Regan asked Burness if he agreed or disagreed with this account. 'All I can say about the statement is that it sounds like journalese to me.' This was hardly the answer Regan wanted.

Tilley, spelled at times by Parmenter, called to the stand a number of veterans to support the story told by Grafftey and Burness. Alfred White, who as a captain had commanded a company of Princess Patricia's Canadian Light Infantry, took the stand on the morning of the ninth day of the trial. Tilley hoped that White's evidence would show that although there had been a determined push to Mons, efforts had been made to minimize casualties. On 9 November 1918 White's company had proceeded from Jemappes on the road running northeasterly towards the Mons-Conde canal. At the point where the road reaches the canal, a forward patrol was fired upon by the enemy. Grenades were fired and the Germans retired. The company then moved to the Pont Canal, where further enemy fire was encountered. 'At that point,' White said, 'I decided the men had earned a rest, so I billeted the men in these houses, mainted a post at this point, and waited until the morning. I anticipated a retirement.'

At 5:00 AM on the tenth, the advance resumed. White received word that the Germans were making a counter-attack, and pulled his men back. At about 8:30 AM, he asked for and got artillery support at a point where the railway crossed the main road, near an enemy machine-gun post. The Germans also had a field gun near the railway station. 'During the rest of the morning the men took all available cover, leaving only posts for observation. The Germans maintained a fair amount of intermittent machine gun fire along the main road from the canal into Mons, and also from the direction of the railway station parallel with the canal.'

At midday, when they were relieved by Captain Grafftey's unit, five of White's men had been wounded. He asked Captain Grafftey if he might be allowed to enter with the movement into Mons. White found billets for his men in Mons at 4:00 AM. He first learned of the armistice at about ten o'clock on the morning of 11 November. 'I heard a band playing ... and I walked along the street and found my regiment marching into the city. I asked the officer where he was going; he said "we are going to the armistice parade," and that was the first I heard of the armistice.'

Richard Symons had served as a corporal with Captain White's Princess Patricia's company and had previously fought in the South African war. At the time of the trial, he was a machinist in Toronto.

On the morning of 10 November 1918, on the way into Mons, Symons's platoon had found two dead Germans and a couple of abandoned field artillery guns which Symons had seen shelling Jemappes during the night. The platoon then met resistance and suffered several casualties. Captain White ordered them to stop, and they were later relieved by other units. Parmenter continued his examination:

Q When did you hear that an armistice was to come into effect?
A I didn't hear anything about an armistice, sir, till nearly dinner time [at noon on 11 November].
Q At pretty near dinner time?
A Yes, sir. It occurred to me after the boys were gone to bed that when the people of Mons woke up there would be a wonderfully good time for everybody, and they would be so pleased at us getting in, and I decided I wouldn't go to bed, I would wait and celebrate.
Q Then you say you didn't hear until nearly dinner time?
A Not till I got back to the company again, pretty near noon. I was out with the Belgians having a good time, sir.

Symons was a scrappy and confident witness who captured the headlines next day: 'DASHING PATS CORPORAL GIVES VIVID ACCOUNT OF CHASING THE GERMANS.'[3] He was a dangerous man to cross-examine, but Regan tried anyway.

Q How often have you gone over this story that you have just told to the court?
A Never, sir.
Q And you are telling us now you went through that story and gave these details?
A Yes, sir.

Q For the first time in ten years?

A First time in ten years. If you had it branded into your mind the same as I have you would do it quite well, too. War is a serious thing, sir.

The outburst of laughter was so loud that the judge intervened without any prompting from Regan. 'I am afraid the crowd is getting a little bit out of hand. I must order the constables, if there is any more disturbance of that sort, to bring some of the disturbers before me to be dealt with.'

Q Mr. Symons, about this armistice; you say you didn't hear about the armistice till noon?

A No, sir.

Q You were having, I suppose, a fairly good time?

A A good time. As good as I could have, yes.

Q You weren't going to let a little thing like an armistice interfere with you?

A Weren't looking for an armistice, in fact – a poor time to stop the war, when we were having it all our own way.

Q Well, that is right, I agree with you. You mean after you got into Mons?

A No, when we were driving them before us and having things our own way. We put up with a lot of misery to put him on the run, and now was the time to punish him, I would say.

Q I suppose you were surprised when you heard about the armistice?

A Yes, sir. I was a little bit sore to hear about the armistice too.

Q Well, I am sorry you were disappointed, in a way. You never heard it discussed before?

A No, sir. I had heard lots of rumours for the past two or three years ... We got used to a lot of rumours. Never took any notice of them. We had enough to attend to our own business, and keep our own hide off the fence.

Q I suppose you were anxious to get into Mons?

A Sure, why wouldn't I be?

Q Absolutely, I agree with you.

A Well, don't you like a good time? I do.

Q Seeing that I am not married, I suppose I can tell you, yes.

A If you had lived in the mud as we had for a long time, why, you would be pleased to get into a city.

Milton Gregg was a lieutenant with the Royal Canadian Regiment. He had been awarded the Victoria Cross for heroic action at Cambrai. Gregg was to have a long public career. He served as sergeant-at-arms for the House of Commons from 1934 to 1939, fought again in the Second World War, and then became the president of the University of New Brunswick. He served as minister of fisheries in the last Mackenzie King government, and subsequently as minister of veterans' affairs and labour under Louis St Laurent. Even at the time of the Currie trial he was well known, and before he was called to the stand a number of spectators had spotted him. Word that a 'VC' was present in court spread around the room, although, as we shall see, Regan did not get the message.

Parmenter started the examination in the same way as he and Tilley had done with several previous witnesses. 'Will you tell the court and the jury what your experiences were on the 10th and 11th November 1918, Mr. Gregg.'

This time, however, Regan objected. 'My Lord, may I rise to take advantage of this occasion? I think it is hardly fair, after putting these witnesses through a lecture down here at the Dunham House [where Currie and most of his witnesses were staying], to come and say, "just tell your story."' Regan had no evidence to justify such a statement, and Justice Rose did not hide his annoyance. 'Mr. Regan, really, if you will persist in making these irregular unauthorized speeches, I shall have to, instead of scolding – I am very tired of scolding – I think I shall have to ask you to let one of the other counsel on your side conduct the case.' Regan sat down, apparently satisfied that he had made his point to the jury, even if it had been at the cost of incurring the judge's wrath.

Gregg proceeded to tell his story. From 1 November 1918 he had served as adjutant of the Royal Canadian Regiment. On 9 November instructions were given for three of the regiment's companies to advance northeast from Jemappes toward Nimy to the east. Heavy machine-gun fire and whizz-bang shelling was encountered. One platoon of 'C' Company attempted to cross the canal at approximately four o'clock in the afternoon, and the platoon commander and three of his men were killed and several others wounded. The advance was stalled until about midnight of 10 November, when 'B' Company was able to enter Mons and occupy some houses.

'What were your total casualties on the 10th, do you know?' Parmenter asked. 'The total casualties of killed or reported to me as adjutant were the four men crossing the canal. There were quite a number wounded; I should say, off hand in the whole three companies, around twenty,' said Gregg. 'Can you say when the last fighting was done on the 10th?' 'The last fighting that was reported to me, on the 10th, where the last severe resistance was at that point – that is the canal, sir – and the very strong resistance from the fosse and some resistance here outside the canal in the afternoon,' the witness replied.

Regan's cross-examination was vigorous and ill-tempered.

Q Can you tell me what brought 'B' Company down into Mons, when Nimy and the suburb of Nimy was their objective?

A I was not there.

Q What brought them into Mons when their objective was right on in another direction altogether? Can you explain?

A No, I cannot. I was not there. I was not commanding the company.

Q It wouldn't be that they wanted to get into Mons too, like one of the companies of the Princess Patricia's south of the canal?

A I imagine they were anxious to get into Mons.

Q Their objective didn't mean a thing to them; what they were anxious about was to get into Mons before the fight ended?

A Their objective meant something to them.

Q What took them from the course which they should have followed to their objective?

A I don't know.

Q Did they suffer any casualties going into Mons?

A They had some wounded around the bridge outside or nearby.

Q Did they have any killed?

A Not that company.

Q Are you sure about that now?

A I am quite sure that there were none killed there, there may have been some died in hospital – I don't know – but there were none killed on the spot.

Gregg was prepared to admit that he 'had heard armistice discussed before ... the conversation and gossip I would take it was an outcome of the various retreats or retirement of the Germans, and the apparent increasing weakness of the Germans.' 'The breakdown of the German resistance?' Regan asked. 'Yes, and the fact that earlier on when we were further behind, we had heard the order that officers bearing a white flag were to be taken care of.' However, Gregg emphasized, 'it was treated as pure stark rumour,' and in his opinion there was no serious talk of an imminent armistice. Regan continued the cross-examination:

Q Now, when [Colonel Ewing] received word that the armistice was signed, he sent out word to his men immediately that no further offensive operations

were to be entered into. You say that was not done with your battalion?
A No.
Q The men were allowed to go on and advance and carry on offensive operations after that hour?
A Company commanders were given the privilege of interpreting that order as they saw fit.
Q They could either fight or not fight, is that correct?
A That is correct ... they would know that they had that discretion under those circumstances.
Q After the armistice was signed, then did they have the discretion to remain where they were and not do any further fighting when the news reached them?
A Yes.

Gregg was openly hostile to Regan, and at one point during the cross-examination Regan retorted sarcastically, 'You are a pretty good man for an adjutant,' a remark that produced audible gasps from the spectators, who were astonished to hear a recipient of the Victoria Cross insulted in this way.

Parmenter cleared up two matters in re-examination. First, as to the so-called Dunham Hotel War College, Gregg explained: 'I have been in Cobourg for several days, and have met a great many old friends here, and we have talked about various phases of the war, pro and con, Cambrai, Valenciennes, Mons and so on.' But he insisted that the only time he had gone over his evidence was with Parmenter three months prior to the trial.

Then, with respect to the armistice rumours and the decision to continue fighting, Gregg offered the following justification: 'My own opinion and the opinion expressed by a great many others, discussed at that time, was that the Germans were simply retiring as a so-called fake to consolidate into a stronger position behind.' 'And if they succeeded in that, what in your judgment as a military man would have been the result?' Parmenter asked. 'If they had succeeded in that without being kept after and hounded, they would have had time to form a strong defensive position before they were pushed out of it,' said Gregg.

After Gregg stepped down from the witness-box, Regan, who had not known of Gregg's decoration, realized that he had blundered. Regan apologized for his insulting remark which, he explained, had been uttered in the heat of the moment and had not been intended to reflect upon a gallant soldier. 'Had I known he was a recipient of the highest honour that His Majesty the King could confer upon the subject for bravery upon the field of battle and a recognition that is only given for the highest evidence of personal courage, I would have rendered him homage rather than criticism.'

Tilley and Parmenter continued to call evidence that the fighting had all but stopped by the early morning of 11 November. Regan fought back with war diary extracts, and suggested that the fighting had been rather more intense than the witnesses allowed. One witness, Roy Russell, a Cobourg taxi-driver who had served in the RCRs, must have driven many officers to and from the station since the trial began. Regan confronted him with the lively account of the scene at Mons on 11 November written by General Edward Morrison, editor-in-chief of the Ottawa *Citizen* before the war, and from 1916 the commanding officer of the Canadian Artillery. Morrison had died three years before the trial, but Regan was determined to put his version of the capture of Mons before the jury. It was a highly questionable means of introducing hearsay evidence under the guise of cross-examination.

Entering Mons by the road we had attempted to follow yesterday we soon came upon dead Boches lying in the gutter and upon the sidewalks. Most of them were the victims of shell fire and were very dead. The capture of the city had been so recent that the place was only partly cleaned up. Fancy Wellington Street on a Dominion Day morning with sprawling bodies, with their loathsome mouse coloured uniforms, dotted along the thoroughfare, while crowds of men, women and children placidly paraded along to get a good place at the military ceremony, either taking no notice of this grim garnishment or grouping about the bodies as if they were an appropriate part of the function. In some instances the sight of them aroused such memories that men whose faces were convulsed with hatred deliberately spat upon them.[4]

Russell said that he had seen only the two dead Germans at the machine-gun post. Regan read on.

There was a tacit understanding that Mons, where the war started so far as the British army is concerned, should be taken by the Canadians before peace intervened. The fight of the night before had been no bloodless victory. The enemy's dead were thick in the suburbs, and especially around the station, where they had made their last stand. The Canadian Infantry had made it a point of honour, notwithstanding the cautions against casualties, to drive the enemy from Mons before the 'cease fire' sounded, and they succeeded at a price. They had not been urged to fight, but rather forbidden and restrained, but it is one of the wonders of the war how men will die for an idea. Their triumph would not have been so sweet had they not celebrated it in the Grand' Place de Mons. The entry of the Corps Commander with his staff mounted, preceded by an escort of cavalry and followed by his battle standard, was a magnificient climax to the day of rejoicing. He literally rode into the captured city along the streets garnished with the enemy dead.

Russell agreed with very little, if anything, of Morrison's account. With specific reference to Currie's entry into Mons, Russell said: 'Well, I know the street that Sir Arthur Currie came in on, and I don't think there was any German dead laying there.'

11

The Generals Take the Stand

Tilley called to the witness-box a parade of senior officers. Colonel Royal Ewing, commander of the Forty-second Battalion, was first. His evidence added little detail to that given by the men who had served under him, but he did describe an important conference at brigade headquarters. 'I went to a conference at Brigade HQ, now I wouldn't be sure whether it was that night [of the tenth] or the following morning, and the question of what was to be done was discussed. We were given detailed verbal orders at the time, to take over from the Patricia's and carry on, and the objective given to us was the high ground east of Mons ... Everybody was in the top of their form, and we didn't want to have casualties if it could be avoided.' 'Were there any instructions given about that?' Tilley asked. 'Quite; the company commanders were told "Now, make your way forward; if you get into trouble sit pat and use your own judgment."'

'Now, when did you hear of the armistice?' Regan asked in cross-examination. 'On the morning of the 11th at 7:45 the message came in,' Ewing replied. 'What did you do then? I suppose it was no news to you?' Ewing insisted that the armistice had come as a surprise: 'If it is any comfort to you, I wakened up the next morning afterwards, and didn't believe it was over.'

There was a good deal of tension between Regan and Ewing, and some pointed questions and answers: 'You were a little better off than some of those who didn't waken up at all.' 'Yes, and some that didn't

go.' Their exchange was punctuated with laughter, nervous and unconscious on Regan's part, quite deliberate on Ewing's.

Regan's suggestion that a sounder and safer strategy would have been
to encircle Mons produced an outburst of knowing laughter from the
officers on the plaintiff's side and from several reporters at the press
table, suggesting to the jury that the lawyer knew little about military
tactics and strategy. 'You know,' Regan complained, 'I don't like this
unseemly laughter here from this bench of notables here on the right,
and I don't think it is fair.'

Regan suggested that it would have been better for the Forty-second
to have remained where it was. Ewing interjected, 'You mean if we
hadn't gone to France at all?' This provoked more laughter at Regan's
expense. He turned very red in the face, and angrily continued:

Q No, no. If you hadn't gone through Mons. You like to be clever, don't you?
A I hope not.
Q Is that remark intended to be cute or entertaining?
A That is for you to decide.
Q Because it is something that is illuminating from a gentleman of your
  rank ... When you got this order about allowing the envoys through, you
  knew then that there was an armistice in the air?
A Well, we might suppose that there was an armistice. We knew that the Ger-
  mans were going back very fast, but how any person that was carrying on
  in the line would know that the show was over I don't know.

Regan turned to a sensitive area. Ewing stated that his officers could
exercise their discretion, and Regan tried to lay a trap for Currie.

Q Is that good military law?
A Absolutely ... We always tried to avoid casualties in the war ... If we were
  carrying on as we were here, with orders to keep in touch, we would, as we
  did, tell them to go on, if you run into trouble step to one side, keep up the
  pressure.
Q But if you had a definite objective, I think you told me, you would take that?
A If we had a definite objective we would go to it.

Ewing said that although his men 'had a definite objective,' the order
was qualified: they were ordered 'to move on to the high ground
beyond Mons, but they were told to take their own time doing it, and
avoid casualties.'

Regan was able to show that Ewing had actually exercised a discretion which Currie had said he could not claim for himself as Corps commander. The battalion war diary showed that upon receipt of the armistice message, 'instructions were immediately sent out to companies that no further offensive operations would take place.' Ewing agreed that this had been done on his instruction. 'Can you explain why Sir Arthur Currie, when he got the armistice message at 6:45 in the morning of the 11th, did not send out the same order that you did when you got it at 7:45?' Regan asked. 'No, I cannot explain anything that Sir Arthur Currie did,' Ewing replied.

Regan wanted to emphasize to the jury that he had scored a point: 'I am very much obliged to you, Colonel. I think you have done more for us than probably you intended.'

Brigadier-General John A. Clark had been the commanding officer of the Seventh Brigade, which included the Royal Canadian Regiment, Princess Patricia's Canadian Light Infantry, and the Forty-second and Forty-ninth battalions. Clark, a Vancouver lawyer, and by 1928 a Conservative member in the House of Commons, years later became the president of the Canadian Bar Association. He was proud of having been at Mons, and in his 'who's who' entry listed as decorations received 'Bar of Mons, Belgium,' and 'Cityoen d'Honneur, City of Mons, Province of Hainault.'

'You were in charge of the units of which many of our recent witnesses were members?' Tilley asked. 'I was,' Clark said. 'And had the oversight and direction with regard to the operations they have described?' 'I did.' Clark described the directions given for the advance towards Mons.

The situation was somewhat obscure; we had not an opportunity to reconnoitre; the advance had been comparatively rapid. Therefore, I took the view that the front line should be manned very lightly, really by a screen of scouts to discover the situation and report upon it, continuing the advance as rapidly as they could ... Instructions were given to the battalion in the line to carry on the advance by night ... If the battalion met opposition in the daylight ... and they were held up, they were not to rush the strong points but were to send information back and we would have them dealt with by artillery fire, and they were to do everything in their power to surround them or outflank them, but to do it at the least possible cost. If they were held up by these strong points during the daylight, then the suggestion was that they should push past them by night, outflank them and capture them, because we figured that confusion would be caused, and surprise, by these night advances.

The Princess Pats were detailed to take over the entire brigade line. They made remarkable progress on 8 November, and only encountered serious opposition on the next day at the railway embankment 1,700 yards west of Mons. That was overcome, and Clark gave an order directing an advance.

The Princess Pats had been going day and night since 7 November, and they needed rest. The advance was continued by the RCRs and the Forty-second on 10 November. The RCRs made good progress, but there were reports of severe artillery and machine-gun fire. The bridges across the canal at the points of entry into Mons were broken down. There was only one possible place from which Mons could be entered over land – a point west of the town immediately south of the Mons-Conde canal at the railway station. Clark continued his testimony:

A As a matter of fact, [Captain Grafftey's] company did succeed, by manoeuvering, to effect an entry into Mons. I got the report around midnight of the 10th–11th that they were actually in Mons, giving the map location, whereupon instructions were given to move carefully with a screen of scouts through Mons, with a view of ascertaining the position of the enemy and to mop up the city and to proceed to their objective beyond Mons.

Q Now, you used an expression, 'mop up' –

A I mean to clear the city of the enemy. For instance, in a city the size of Mons, which was a railway centre and a road centre, there might easily have been concentrated there a strong unit of motor machine guns.

Q [Tilley referred to Regan's suggestion that Mons should have been surrounded.] We have had evidence as to the casualties; what do you say might be the risks if you had proceeded by other means?

A Well, the risks were proven most clearly. The troops on either side of the city, on either flank of the city, suffered much heavier casualties than the troops which were immediately in front and went through the city. [Clark got the armistice message at about 6:45 or 7:00 AM.] When I received the armistice order the first thing I did, I took a map and I marked on it a further objective and issued orders for the 5th Lancers, a British unit attached to us, to go through the infantry and to establish themselves on that line if possible before 11:00, and then arranged immediately with the divisional commander for the relief of our infantry, which was immediately arranged.

Q Then do I understand that when you got the armistice order, you substituted, so far as further progress went, you substituted the mounted troops for the infantry?

A Yes, exactly.

Q Were they Canadian or Imperial?
A The 5th Lancers were Imperial.

Regan's cross-examination of this important witness lacked direction. Clark was often able to make points even more effectively than he had in his examination in chief.

Q There were, I understand few, if any, casualties?
A Well, there were remarkably few casualties at any time during this operation.
Q And that was due, I suppose, in part to the men's natural ability and to your orders not to expose themselves needlessly?
A Yes, and to the rapidity with which they advanced ... The very moment we stopped [the Germans] would have the opportunity of taking up gun positions and shelling our men.

The extract from the First Army report was read again: 'On the outskirts of Mons the enemy showed that he intended to resist our entry into the town to the utmost.' Clark agreed with the statement, and that there were numerous enemy machine-gun posts.

Q And they intended to hold out, according to the 3rd Division to the utmost?
A If they were like our men, they would.
Q And I suppose they did, because, reading on here, in the First Army Report it says, 'the crews of which were all either killed or captured.'
A Well, I don't know; I wasn't there. That is a detail.
Q I know, but that would indicate, if this report is right, that they did hold out to the last?
A Well, they held us back from the night of the 9th, remember, 24 hours they held us back.

When Clark was uncertain about how many Germans had been killed or captured, Regan again attempted to tender inadmissible evidence: 'You, coming from the House of Commons ... can give us some information about a picture that is hung in the House of Commons.' Clark was not sure what picture Regan was talking about, and Regan produced a photograph taken from a newspaper. The caption read, 'Huge canvas of Mons victory is hung at Ottawa. Famous painting of Canadians last battle.'[1] Tilley objected, and Justice Rose agreed that the picture could not be put before the jury. Regan said that he just wanted to see 'if the witness disagreed with the picture,' and protested,

'It is a lovely picture.' The judge commented, 'He will be able to see the original when he goes to Ottawa.' But Regan persisted.

Q Haven't you seen it yet?
A Not to my knowledge.
Q Because there are dead German soldiers in the picture.
A You might show it to me this afternoon when we are through.
Q All right, I will be glad to, because the picture shows dead German soldiers.
Q [Clark was then questioned about the armistice message.] Now then, when you got this order at 7:00 o'clock or approximately, did you issue any order to your troops in respect of any further offensive operations between the hour that you got the order and 11:00 o'clock?
A On receipt of that message I issued an order for the 5th Lancers to advance and take up the line, which was taken up.
Q Advancing which might result in casualties?
A Yes.
Q Now, why did you not do what Colonel Ewing did with his men when he got word of the armistice, I think around 9:00 o'clock, at the Grand'Place, the Hôtel de Ville in Mons?
A The 42nd Battalion had reached its objective. The 7th Brigade had not.
Q Why did you not send out the order that no further offensive operations should take place?
A Because I would have been disobeying an order.
Q Don't you think you would be justified in disobeying an order at that late hour when you knew that hostilities would cease at 11:00 o'clock, because in obeying it casualties might occur?
A Treason is never justified.
Q You think it is treason then to have disobeyed that order?
A Absolutely.
Q That is a very strong statement, General.
A I can't make it too strong.
Q You are an educated man, General, a Member of Parliament. Do you recall when Nelson disobeyed an order at Copenhagen? Was he guilty of treason?
A I can't answer. I don't know the circumstances.

Clark insisted that his brigade had suffered no casualties on the eleventh. 'Supposing they had,' asked Regan. 'Would the advantage gained have been justified?'

A Yes, I say yes, because the line taken up was 5 miles beyond Mons, and there was a decided advantge in the position occupied, because it occupied higher ground than existed in front of Mons, and, more important than that, I realized that my troops would be billeted in Mons. It was a very fine billeting area. There were 30,000 civilians there, and it was my duty in case hostilities resumed to secure a position from which that thickly populated area could be protected from enemy shell fire, and defense generally maintained.

Q Well, when hostilities were going to cease, wouldn't that have been the time that you might have stood fast?

A When I received the armistice telegram? Certainly not.

Q Press until the last moment?

A My orders were –the orders are there, and the orders are perfectly clear, and I did my utmost to carry them out in a reasonable manner.

Regan suggested that Clark did have the discretion to hold back in the light of the circumstances. He read from the Field Service Regulations. 'A departure from either the spirit or the letter of the Order is justified if the subordinate who assumes the responsibility bases his decision on some fact which could not be known to the officer who issued the order and if he is conscientiously satisfied that he is acting as his superior, if present, would order him to act.' Regan then asked, 'When Sir Arthur issued the order on November 9th [under which Clark was acting] he did not know that an armistice would be signed at 5:00 o'clock on the 11th?' 'Well, you will have to ask Sir Arthur,' Clark answered.

Clark insisted that the armistice message itself constituted an order to continue. 'It says, hostilities will cease at 11:00 o'clock. It might just as well have said, "hostilities will continue until then"; it would mean the same thing.' Regan asked why the armistice had been delayed until eleven o'clock. 'My opinion is that as the armistice was signed only a few hours before, it would be a very difficult matter to get the information to all the front line troops, and furthermore, it would give the troops the opportunity to adjust their lines tactically according to the situation as it existed then. For instance, in my own case it gave me the opportunity to put my line five miles beyond Mons, and thereby protect the main body and the civilians from shell fire in case of the resumption of hostilities. That is my interpretation.'

Preston decided to put a few questions to Clark, but he hardly helped his case. He asked whether Clark had heard anything of the armistice message Lingard claimed to have received by radio on the night of 10 November. Clark thought it impossible that such a message could have been sent: 'I would say it is ridiculous.'

Q You were a general having large responsibilities. Had you ever heard that an armistice was likely to come into operation?

A No, sir.

Q Not a shadow of a hint?

A Not a shadow of a hint.

Q Never heard it mentioned?

A Well, of course, when you speak of gossip, I wouldn't say that; any gossip that there may have been did not impress itself on my mind. I had one job to do, and I wasn't thinking very much about gossip.

Major-General Frederick Loomis, who had been the commanding officer of the Third Canadian Division on 11 November 1918, was called to the stand. Before the war Loomis had been in the contracting business in Sherbrooke. He went overseas in 1914 as a battalion commander and became a brigadier-general in 1916 and a major-general in 1918. Loomis returned to a business career in Montreal after the war. He was knighted in 1919, and his name was closely linked in the public mind with the capture of Mons. Tilley questioned him:

Q Now, did you have any conference with Sir Arthur Currie just prior to the 11th?

A Yes.

Q With regard to the proper course to pursue?

A Yes, I had a conference with him ... on the morning of the 10th.

Q What was the nature of that conference?

A Well, I think Sir Arthur visited me to impress on me the necessity of not shelling Mons heavily ... and to not undertake any serious offensive in the way of a heavy attack or a set piece with artillery; in other words, to avoid casualties and losses.

Q Was that his instruction to you?

A Yes, definitely.

Q And that was carried out?

A Yes.

Q I don't want to go over the whole story again, but it is suggested that there was an attack on Mons or an assault on Mons; what do you say?

A Well, there certainly was an attack on Mons.

Q What do you mean by an attack?

A Well, we were pressing the enemy, we were in touch with the enemy, and we were fighting the enemy, we were pressing him back ... The orders to the troops who were attacking were to press forward, get forward as rapidly as they could, but they were not to undertake any operation which would bring about losses. If they met with serious opposition they were not to proceed and attack them without referring to higher authority.

Q Now, was that a special order as to Mons, or your whole front?

A That was an order as to the whole front, as far as the 3rd Canadian Division is concerned.

Q Not specially as to Mons?

A No, not specially as to Mons. The only thing specially as to Mons was the question of shelling.

In an attempt to show that Currie had not sought glory in the taking of Mons, Tilley asked who had been responsible for arranging the victory parade at Mons on 11 November.

A I think I had a great deal to do with it. I think I influenced Sir Arthur to carry out the afternoon parade as well.

Q And was it any idea of his that there should be a parade?

A No, none whatsoever, he didn't want to carry out the parade.

Q What do you say as to the result of the two parades?

A Well, it was my opinion that those parades fitted the occasion. A ceremony of that kind is quite the usual thing under the circumstances, and that was a time for my division to do anything of that kind; they had to do it then or never.

Tilley then asked whether Loomis thought it would have been better not to go through Mons at all, but to pass to the north and south as Regan had suggested. Loomis was reluctant to answer. Regan objected that Tilley was leading the witness. Loomis insisted, 'I would have to know what the suggested operation would be before I could pass any judgment.' Tilley extricated himself neatly: 'Well, then, Mr. Regan can explain it to you.'

Regan's cross-examination of Loomis was perhaps his most effective to this point in the trial.

Q You commanded the division that captured Mons, General?

A Yes.

Q And was it an occasion for congratulation?

A Our success was.

Q This is what Sir Arthur thought when he learned about what had happened at Mons [referring to the message Currie sent Loomis on 11 November]: 'Warmest congratulations on having recaptured the historic battlefield of Mons before the cessation of hostilities.' What is the justification for that message, when all your troops had to do, as they have all sworn here, was to walk through Mons without a shot being fired or the loss of one life?

A That is ridiculous, walking through Mons without an opposition ... there was no walking through Mons without attacking Mons.

Q You said there was an attack on Mons?

A Yes.

Q Was there fighting?

A Yes.

Q Were there any Germans in Mons?

A Certainly.

Q There was fighting between the Germans in Mons and the Canadian troops outside?

A Yes.

Q And then you reply to Sir Arthur Currie: 'Many thanks for your congratulations on the recapture of the historic battlefield and town of Mons.' I can't understand for the life of me what all these wires were congratulating each other on the capture of Mons, when there was no fighting to get into Mons?

A I don't agree with you about the fighting

Q [Reading from the First Army report] 'All Ranks felt the impulse to drive the enemy as far as possible before the armistice was signed.' Does that apply to your troops?

A I think so.

Q 'The Canadians had the additional incentive of recapturing Mons before the close of hostilities.' Does that apply to your troops?

A I think so.

Q Was it true as far as you yourself are concerned?

A I should think so, yes.

Q Then you did have an additional incentive to capture Mons before the close of hostilities?

A I should say so, yes.

Regan then turned to the Third Division narrative, Loomis's own report. '"One platoon was sent through the north and one through the centre of town, joining up on the east side of it. A third attacked an enemy machine gun post, and after a short, sharp fight with Lewis guns and grenades, captured gun and crew."' Regan recalled Grafftey's statement that there had been no fighting in Mons at all. Loomis's report appeared to contradict that statement. When pressed, he replied disdainfully, 'Your Lordship, I have no particular remembrance of this particular small affair.'

Loomis got the armistice message at about 6:45. He was in bed when it was received.

Q Now, as a result of the receipt of that information, did you issue any orders to your troops with reference to any further offensive operations?

A Yes, I issued further orders. They were to carry out the operations that we were under orders to carry out, and with regard to the armistice order, what you call the armistice order, to carry out the requirements of that order. Those were issued. Now the details of those orders were given to the brigade.

Q Major General Clark takes the position that the armistice order was an order which justified him in advancing, to proceed to advance—

A Yes.

Q To carry on an offensive operation if it was necessary in the course of that advance to do so. Do you agree with that?

A We already had the operation order; we already had the operation order to carry on ... He was already required and ordered to advance. The armistice order was to tell them when to stop.

Q Now, you heard about this armistice some time before, the probability of an armistice being signed?

A I may have done so; I may have heard of it. I may have heard of things that were published in the papers at that time. We got papers occasionally, and I may have seen something about the pending armistice, and negotiations that were pending. I may have heard about it, yes.

Beyond that Loomis would not go. He had no recollection of reading about the Kaiser's abdication, and no specific information as to the likelihood of an armistice.

Sir Arthur Currie himself took the witness stand on the eleventh day of the trial. Despite the strain he was under, he looked robust as he entered the box. His civilian attire and heavy spectacles suggested the university principal rather than the warrior. The courtroom was packed. Every seat was taken, and even the aisles and passages were congested. Up to this point his case had gone well, very well. However, it could still be lost. So much would depend on how he appeared to the jury. Even if he could refute the specific allegation about Mons, any appearance of callousness or of seeking self-glory could turn the jury against him.

Tilley's examination in chief was a masterpiece of brevity and clarity.

Q General Currie, extended extracts have been read from your examination for discovery and are now before the jury, so that I shall not go over all the material matters by way of repetition, but I want to ask you about the orders of the 2nd, 9th and the 10th of November 1918, and follow on from there. Have you the orders before you?

A Yes.

Q Now, those three orders are all from the First Army?

A Yes.

Q And that means they are orders that would come to you rather than orders that would be issued by you?

A They would be orders issued to me.

Q Now, will you just describe your position – when I say your position, I mean the position of the Canadian troops – with respect to the First Army? What did the First Army consist of?

A At that time it consisted of three corps; the 8th Corps, the 22nd Corps and the Canadian Corps; the Canadian Corps being the centre corps.

Q The 8th Corps was to the north of you?

A Yes.

Q And the 22nd to the south?

A Yes.

Currie testified that an order had been issued on 2 November to the First Army, of which the Canadian Corps formed a part, and to the Third and Fourth armies on the southern flank of the First. The objective for all three armies was 'the Avesnes-Maubeuge-Mons line,' Maubeuge and Avesnes being towns directly south of Mons.

Q Now, then, that being the order of the 2nd of November, let us go to the order of the 9th of November, Exhibit 20. Now, would you read that order?

A It is from the First Army to the Canadian Corps, issued at 15:30, that is 3:30 in the afternoon. It says: 'Advance will continue tomorrow. 22nd Corps to the line of the Maubeuge-Mons Road and establish itself east of it, sending mounted troops and advance guards forward to keep touch with the enemy. Canadian Corps to the high ground east and northeast of Mons, sending mounted troops and advance guards forward to keep touch with the enemy south of the Canal du Centre. 8th Corps' – who were in the north – 'will push forward cavalry and troops on to the objective of the Mons-Jurbise Road, using buses and lorries to carry up supporting infantry so as to be up to the line of the left of the Canadian Corps as soon as possible. The Canadian Corps will give facilities to the 8th Corps to pass troops in buses along Valenciennes-Mons Road so as to take over from Canadian Corps as far east as possible north of Conde canal.'

Q Then that also would be an order to you as representing the Canadian Corps?

A Yes.

Q Did you [then] issue an order?

A Yes, sir. This is the Canadian Corps operation order sent to the 2nd and 3rd Divisions, the divisions that were in the line. 'Advance will be continued tomorrow in conjunction with the 22nd Corps on the right and 8th corps on the left. 2nd Canadian Division will capture the high ground east of Mons. 3rd Canadian Division will capture high ground in Q.4 central and the suburb of Nimy.' Also that 'mounted troops and advance guards will push forward east of above objectives to maintain touch with the enemy south of the Canal du Centre.'

Q Then, that being the order for the 9th, we come to the order of the 10th, issued to you?

A Yes.

Q Now will you read that?

A This is an order from the First Army to the 8th, the 22nd and the Canadian Corps, and it orders the Corps – it says: 'Corps will act as directed in G.215' – that was their order of the day before – 'of 9th inst. No operation orders will be issued tonight.'

Q Now then, I want to ask you this, General Currie: Would those two orders issued by the Army to you, would they be issued without consultation with you or after consultation with you?

A No, not after consultation with me; it would be the Army instructions.

Q Army instructions to you?

A Yes.

Q Then what was sent out following this is the order of the 10th of November?

A Yes.

Q Will you read it, please?

A 'Objectives for tomorrow as for today. No further operation orders will be issued.'

Q And that is the way the matter stood, so far as orders were concerned, at the end of the 10th?

A Yes.

Q Now then, on the 11th you received what we have called the armistice message, did you?

A Yes.

Q From the First Army?

A Yes. To Canadian Corps, dated the 11th: 'Hostilities will cease at 11:00 November 11th. Troops will stand fast on the line reached at that hour which will be reported to Army Headquarters. Defensive precautions will be maintained. There will be no intercourse of any description with the enemy. Further instructions follow.'

Q Now, having repeated that message, the armistice message, did you do anything further by way of issuing a further order?

A No.

Q That is to say, you transmitted that message to the divisions just as you had been instructed yourself?

A Yes.

Q Now, is that the way matters stood so far as you were concerned until eleven o'clock?

A Yes.

Q Did you during the 9th, 10th or 11th order any advance other than as indicated in the messages we have already read?

A No.

Q Was that the first message you had that armistice was signed, the one of the 11th, that we have read, the one that Mr. Magee got?

A That is the first intimation I had.

Q The first intimation you had?

A Yes, of any sort or description.

Q Why did you not issue any order other than these?

A These are clear and definite. It indicates what was to be done.

Q What was it?

A That hostilities would not cease until 11:00 o'clock. If it had meant they would cease earlier, it would have said so. It said, 'Troops will stand fast on the line reached at that hour,' which to me means that the advance would be continued, and when they reached that line they will take defensive precautions and maintain them, and they were to have no intercourse with the enemy, of any description.

Q So far as you are concerned, or your knowledge goes, were those orders carried out?

A Yes.

Q So far as you are aware, were they departed from in any way?

A No.

Q Now then, had you down to eleven o'clock on the 11th received any information as to the terms of armistice other than as indicated in the cable or the order?

A No.

Q But I mean, did you down to eleven o'clock, when the armistice became effective, know what the terms of armistice were except as indicated in the orders we have read?

A No.

Currie then explained that on 8 or 9 November, after the German envoys had been through the lines to discuss the possibility of an armistice, General Henry Horne, commander of the First Army, instructed him that there was to be no relaxation of the pressure on the retreating German forces.

Q Now, General Currie, was there any ... particular line ... on the German side ... that would offer special facilities for the Germans in taking up a defensive position?

A Yes.

Q Where?

A What we used to call the line of the Meuse.

Q Can you fix approximately how far back that would be from the line as of November 11th?

A I think thirty or forty kilometres – twenty-five miles.

Q In Belgian or German territory?

A That is in Belgian territory.

Q And how fast were the Germans receding?

A Some days they retired very much more rapidly than others ... They would leave their advance guards, a small delaying force, and the main body of the troops would retire rapidly and take up another position. Then as soon as we swept away the advance guards we would be allowed to go on quite rapidly until we came up against their next line of resistance. Some days we made four and five miles, some days only eighteen hundred yards, but in no case did we allow them to get away.

Q Then I think it has been suggested that the method of procedure at Mons was improper, that the advance should have been made north and south of Mons, something to that effect. What do you say about that?

A I disagree with that suggestion ... It is a fact that the troops proceeding on the south ran into far more opposition, had to overcome far more difficult obstacles and met with far more casualties, showing that that as a means, if its sole purpose was the taking of Mons, was a very poor way to take it, or was an expensive way. Now, these troops that went up ... to the north, also met with obstacles. It is more open country. As they attempted to cross the country they came under shellfire and machine gun fire ... Now, troops that are ordered to advance keep generally testing the line, always, and the place to pierce a point is at its weakest point – that is surely sound military tactics – and in this pressure the weakest point was disclosed right at the railway station, right there, and troops entered, and in a few hours afterwards had gone through the city and out on the other side.

Q Then were there at any time special instructions given to you to capture Mons except as carrying foward to these objectives?

A No.

Q Or were any instructions of that kind given by you to those under you?

A No.

Q Was there any purpose or object that you were serving in what was done on the 10th and the 11th except to carry out orders?

A No.

Q Received from the First Army?

A Yes.

Q That is all, thank you.

Currie had entered the witness box at 9:45 in the morning, and he answered Tilley's last question at 10:29. Regan was startled by the brevity of Tilley's examination in chief, but rose confidently from his chair to confront and, he hoped, to destroy Sir Arthur Currie in cross-examination.

12

General Currie under Fire

Frank Regan's cross-examination of Sir Arthur Currie was a dramatic confrontation between the combative, scrappy lawyer and the tense but confident general. It was the climax of the trial.

Q Do you think, Sir Arthur, that the story you have told Mr. Tilley a few minutes ago, and which took about ten minutes, is a complete story or all that the jury should have heard about Mons?

A We have had a great deal for the last ten days or more. I think mine supplements and makes the story complete.

Q Well, I wanted to get your view on it.

A Because you say that I ordered an attack on Mons after I knew the armistice was coming into effect.

Q We don't say you did.

A Yes, you do.

Q Oh, no. That is where we differ on the article.

A Well, all right.

Q I will get you to explain.

A You say there were appalling losses of life after I had this knowledge of the armistice coming into effect. The evidence of recent days may prove otherwise.

Q Did you give an interview to the *Star Weekly* of November 5th, 1927, reported by Charles E. Vining?

A Yes.

Q And continued in the issue of November 12th, 1927?

A Yes.

Q And did you tell them the story of Mons?

A Yes.

Q Did you notice the date that your writ was issued? ... About three weeks before you gave these interviews and told your story of this case to the world through the *Star Weekly*?

A Yes.

Q Standing in the box there today, Sir Arthur, as Principal of McGill University, will you say that that was an honourable thing to do?

A Yes. I did not know that there was any reason why I shouldn't. It was not the first story of the war I had given to the *Star* ... No thought came to me that I was doing an improper thing.

Q You don't know that might be considered by some courts as contempt of court?

A Well, I did not know that, and I would be the last person in the world to do it if I did.

Q Did you make this statement in this article? It is in connection, I think, with Cambrai and General Byng, you said these words: 'We went on with our plans, and a couple of days before the attack General Byng, who was commanding the Third Army, came to me. He said, "Currie, I have read over your plans and I know they are as good as they can be made, but can you do it?" I said, "Yes," and Byng answered, "Do you realize that you are attempting the most difficult operation that has been tried in the war? If anybody can do it the Canadians can do it, but if you fail it means home for you."' Do you remember making that statement?

A Not definitely in those words. That may be the sense of something I said.

Regan read more from the article: '"Cambrai. That is where the lives of the Canadian Corps were risked, and where Lord Byng felt so serious about doing it that he came to Sir Arthur and pointed out to him the seriousness of what he was doing. But in the face of that, Sir Arthur went on, and succeeded."' Currie interjected, 'In what is generally regarded as one of the most brilliant operations in the war.' Regan continued:

Q 'The night before the attack General Horne, our Army Commander, came to me and we went over the plans together. He was very anxious concerning the outcome, quite realizing, as I did, the risks we were taking. I was told afterwards that after he had said good-bye to me and was riding home, he more than once thought of turning back and cancelling the attack, but the thought came to him that the Canadians had never failed, and so the attack went on next morning at dawn.' I suppose these words represent what was said?

A Yes.

Q Then, Sir Arthur, the reporter asked you a question, and this is a rather significant question he put to you, after that attack, the most brilliant attack, you say,. of the whole war?

A One of the most.

Q One of the most; I thought perhaps it was the most from what you said. 'The end must have been in sight now.' Do you remember him asking you that question? ... Let me read you what he said you said when he asked you that question. 'Yes, I think we all knew then, even Ludendorff knew.' Did you make that statement?

A I may have.

Q So that after the battle was over, on the 9th of October, at least we can say the middle of October, to give you a good wide margin, you knew then that the end was in sight.

A I felt that we would defeat Germany.

Q Now then, were you asked this: 'The next month was chiefly a business of chasing the enemy ... with sharp local fighting, and one stop for the capture of Mont Houy and Valenciennes by the 4th Division'?

A Yes.

Q This was on November 1st?

A Yes.

Q Ten days before Mons. 'It was a smaller battle, but it was important, and in its execution it was the most deadly and efficient attack of the whole war.' That statement, of course, is true?

A I think so.

Q Now then, the reporter says you used these words: 'I told Andy MacNaughton, that is, the General Officer Commanding Heavy Artillery, that I thought this would be the last barrage I would ask him to put on in the war, and Andy said, "Well, by Jove, it will be a good one." And it was. It was terrible. The 4th Division's total casualties were sixty killed; of the enemy we buried over eight hundred dead and took thirteen hundred prisoners. I don't believe one of them escaped.' Is that statement true?

A Yes.

Q That statement is true, that when you asked MacNaughton to put on the barrage around November 1st, that you told him it would likely be the last barrage of the war?

A The last set-piece attack.

Q Why did you make that statement, then, unless you knew, Sir Arthur Currie, that the war was over, as far as putting on barrages was concerned?

A I felt that we were getting on. We were driving the enemy before us ... and I thought it was possible that was the last set-piece attack, that is, organized attack –

Q How did you think that was possible, when you swore a moment ago that you were afraid the Germans were going to retire to the line of the Meuse?

A There is no inconsistency.

Q Isn't there?

A No.

Q Well, if they retired and took up that position on the Meuse, wouldn't a barrage be the most necessary of all things?

A Yes, but we were not going to let them do that ... We were not going to let them disengage. We were going to follow them.

Q That is perfectly true, but your fear was that unless you did keep driving them and capturing Mons, that they would get back to the Meuse, and a barrage would be necessary?

A Leave out the words 'and capture Mons' and I will agree with you. We were not going to let them get away from us. We were going to keep pressing them ... They wanted to disengage to get back and it was the general belief in the army that were they allowed to do that they would retire behind the Meuse, which constitutes a very difficult obstacle, a river, the bridges over which would be blown, and we might well have been into a few months of war in the winter.

Q But you knew in your heart, Sir Arthur, when you made that statement, that the Germans would never be able to take up that line on the Meuse ... You knew that they wouldn't be able to take up that line on the Meuse because you said to MacNaughton, 'This will be the last barrage I will ask you to put on in the war.' You tell us now that you did not know absolutely in your own mind when you made that statement, that the Germans would never be able to take up this line on the Meuse?

A No, I didn't.

Q Now then, I will read what this reporter, Mr. Vining, has said that you said: 'After Mont Houy there were ten more days of pursuit, strenuous days.'

A Yes.

Q 'There was simply a general Army Order to press the enemy as hard as possible, and our advance was swift.'

A Yes.

Q You made that statement. 'After Cambrai in thirty days or so the Corps pushed the enemy back ninety-one thousand yards, or about fifty-two miles.' You made that statement?

A Yes.

Q That statement is true?

A Yes.

Q 'There has been some foolish talk about my ordering an attack on Mons after the armistice came.' Do you remember making that statement?

A Yes. There had been for ten years.

Q And everybody had been talking about it?

A I don't say everybody.

Q Well, for ten years this discussion had been going on, backwards and forwards, about this attack on Mons?

A Yes.

Q People had said that you should not have made the attack?

A No.

Q Well, what did they say?

A That I made the attack after I knew the armistice had come into effect.

Q And that had been going on for ten years?

A Yes.

Q So that when we wrote the article we were only simply saying something that had been said for the past ten years?

A You put it in print.

Q Yes, put it in print. Of course, others had put it in print, Sir Sam Hughes had done that in the House of Commons, hadn't he?

A Yes.

Q And he said that if he had been Minister for six weeks longer, he would have had you court martialed?

A He couldn't court martial me.

Q I know, but he made that statement?

A Yes.

Tilley might have objected at this point, but he remained in his chair. He had decided that Currie could handle whatever Regan threw at him. It was going to be an unrestrained fight to the finish.

Q Just let me see what he did say. This is what Sir Sam Hughes said: 'I have just this to say about Mons: were I in authority, the officer who, four hours before the armistice was signed, although he had been notified beforehand that the armistice was to begin at eleven o'clock, ordered the attack on Mons, thus needlessly sacrificing the lives of Canadian soldiers, would be tried summarily by court martial and punished so far as the law would allow. There is no glory to be gained, and you cannot find one Canadian soldier returning from France who will not curse the name of the officer who ordered the attack on Mons. What was in it? They did not take the town, which was only a little one-horse town anyway. It had no strategic value, and the attack was only a bit of bravado, as the Canadians had already passed it. What should have been done was to go around these places and take the Germans prisoner, then make the Germans go in and remove the booby-traps, instead of having our boys blown up in hundreds, as they were in Cambrai.' That is what Sir Sam Hughes said about ten years after?

A Yes.

Q [Regan again quoted from the *Star Weekly* article.] Now, then: 'As a matter of fact, I never ordered an attack at all on Mons.'

A Not on Mons as a unit.

Q You ordered an advance?

A Yes.

Q And if Mons resisted then you knew it would have to be attacked and carried in order to get to your objectives? That is true, is it not?

A Our objective embraced Mons.

Q And if there was resistance it would have to be overcome?

A In those days our instructions were not to force in case of too strenuous opposition.

Q Well, just how strenuous did it have to be, Sir Arthur, before you would pass it by?

A Well, it had to be continuous machine gun fire and very severe shellfire and –

Q That is precisely what happened at Mons, according to your story. Let us see what you say about it: 'On the outskirts of Mons the enemy showed that he intended to resist our entry into the town to the utmost.'

A Yes.

Q That indicates pretty severe opposition?

A There was, Sunday morning, the morning of the 10th ... Up to the afternoon.

Q I don't care when it is. That kind of opposition that is mentioned here would necessitate an attack, would it not?

A The opposition mentioned there would necessitate our halting – not an attack.

Q How was it going to be overcome?

A We did halt when we met that opposition, and we waited until that opposition disappeared.

Q How did it disappear, now?

A Well, the Germans retired.

Q So then you met with no opposition when you went to enter the town? Say yes or no.

A Oh, yes; any time that there was any movement [it] would be greeted with machine gun fire, and in face of that the troops stopped.

Q That is perfectly true, but then when you came to enter the town you say the Germans had retired and you met with no opposition?

A When we entered the town at the railway station there was no opposition.

Q [Regan again read from the report of Currie's remarks in the *Star Weekly*.] 'And by six o'clock' – that is on the 11th – 'the 7th Brigade had cleared the enemy from the city.' Was that statement correct?

A Yes.

Q How do you reconcile that statement with the one you made a few minutes ago, that the Germans had retired out of Mons and that when your troops entered they met with no opposition?

A The main body of the Germans in there had got out, but there were some people left behind.

Q Did you mean, when you used the word 'evacuate,' to refer to the main body of the Germans?

A Yes.

Q Then will you admit that there were some of the rearguard still remaining in Mons when you went to enter the city shortly before midnight?

A Yes.

Q Left there, I suppose, for the purpose of defending the entry of your troops into Mons?

A Yes, as long as they manned their machine guns they were left there for that purpose. When they left they evacuated the town.

Q Well, of course, some did not leave, according to the First Army report and according to your own evidence?

A Yes, some did not leave.

Q [Regan quoted from the *Star Weekly*.] 'I have heard stories of our heavy casualties on Armistice Day and how I rode into Mons like a conqueror through the dead Canadians along the road. The fact is that not a Canadian was killed on November 11th. Our records prove it, and the only dead I saw on entering Mons that day was one man; he was a German.' Did you make these statements?

A I may have, yes.

Q And if you made them, I suppose you believed them to be true?

A Yes.

Q Do you still believe them?

A With the exception of one man.

Q Now, let us see: 'I have heard stories of our heavy casualties on Armistice Day' ... I suppose that is the silly talk you referred to back in another paragraph?

A Yes.

Q ' ... and how I rode into Mons like a conqueror ... ' How did you ride into
   Mons? As a conqueror of Mons?
A I rode into Mons as the General Officer commanding the Canadian Corps.
Q Which had captured Mons?
A Yes.
Q Conquered the German resistance?
A Yes, overcame it.
Q Through the dead Canadians along the road?
A No.
Q Twenty-five or thirty witnesses of ours, Sir Arthur, have gone in the witness
   box, privates who had the courage to stand up in front of you and the other
   high officers of the army who you brought here and say that they saw dead
   on their way into and in Mons; you say you did not see any?
A I did not see any.
Q 'The fact is that not a Canadian was killed on November 11th.' After hearing
   what these twenty-five or thirty witnesses have sworn, with the exception
   of Price, do you still take that attitude?
A I do most positively take that attitude, with the exception of poor Price.
Q Now, were you asked this question? 'Where were you, Sir Arthur, when word
   came of the armistice?'
A I dare say, yes.
Q Did you make this answer: 'Corps Headquarters by that time were in Valen-
   ciennes.'
A Yes.
Q 'When word came from the Army Headquarters I was sitting in my bathtub,
   an old canvas bath that I carried with me throughout the war, and still have
   upstairs. It was twenty minutes after seven.'
A Yes, a good thing to have in the morning.
Q Something more than the privates were doing in the front line that morn-
   ing?
A They were not.
Q Was it twenty minutes after seven?
A I think now it was earlier.
Q How did you come to change your mind? Because there is a vast difference
   between 7:20 and 6:45?
A Yes.
Q How did you come to make the statement that it was twenty minutes after
   seven? Now, that is a definite time, Sir Arthur, made by the Principal of
   McGill University to a newspaper that is to go out to the world.
A That was my recollection of something that happened ten years before. Ap-

parently I was out about thirty-five minutes. It is since we have gone into the detail of this case, I think that my twenty minutes past seven was a little late. I think I was up earlier that morning than I thought I was.

Q When did you get the first message? 7:20 you say is not right; when did you get it? The hour and the minute?

A Oh, I can't tell you that.

Q Give me the day, can you?

A 11th November.

Q When did you get it on the 11th?

A Shortly after 6:45.

Q Your statement that you swore to on your examination for discovery, then, was not correct, when you said it was 6:45?

A Well, I will say that now, then.

Q You will change your story again?

A No, I am not changing the story.

Q Well, you said a moment ago it was shortly after 6:45. When was it?,

A We will say it was 6:45.

Q Don't say 'we will say' –

A I can't say thirty seconds one way or another, and I don't think anybody is confused as to what I mean when I say 6:45.

Q Well, we will see. Now then, you were asked this question: 'Did you finish your bath?'

A I don't know; I don't know that. I probably did finish it; I am not at it yet, so I must have.

Q 'I could not feel excited about the armistice'?

A No.

Q The mere fact that the war was going to stop didn't interfere with your ablutions?

A That is not at all right, Mr. Regan. You are asking me to be careful about my insinuations. I suggest that you obey your own behest.

Q I will be delighted, Sir Arthur, to meet you in every way.

A You don't apparently appreciate the feeling of men who were there, and I don't remember anybody being vastly excited about the armistice. The feeling was too deep. I can't describe it. It seemed to me that there was nothing unusual. It seemed days before you appreciated that this thing had ended. I don't remember any incident of men rejoicing. I remember very well, being with the 1st Brigade at eleven o'clock, and I remember very well how they felt. It was a solemn seriousness.

Q [Reading from the *Star Weekly* article] 'We didn't know the war was going to end so soon. When the news came through I got old Mac [Major-General Sir A.C. Macdonnell, commander of the First Division] on the telephone and told him about it, and I said, "I suppose I had better call off the inspection [of the First Brigade]" but he said he wanted me to come, so I drove over to the brigade just before eleven o'clock and inspected them.' Is that what you did on the morning of the 11th?

A Yes.

Q You did not go up to where the fighting was; you went over to hold an inspection?

A Yes.

Q Didn't you think it was your first duty to get word to these men in the front line who were doing the fighting, that the armistice was going to come into effect at eleven o'clock, and if possible prevent any casualties which might be incurred by a misunderstanding of orders or a misconception of duty or a desire to push forward too fast?

A No.

Q Or to fire the last shot in the war?

A No.

Q You felt your duty was in the opposite direction from the front?

A Yes. I could not hurry the distribution of that armistice message, in any way by going anywhere, because there is a very complete organization in the army for the distribution of information, and that machinery had been put into effect.

Q Now, did you make this statement, after you went over and reviewed the parade, the 1st Division: 'After that I watched them march off parade, and I will never forget standing there as they marched down the road so proud, so glad, so magnificent in their bearing. Those men. It was perhaps wrong of me, but I remember I could not help thinking inside as they went, "By God, I'd like to see them at the Boche again."' Did you make that statement?

A I don't remember making that statement. I remember very well, though, the feeling of pride I had in the bearing of those men as they marched away, and I suppose any general when he sees men like that thinks of the purpose for which they are there, that was to fight and overcome an enemy.

Q You were not satisfied with the fact that there had been in the Canadian Corps 215,542 casualties?

A Yes, I was, yes, I was there through all the months.

Q You were not willing to quit with half of your Corps casualties, you wanted another fight?

A No, I did not.

Q I will read it to you.

A What I said did not intimate I wanted them to fight again.

Q 'God, I'd like to see them at the Boche again.' Look at me and tell me what you meant by it – 'God, I'd like to see them at the Boche again' – with a quarter of a million casualties, approximately, in your Corps. Weren't you satisfied they had done enough fighting?

A Absolutely satisfied, and I know a great deal more about the casualties, Mr. Regan, than you do.

Q Do you?

A Yes, I lived through the months of war there, I saw those magnificent battalions go into battle and come out badly decimated, and I have feelings about it that you can never appreciate.

Q In describing the career of the Corps you used these words: 'Along the road of 100 days to that day in Mons nine years ago, the men of Canada fought three great battles, at Amiens, at Arras, at Cambrai. They led the attack, they never failed. They broke the Hindenburg Line, they took over thirty thousand prisoners, they freed over two hundred cities and towns and five hundred square miles of France and Belgium. They met and crushed forty-seven divisions of the enemy, one Corps of Canadians, four divisons – four against forty-seven.' Is that statement correct?

A Yes.

Q Don't you think, Sir Arthur, that in the dying hours of the war you might have spared your men a trifle more than you did?

A No. You are the man that is suggesting that those men who did that should lie down and quit within two days of the final victory.

Q I didn't say that.

A Oh, yes, you say spare them, you say quit.

Q I don't mean to lie down and quit.

A Well, that is what you are suggesting.

Q No, it isn't.

A Yes, it is.

Q If the men had been allowed to remain there [where they had reached on 10 November] without going into that town, Mons would have fallen without the firing of a shot?

A They didn't suffer any casualties.

Q That is what you say, but that is not what our witnesses say.

A Well, your witnesses were not there.

Q Well, they were a lot closer to it, Sir Arthur, than you were?

A No; I was up there.

Q You didn't get in till half-past three?

A No.

Q Those men got in, and some of them were repairing bridges that had been shot down.

A Well, it isn't my job to make bridges.

Q Would you say that man was not there?

A Yes, he was there.

Q He saw them pulling a dead soldier out of the canal crossing into the city?

A Yes.

Q You do not suggest he came here and said something that was mistaken?

A No.

Q Now, wouldn't it have been better, after having defeated forty-seven divisions, for you to have allowed these troops to remain west of Mons for a few hours, in which case Mons would have been in your possession?

A No, no; you would have them disobey an order; you would have them mutiny, practically; you would have them be guilty of treason, disregard the instructions of the Commander in Chief, disregard the instruction of Marshal Foch, and act in an unsoldierly way, right at the very last. Those were not the men who did that sort of thing.

Currie spoke with intensity and emotion. The tension in the courtroom broke. There was a prolonged outburst of applause, which lasted until the sheriff called for order.[1]

Q You say they would be guilty of treason, to disobey an order?

A Yes.

Q [Quoting from the newspaper report of the unveiling of the Mons monument in 1927] 'But the most impressive function was the public funeral accorded to the men of the Canadian corps who fell in the fighting for the town.' True or untrue, is that statement?

A I would say that is poetic license. You must understand Sir Rodolphe [Lemieux, speaker of the House of Commons, who delivered the address] was ... on Belgian soil.

Q In Mons?

A Yes.

Q You think he was drawing upon his imagination or resorting to poetic license when he made this statement, that the most impressive function was the public funeral accorded to the men of the Canadian Corps who fell in the fighting for the town?

A Yes, I would say that would leave a wrong impression in a strictly military sense, that they fell in the fighting for the town. The fighting, as I have pointed out to you, was not for that particular town.

Q You are denying the right to these men who fell and who were buried in Mons, the honour of having it said of them, they fell in the fighting for Mons?

A No, I am not denying them that right at all.

Q Then will you admit it?

A I think that a man who fell on any field of battle is entitled to just as much honour as the man who fell on what you call the field of Mons.

Q Will you admit it, then, that they fell –

A There is no more honour in falling in the fighting of Mons than there is in falling on any other field of honour.

Q That is perfectly true.

A Yes. I am not trying to deny them any particular honour.

Q Then why deny to these men who fell in the fighting for the town the same honour that you have accorded to every other soldier, if I may put it that way, who fell in fighting for any other place?

A I can't understand you saying that I am denying them an honour. I will not admit that the ten men who were buried fell in any particular action in Mons. They fell in the advance for Mons which was preceding the advance to their objective.

Q Well, you will admit, then, that they fell in fighting for the town?

A That fighting was not particularly for the town. The trouble with you, Mr. Regan, you are trying to make every military activity that went on in those few days centre on Mons.

Q And that is true, is it not?

A It is not.

Q That is where you were going?

A That is not true.

Q That is where you swore to be before the war ended?

A That is not true.

Q You deny this?

A Absolutely.

Q [Regan began to read from newspaper reports of the capture of Mons.] 'The Canadians, with an inspired sense of historic fitness, had sworn to be in Mons while the war lasted.'

A I have never heard it.

Q Do you deny this: 'The revenge is perfect, wrote the *Times* Correspondent, describing the Canadians' entry into Mons at Armistice Day.'

A Absolutely.

Q You deny that absolutely?

A Yes; at least that is not my opinion.

Q Are these other statements ... not true? 'A plot in the cemetery was dedicated to Canada, and orations were delivered at the graveside by representatives of the town of Mons, and of the Province of Hainault, giving eloquent expressions to the feeling of populace. They extended sympathy to the relatives of the fallen, and gave an assurance that the memory of these noble sons of Canada, whose bodies now rest in Belgian soil, would not be only perpetuated in stone and bronze, but also by the more enduring tradition which each father would transmit to his son, each mother to her child, throught the years to come because, in Mons, the name of Canada would ever remain synonymous with honour, loyalty and heroism –'

A [Interrupting] Not if you have your way.

Q You are the man, Sir Arthur, that denies to these men who fell at Mons –

A Not so.

Q You are the man who denies to these men the right to be known as having fallen in the capture of Mons?

A Never, never.

Q You don't admit it, you don't admit it. And because Wilson and Preston are men enough to get up and say that these men did fall in the capture of Mons in the dying hours of the war, and that their sacrifice was needless, you sue them for fifty thousand dollars.

A No, the statement here is that after I knew an armistice was coming into effect – that is, 6:45 in the morning – I ordered an attack which resulted in an appalling loss of life. That is not true.

Q [Reading from the Port Hope *Evening Guide* article] 'This is an event which might very properly be allowed to pass into oblivion, very much regretted rather than glorified.' Do you disagree with that?

A Yes.

Q You think it should be glorified?

A I don't say that. I don't think it should be allowed to pass into oblivion. I wouldn't ask that the giving up of life of a single soldier should be something that should be allowed to pass into oblivion – not at all. I believe the memory of these men should be commemorated.

Q But you are denying to them, Sir Arthur, the right to say that they fell in fighting for the town in the capture of Mons?

A I have repeatedly said that it is no more honourable to fall in Mons than in any other field.

Q Please don't twist a thing like that.

A I am not twisting; you are twisting.

Q You are the Principal of McGill University. I say you deny to these men who fell on the 9th, 10th and 11th of November the right to have it said of them, they gave up their life for the capture of Mons.

A Then you are admitting then that it is an honourable thing?

Q Did you ever think for a moment that I didn't? Did you?

A I thought it was only for my glorification that they fell.

Q Oh, no. Did you think for a moment that we didn't think it was an honourable thing for these men to die?

A You said it was for my glorification; that is what your article says.

Q That is not answering my question. Will you suggest for a moment that Preston and Wilson, the defendants in this action, say that it was not honourable for these men to die?

A I cannot gather that from anything they wrote in this article.

Q You take the position that they did think it was dishonourable? I just want to see how far you go.

A They say to every mother whose only comfort and solace has been that her son fell in the performance of his duty, they say to her, 'Now, that is not so. Your son fell to glorify General Currie, and that was his object.'

Q What was the result from a military standpoint of the capture of Mons? Did it lessen or affect or hasten the end of the war for one brief minute?

A It was a proper military operation.

Q That is all very well; did it affect or hasten the end of the war for one minute?

A That is not a fair question.

Q You answered it on your examination for discovery.

A Well, I say no, it did not.

Q No, of course it didn't.

A If Mons had not been taken or occupied the war would have ended just when it did.

Q Just the same?

A Yes.

Q And we can tell the fathers and mothers of these boys who did fall in Mons that their fall was because you felt it would be treason not to carry out your orders to advance through Mons? That is what we are going to tell them, is it?

A I am quite sure that the Canadian troops would have felt it a very great disgrace if they had been the only troops on the whole battle line that had quit within twenty-four hours of the finish.

Q I am not saying to quit within twenty-four hours.

A That is what you are suggesting.

Q Now, you don't suggest for a moment that that article meant or could possibly mean that it was the last minute before eleven o'clock that the mad idea was conceived, just looking at that sentence.

A That makes it doubly diabolical to put in someting which you say has no meaning, and yet convey the impression that I, to glorify myself, ordered an attack.

Q You say it is doubly diabolical?

A Yes.

Q And that it would mislead people to have a statement made that would be absolutely impossible?

A Yes.

Q If somebody said that you jumped over the moon, something that could not possibly be true, that it would hurt you?

A That would make it all the worse.

Q Now, when did you get your appointment to McGill University?

A About April, 1920.

Q Now, all this talk that has taken place this last ten years, charging precisely the same thing as we did about the loss of life at Mons has not affected you in your position as Principal of McGill University?

A Not up to the present. I don't know how it will in the future.

Q Well, up until now?

A No.

Q Until this little Port Hope *Guide* told the same story?

A Oh, well, that started it in print.

Q Oh, it was in print before; Sir Sam Hughes had it in print.

A Privileged circumstances.

Q Is it not true that you and General Horne, Commander of the First Army, had a conference on November 9th before he issued his order from the First Army to you and you issued your order to the Canadian Corps?

A I think I had a conference with General Horne on November 9th, because then it was that he told me that there should be no relaxation of the pressure; that is the message he brought to me.

Q And you both knew that the [German] envoys at that time were down with Foch?

A Yes.

Q And that, in the language of the First Army, if you care to go that far now, that an armistice would probably be signed within a few days?

A I stick to what I said, that I hoped it would.

Q And then Horne orders you and you order the troops, giving them definite objectives ... which would necessitate the capture of Mons?

A Yes.

Q Is it unfair to suggest to you that at that conference between you and Horne on November 9th, when you learned that the envoys were with Foch, that you decided to name objectives for your forces that would enable them to capture Mons before it would be time for the armistice, if any, to come into effect?

A Most unfair.

Q Most unfair?

A Yes.

Q Then why, Sir Arthur, did you on November 9th give definite objectives to your troops ... to proceed through Mons, which at that time was filled with German troops?

A I was ordered to.

Q That is your reason?

A Yes.

Q Now then, it didn't occur to you that it would be possible for you to disobey that order?

A No.

Q You had no discretion in that matter?

A No.

Q [Reading from the Field Service Regulations] 'A departure from either the spirit or the letter of an order is justified if the subordinate who assumes the responsibility bases his decision on some fact which could not be known to the officer who issued the order and if he is conscientiously satisfied that he is acting as his superior if present would order him to act.' In that case he has discretion?

A It doesn't apply to this at all.

Q [From the Field Service Regulations] 'If a subordinate in the absence of a superior neglects to depart from the letter of his orders when such departure is clearly demanded by circumstances, and failure ensues, he will be held responsible for such failure. Should a subordinate find it necessary to depart from an order he should at once inform the issuer of it and the commanders of any neighbouring units likely to be affected.' Here you say you had no discretion?

A [An officer] has a certain amount of discretion, mind you, but generally ... he should never depart from a formal order either in letter or spirit.

Q If a subordinate in the absence of a superior neglects to depart from the letter of his orders when such departure is clearly demanded by circumstances, and failure ensues, he will be held responsible for such failure?

A Yes.

Q Now then, on November 9th, when Horne ... ordered you to make this advance, and you learned what was in front of you, why did you not go to him and say –

A Oh, there was no reason in the world why I should go to him. There was nothing unusual in front of me. We were simply advancing. I fully agreed with that order. I fully agreed with the instructions that come from Marshal Foch, to keep on pressing this enemy.

Q Well, how far did you go from – say from six o'clock on the 9th until six o'clock on the 10th, as far as Mons was concerned?

A Not very far.

Q In the language of the 3rd Division, Sir Arthur, if you will allow me to read it: 'On the outskirts of Mons the enemy showed that he intended to resist our entry into the town to the utmost.' That is why the Princess Patricia's stopped?

A Yes.

Q And stayed there?

A Yes.

Q What sort of opposition did you figure on encountering when you issued that order of November 9th, when the town was filled with German soldiers? If your troops had carried out your instructions, Sir Arthur, issued to them at half-past six o'clock on the evening of the 9th, and had attacked Mons, or had rather proceeded to walk through it, what would have happened to them?

A If they had gone up against that severe machine gun fire they would have been decimated.

Regan then read the account, now familiar to all, contained in the reports of the First Army and of the Third Division and the diary of the Seventh Brigade, all of which spoke of determined enemy resistance at Mons. Currie adopted a dismissive tone: 'Oh, I think it is quite probable that the report of the opposition is just a little exaggerated in the writing up of the reports.'

Q Well, whose story are we to believe about Mons? Is it the First Army story, your story, the 3rd Division story, the 7th Brigade story, or the story of those men who come in here and who say there was not a sign of an enemy?

A I think the best story will be the story we can write after this trial is ended.

Q The story, I suppose, that we can quite properly style 'The Fifty Thousand Dollar story.' Do you agree with me there?

A If I write it I won't head it that way.

Regan pulled out the proclamation that had been posted up on Armistice Day in Mons. This time Tilley did not object. 'Can you read that?' Regan asked. 'Not very well,' said Currie. 'You read it.' 'Well, I thought perhaps, coming from Montreal, that you would be able to read French better than I could, Sir Arthur. I am only an Irishman from Toronto.'

After some discussion of what should be read, Currie read a translation of the proclamation: '"The 3rd Canadian Division, at the price of bloody sacrifices, penetrated – entered the town – at three o'clock this morning."' Regan responded:

Q I have the translation here; if you would just see if this translation compares with yours: 'The 3rd Canadian Division, at the cost of heavy sacrifices, entered the city at three o'clock this morning, thus avenging by a striking success the retreat of 1914. Honour and thanks be to it.' Is that a fair translation of what is written in there?

A Yes.

Q Do you agree or disagree with that statement?

A I disagree with that.

Q Will you tell the world, Sir Arthur, now where these men got all this information which is written down in the war diaries, army reports, reports by yourself, histories written by reputable, honourable men, statements made by a dead Major-General, if you differ with them all? Where did they get the information on which to base these?

A I don't know.

Q Do you think that man, who lost a leg, who is going now for the remainder of his life without a leg, that was justified.

A Yes.

Q Then there were gold medals issued by Mons for the officers and silver medals or aluminum medals for the men?

A I got a gold medal; I have heard of other gold medals.

Q Is it true that the British Officers wore what is known as battle honours as a result of the capture of Mons by the Canadian troops?

A Well, when you have a medal you get bars from it, you get a bar for every engagement which the Battle Honour Committee or the War Office consider entitles you to it. For instance, we would get a battle honour called Ypres, and you would wear that as a bar on your medal ribbon; there would be another for Vimy, there would be another for Amiens, and so on. I don't know how many there are – probably ten or so – and in the last eleven days or so there was a battle the British fought called the Somme; that would be normally their battle honour. Well, the Somme doesn't mean anything to the Canadians, and the Canadians asked that their battle honour for that be called Mons ... A regiment that has a flag, a regimental colour, can have those names engraved on the colour.

Q The only thing I didn't understand, if there was no attack or fighting in Mons, why there would be a battle honour issued in connection with it? There is none issued as far as Jemappes –

A The battle honour named Mons applies to all the fighting that took place from the 1st of November to November 11th.

Q Why didn't they call it Jemappes?

A Because Mons is an historic place. The old Battle of Malplaquet is right south of it, and many battles having been fought in that area, makes it an historic place.

Q [Regan turned to the funeral at Mons for the dead Canadians.] Of course, it didn't occur to you, I suppose, to attend the funeral?

A No. I had no communication regarding that funeral at all.

Q Don't you think it would have come with a good grace if you had attended the funeral?

A I have attended hundreds of funerals in France, Mr. Regan, and I had no communication regarding that funeral. Now, how could I reasonably be expected to attend something which I didn't know was taking place?

Q Well, I would have thought that when the Belgian people, the kindly Belgian people, thought it was incumbent upon them to go and get coffins for these men and hold a military funeral, attended by some of the highest officers in the county, that it would have been a splendid thing and a proper thing for you to have been there.

A But how could I be there if I had no communication of it? Now, please be reasonable.

Q Now, tell me, just one more question; you are suing in your writ for fifty thousand dollars?

A Yes.

Q I think you told me this morning that you had not suffered any damages from a financial standpoint at least, from anything that had been said heretofore about you or about Mons, apart from this article?

A No, if you will let me –

Q Listen to me; I am not going to let you make any speeches; I want to get through, because everybody is getting tired. You can say yes or no, Sir Arthur?

A I don't know.

Q You don't know.

A No.

Q That is all.

It was now time for Preston to cross-examine. He began by taking Sir Arthur back to his pre-war days in the militia out in Victoria. As he gradually came to the matter of the irregularity in the regimental accounts, Currie must have suffered almost unbearable tension. Would the indiscretion that already had caused him so much private embarrassment be revealed to all? Then the question came.

'Now, I want to be perfectly fair with respect to a question which I am going to ask you, if I am permitted, regarding the organization of the 50th Battalion –' Tilley sensed what Preston was leading up to, and quickly came to Currie's rescue: 'My Lord, are we concerned with the organization of the 50th Battalion?' Justice Rose agreed. 'I don't know what in the world we have got to do with the 50th Battalion. We have got to do with Mons and your article, Mr. Preston.'

Preston let the matter pass. He continued his questioning in a quiet, level tone of voice. At times, Currie's replies contained a note of indignation.

Q Had you during the previous eight or nine years heard from any particular source or from various sources criticism of the action of what is known as the Battle of Mons?

A Yes.

Q When did you first hear complaints as to your alleged course in connection with Mons?

A I dare say the first was the criticism uttered in the House of Commons.

Q Can you fix the time?

A 1919, 20; I think it was made in 1919 and repeated in 1920.

Q Can you say generally what that criticism was?

A That I had needlessly sacrificed Canadian lives, with particular reference to Mons; that I had ordered an attack after I knew the armistice was coming into effect at eleven o'clock. I don't know whether it used the words 'for my own glorification' or not.

Q Now, if I am in order I would ask you who was the special particular person who made these complaints?

A Sir Sam Hughes.

Q Sir Sam Hughes had occupied what position— What position was he occupying when he made the complaint?

A Private Member of the House.

Q What position had he previously occupied?

A Minister of Militia.

Q For an extended period?

A I think from 1911.

Q Had you occasion to learn whether Sir Sam Hughes was taking much of a personal interest in the war?

A I think he did.

Q In all the events of the war?

A That would probably be true.

Tilley had allowed Regan to cross-examine Currie on Hughes's statements, but, perhaps sensing that Preston was less likely to wrangle over each point, he challenged the relevance of the line being taken. Justice Rose seemed to agree. But Preston was not without ingenuity: 'They are admissible, if these speeches have come to the attention of the plaintiff for years, and there has been no reply by him to them, no attempt or effort on his part to prove their falsity ... I submit I am quite in my line to ask what reply ... has he made to these, or has he made any reply.' The judge ruled that Preston had a right to ask the question, and Preston continued:

Q Then, General Currie, what reply have you made to these suggestions, in their wider or their narrower sphere, if you like, which you say you have been acquainted with for nine years, eight years?

A In no other way than telling the story of Mons, the true story, from different platforms in Canada, to audiences I was addressing.

Q Where else did you speak than in Massey Hall in 1919 on this question?

A I cannot definitely say that.

Q Did you speak anywhere where the public would have an opportunity of having you reply to these rumours, largely based perhaps on what Sir Sam Hughes had said?

A I don't know any place.

Q Will you give me a copy of any remarks which you have made on that question?

A No.

Q Were there not channels by which you could have made your defence clear, unmistakably clear, that a needless loss of life did not take place, so that the general public and everyone could hear it? ... Was there no channel of communication to the public which you could have availed yourself of that would have placed your case beyond question?

A I don't know how I could have done it.

Q Could you not have written a communication to someone to read in the House of Commons?

A I might have done that, yes.

Q Remember that we are all subject to attacks in the House of Commons; I have been for forty years, but I have managed to get a reply made every time. Did you take any such steps?

A No. I had come back to my own country after four years of war, and I did not think that I should be called upon to defend every charge that anybody made against me ... I felt too hurt to enter into any conflict of that kind at that time. I did not think the thing would be believed, but apparently it has for ten years.

Q But you have been running up against it for ten years?

A Yes.

Q Has it done you any harm?

A Yes.

Q And still you do not think it was of sufficient importance to contradict?

A I didn't know how I can contradict rumour.

Q And you preferred to remain under a cloud of that kind rather than defend yourself?

A I didn't know how I could dispel it.

Q My dear General, that is testing credulity; pardon me for saying so.

A Well, you are speaking from the vastness of your experience.

Preston hoped to minimize the damages by showing that his article had been published elsewhere.

Q Now, was this published anywhere else?

A I have been told so.

Q What do your pleadings say?

A I think it was published in an Ottawa paper.

Q I think it was brought out in evidence that the Port Hope *Guide* has a circulation of about a thousand. Have you got any idea what circulation the Ottawa *Citizen* has?

A No.

Q Do you know that it is one of the largest, I might say the most influential newspaper[s] in the Dominion of Canada?

A I do not know that.

Q Do you know that it is owned by a multi-millionaire?

A By the Southams, yes.

Q Do you know that they have a chain of newspapers extending from Ottawa to Calgary in all the principal cities?

A Yes.

Q Knowing probably what you do about the circumstances of the Port Hope *Guide* and my humble self, don't you think if you had a good case and fifty thousand dollars you had a better opportunity of getting it from there than you have here?

A You were the publisher, you were the people that started this, put it in print, and I wanted you to take it back.

Q But don't you know that the Ottawa *Citizen* in law is [as responsible as] the Port Hope *Guide*?

A I don't know.

Q Then consult your solicitor. Don't you know you could have made the Ottawa *Citizen* ... a party to your action?

A I did not know that.

Q It never occurred to you that a multi-millionaire living in the capital of Canada might possibly have a very much better opportunity, for very many reasons of defending a libel suit than Mr. Wilson and myself?

A Mr. Preston, if I may be allowed to interrupt, I am not after money ... Fifty thousand dollars, or five times fifty thousand dollars, would not compensate me if such a charge could be substantiated.

The suggestion that Currie had avoided the more powerful Southam chain to go after the Port Hope *Evening Guide* might well cause the jury to feel protective of their local paper and editor. In fact, however, the *Guide*'s article was not repeated by the Ottawa *Citizen*, as F.N. Southam forcefully pointed out to Currie as soon as he read reports of Preston's cross-examination.[2] Two weeks after the *Guide* had published its Mons article, the Ottawa *Journal* – not the *Citizen* – had condemned Preston for writing it. In an editorial headed 'W.T.R. Preston Again,' the *Journal* did repeat a substantial part of 'Mons,' but went on to censure its author:

It would be impossible to do worse violence to the truth. There is not a Canadian who was in Mons on that historic day who cannot testify to that. They know that there was practically no bloodshed; that the Canadian advance was made upon orders, from orders from the Commander-in-Chief of the Allied Armies; and that the Burgomaster at Mons issued a proclamation congratulating the Canadians for refraining from the use of shell-fire, thus preventing loss of life.

It is a great pity that there is not some law in this country to protect men who have rendered national service from such scurrilous and outrageous abuse.[3]

The sentiment of the *Journal* editorial writer inspired a similar outburst from the St Catharines *Standard*, which also reprinted a substantial extract from Preston's 'Mons' article under the heading 'W.T.R. Preston Again Breaks Out': 'Why should men who served and sacrificed be libelled by Preston years after the event? ... It is a pity that war time regulations do not always prevail for the Preston type. Brave men would not then be slandered.'[4]

When he initiated the proceedings against Wilson and Preston, Currie was unaware that these editorials had appeared; but even if he had read them, they would have given him no reason to take action. For some reason, this important matter had not been properly investigated by

Currie's lawyers, and Tilley offered no response to Preston on the point. The jury would retire to decide the case thinking that Currie had tackled the Port Hope *Guide* but had shied away from the powerful Southams.

The trial had come to the end of its second Friday. Currie had faced six and a half hours of cross-examination by Regan, and then more from Preston. It had perhaps been the longest day of his life. Currie probably was paying little attention when the arrangements for a Saturday sitting were made. Tilley was openly exasperated by the length of the trial, and accused Regan of deliberately prolonging the matter. When Regan complained that Tilley was being unfair, Tilley replied, 'Oh, I state that deliberately.'

Regan was annoyed. 'The idea of Mr. Tilley saying that he gets up here and he talks to Currie ten minutes, and expects the jury to give him fifty thousand dollars for a story like that – now, that is just about the size of it – and then because I have to cross-examine him –'

Tilley played on his suspicion that the jurors were getting restless: 'I expect the jury to give me more money the less time I take. I am expecting the jury would have some appreciation of shortening up a case.' Regan did not let this go unchallenged. 'I tell you, they know how hard it is to earn fifty thousand dollars.'

But Tilley had the last word: 'Well, they don't think it is earned by just talking.'

13

Verdict

When the trial resumed on Saturday morning, Regan was not at the counsel table. He had slept in; perhaps he had been drinking the night before, after his prolonged duel with Currie.

Tilley was determined to complete his case before the day was over. He called to the stand Walter Gow, a member of the well-known Toronto law firm of Blake, Lash, Anglin and Cassels. Gow had served as deputy minister of overseas military forces in London from 1917 to 1918. He had been in Mons on 11 November 1918. Tilley's reason for calling him quickly became evident.

'Whom did you go into Mons with?' 'The late Sir Edward Morrison, Major-General Sir Edward Morrison, Commander of the Canadian Corps Artillery.' (Regan had made much of Morrison's account of Mons on Armistice Day when cross-examining Currie's witnesses.) Tilley continued:

Q Is that the person that wrote something with regard to the War?
A Yes, he has written a good deal, I think, prior to his demise.
Q A journalist?
A He was a journalist in civil life.
Q Now then, some reference has been made to what he said in some writings with regard to what dead bodies were seen, or what dead bodies were in Mons. Will you just tell the Court and jury what [you saw]?
A I accompanied General Morrison into Mons on the morning of Armistice

Day, I should think about nine o'clock, possibly a little earlier, although I am not very sure after ten years. We drove in the General's motor. We went in over the road which leads from Mons to Maubeuge ... We had come from Valenciennes, Corps Headquarters, and enter[ed] Mons on the southern most point, going from there to the Grand'Place. We saw on that road, which was the main entry to Mons in that district, three or possibly four dead German bodies.

Q Was that all?
A That was all – lying on the road.
Q Did you see any Canadians?
A None whatever.
Q That is all, thank you.

Regan, who by this time had arrived in court, tried to turn Gow's testimony to his advantage. In response to Regan's question, Gow agreed that the German bodies were on the boulevard surrounding Mons and on the adjacent streets. 'Would that have indicated to you that there had been a fight between Germans and Canadian soldiers at that particular spot?' Regan asked. 'Not necessarily,' Gow replied. 'It indicated to me that there were three or more dead men there, that is all. How they were killed, how they got there, I don't know.'

Regan again read General Morrison's account of his entry into Mons on the eleventh, with its emphasis on the determination of the Canadians to take Mons and the price they had paid. Gow would not say explicitly that he disagreed with Morrison's account, but the implication was clear. He had been with Morrison throughout the day, and the only dead he had seen himself were those few German bodies at the edge of Mons.

The plaintiff's next witness was Sir Richard Turner, who had served as chief of the Canadian general staff in London for the last two years of the war, and who at one time had been Currie's rival for the post of commander of the Canadian Corps. His willingness to testify on Currie's behalf was significant, for the two men had not always seen eye to eye. Turner was close to both Sam and Garnet Hughes, and Currie had once suspected that Turner might be the source of some of the charges made against him at the close of the war. But his responses to Tilley's questions were unequivocal:

Q Do you know General Currie?
A I do, sir.

Q Do you know his reputation?

A I do.

Q As a military man?

A I do.

Q What is it?

A Well, I should say that any man that could have a military reputation such as General Currie would be envied.

Turner went on to say, without reference to his own aspirations, that Currie had been recommended for the position of Corps commander by both Byng and Haig.

Q And what would you say as to his qualification for that position?

A I might make a comparison. If I was a farmer, and I had good buildings and well-tilled fields and cattle, and so on, in good shape, I would say that man was on his job. You went out to Canadian Headquarters and you visited the Corps, and you found the battalions and divisions and everything right up in good fettle and ready for their work. At General Headquarters in France, to which I had access at all times, because my work did take me out to France about once every month, I had the opportunity of speaking to officers, and I know the high esteem that they had for Sir Arthur Currie.

Turner agreed with Tilley's suggestion that the proper course when following up a retiring enemy was to 'press his rearguards for all it was worth. If you allow him to slip away from you, you enable him to get away his war material, get out of any net that is being set for him.'

Regan's cross-examination, which was somewhat hampered by Turner's slight deafness, made little headway. He tried to draw Turner out on tactics and on the need for further fighting once the enemy seemed beaten, but despite his flattery – 'I understand you are perhaps one of the most distinguished soldiers in the British Army' – Turner stood fast.

The precise terms of the order made by Marshal Foch on 9 November 1918 had not yet been put in evidence. Tilley wanted the jury to see the order because it emphasized the need for concentrated and co-ordinated action: 'The enemy, disorganized by our repeated attacks, retreats along the entire front. It is important to co-ordinate and expedite our movements. I appeal to the energy and the initiative of the Commanders-in-Chief and of their armies to make decisive the results obtained.'

The only source Tilley had for the order was a book written by Foch in 1923. Tilley tried to introduce the book through James H. MacBrien, who had served as brigadier-general in command of the Twelfth Brigade for the last two and a half years of the war. He was a much-decorated and well-liked soldier who after the war was promoted to the rank of major-general and served as chief of the general staff of the Canadian militia; he would be appointed commissioner of the Royal Canadian Mounted Police in 1931.

Regan objected to Foch's order being read. He had been refused the right to lead evidence of the remarks Sam Hughes had made in Parliament, and he contended that Foch's book fell into the same category. Tilley did not press the point, but then was astonished as Regan began his cross-examination by asking MacBrien whether Foch's order made any explicit reference to 'pressure' on the enemy. Regan could no longer object, having referred to the words of the order himself; Tilley seized the opportunity, and read the entire text of the order in re-examination.

Regan then asked MacBrien about remarks he had made at a recent dinner held in Ottawa to celebrate the battle of Vimy Ridge. 'Did you mention Sir Arthur Currie?' 'I did,' said MacBrien. 'I said that he was fighting a battle for all the officers of the Canadian Corps.' Regan suggested that it had been improper to make such a comment on the eve of the trial, and then emphasized that MacBrien had referred only to officers.

Q You left out the privates?
A Yes, leave out the privates, because they haven't the responsibility.
Q They do the fighting, the dying ... ?
A Along with the officers and non-commissioned officers ... I said that it was sometimes considered the mark of a very storng people to show ingratitude to their great men, and such I considered was being done at the present time in the attacks that were being made upon General Sir Arthur Currie and the other officers of the Canadian Corps.
Q Anything else you said?
Q That he was fighting our battles for us again in peace as he had done them in war.

The last witness in the trial was George G.D. Kilpatrick, a United Church minister, who had been senior chaplain to the Third Canadian

Division. He was asked how the troops had taken the news of the armistice.

A I think we all were much struck by the total absence of any evidence of joy or delight on the part of the troops. We went about ... with a sense of strange unreality at the whole business, and through that day in Mons, and particularly through the evening, the soldiers did not celebrate in any way ... The celebration was of the formal type in which we held parades, and the bands were playing, but the manifestations of joy were all on the part of the citizens.

Q Now, then did you officiate at the burial on the 13th?

A I did, sir.

Q It is said that there were ten buried that day. Were the original arrangements for ten?

A No, sir; the original arrangements were for eight, and subsequently, when it was made known that this funeral was being given by the city, two bodies were brought in from the right flank, 2nd Division men, making a total of ten. [Kilpatrick explained that Mons civic officials had asked for the privilege of giving a public burial for the Canadian dead.]

Q The Canadian dead where?

A Those available in the district of Mons.

Kilpatrick then described the funeral arrangements. The city officials had arranged for the bodies to be collected. The dead were brought in carts to the mortuary, where they were put in the most elaborate coffins available. They were then conveyed into a large room in the city hall, which was draped in black and silver and lit with candles. The citizens of Mons were invited to pay tribute, which they did by the thousands, filling the room with bay-leaf wreaths. On 13 November at three o'clock a procession left the hall, the Forty-second Pipe Band leading the cortège of coffins and the RCR Band, followed by the chaplain, officers, city officials, and a rather pathetic group of old men, Belgian veterans of the war of 1870. Kilpatrick's quiet manner did not conceal his emotion, and his description of the funeral made a strong impression on the crowd in the courtroom.

Then came the citizens, not in column of route, but surrounding the cortège on either side, and there must have been four or five thousand citizens accompanied us to the cemetery, where the graves were already prepared, and after the religious service which is customary in the army, the representative of the Province of Hainault and the Mayor of the City delivered very eloquent addresses, part of which Mr. Regan quoted from. One sentence which, if I might be permitted to give, I have from memory: 'There are those in your land who sorrow this day. Tell them that their sons are in our keeping. They rest in a corner of Belgium which is forever Canada.'

The trial started its third week on Monday, 30 April. The concluding arguments were anxiously awaited. The session was not scheduled to start until 1:30 in the afternoon, but by 10:00 AM many spectators had claimed the best seats. By the time Justice Rose took his place, the courtroom was crammed. The main doors were left open so that the disappointed spectators who crowded into the main lobby could listen.

Regan took the lead. He began on an ingratiating note, admitting that he had tried the judge's patience during the last two weeks. He asked forgiveness, maintained that he acted in good faith and in the interest of getting into the record evidence he thought to be relevant, and drew attention once again to the fact that the legal rules of evidence excluded much of the material he wanted to present.

Regan's basic strategy in argument was the same as it had been during the trial – to try to escape having to prove the literal truth of everything in the article. The last minute of the war, he contended, must mean the last days of the war. The word 'Mons' as used in the article must be taken to mean the territory surrounding Mons as well as the city itself. Despite the orders Sir Arthur Currie had received, he had had it within his power to prevent needless loss of life. Currie must have known that the German army was finished and that peace was imminent. The order to permit the German envoys to pass through the line had been received on 7 November; how could anyone, in the face of that, say that an armistice was not imminent?

Currie himself had said that after Cambrai he knew the end was near, and the war diaries showed that there was constant talk of an armistice. The First Army report stated that from the first days of November all ranks knew that an armistice would be signed shortly. Regan reminded the jury of Nickle's evidence concerning the order not to send more troops to France. All of this, he contended, should lead the jury to conclude that the German retreat was in reality a rout, and that the Germans could not have attempted to consolidate a position at the Meuse or anywhere else.

Despite the mauling he had received when he put the suggestion to the witnesses, Regan repeated that Mons should have been surrounded so as to avoid loss of life. There had been a direct attack on Mons, he said, and he reminded the jury of Currie's conference with General Horne a few days before the end when the final strategy was settled. The diaries of the units involved were to be believed, not the officers' recollections ten years later, and those diaries spoke of stubborn enemy resistance. The enemy positions had been manned with machine-guns. The jury, Regan suggested, could well imagine the slaughter that ensued when the Canadians rushed these positions while firing hundreds of shots per minute. Even Sir Arthur's own report mentioned resistance, and the jury should not conclude that there was no fighting or that the Canadians had suffered no casualties. German machine-gun positions could not be taken without loss of life.

Regan reminded the jury that the casualties of the last three days of the war were all entered in the records as having occurred on 9 November. This had been done because the officers were ashamed to face the world and to say that at the last moment men had been ordered into battle and suffered appalling casualties. Defence witnesses swore that they had seen dead Canadians in and near Mons; if their accounts were taken together, there was evidence that at least thirty-nine Canadian bodies had been seen. All of these witnesses had been privates: 'You know, gentlemen, what discipline is in the Army. What an effort to stand in that box, face the Corps Commander, and give that evidence. I'm going to ask you to believe every one of our witnesses.' Regan's own reckoning was that seventy-three Canadians had been killed in taking the high ground east of Mons; the official records were not to be believed in the face of the evidence he had provided.

Lives had been lost in the taking of Mons, Regan said, and the jury would surely not like to think that those men buried in Mons did not die in the glorious taking of the city. How would a member of the jury feel if he had lost a brother or a son only to be told that his relative did not die in the taking of Mons? Holding a picture of the funeral for the fallen Canadians at Mons, Regan spoke emotionally: 'All that old man Wilson – brave man that he is, asked for – that these brave men be given their share of the glory of Mons ... Who is a traitor in his country – the man who will stand up to Foch and say "I will not send my men in to the fighting in the last minute" or the man who sends his men in to be killed? I wonder who was [the] traitor, Colonel Ewing, who ordered his men to stop, or those officers who pushed their men on so they could have their line nice and straight.'

Regan pointed out that Foch's order said nothing about any specific operation around Mons. 'Keeping in touch with the enemy, as ordered, does not necessitate sending battalion after battalion of men against fortified positions.' Regan was interrupted by both Rose and Tilley: there was no evidence to support his statement. But Regan was in full flight. Only at Mons were celebrations held, he said; there was no report of celebrations in any other place. The officers had been awarded gold medals, the men aluminum: 'Glory for the officers, but graves for the men.' Neither Marshal Foch nor General Horne knew, when they issued their orders, that there were officers in the army who would deliberately send their men in to fight when there was no need for fighting.

Why had Sir Arthur taken action against the Port Hope *Guide* instead of the two other larger papers that had also published the article? Regan concluded dramatically: 'Don't give him a dollar, for a dollar means about $15,000 in costs. Bring in a verdict for the defendants, for usually the costs go with the verdict. We have tried to do our duty to the living. We have tried to do our duty to the dead, and because we have the temerity to say it, Sir Arthur comes and demands $50,000.'

Preston was next to address the jury. He had chosen not to testify under oath, but he was not about to pass up the chance to speak now. The libel action, he asserted, was unprecedented in British legal annals. He shirked no responsibility for what he had done. His actions had been taken in the public interest, and he budged not one inch from his position of a year ago when he wrote the article. The evidence, Preston contended boldly, supported every word he had written. The article was based on the speech made by Sir Sam Hughes in Parliament, and Hughes had been in a position to know what he was talking about. As minister of militia he had been familiar with every phase of the war and was especially well placed to secure knowledge of events overseas. Currie had admitted that he had learned of the speech when it had been made. Hughes was Currie's accuser. Why, Preston asked, was no response made either by Currie himself or by someone on his behalf in the House? 'A cat can look at a king, and the humblest citizen of Canada could have applied to Parliament for an investigation.' Rather than take on Sir Sam Hughes, Currie had waited for ten years, done nothing, and then attacked two unassuming persons, himself and Wilson.

Preston asked the jury to consider what Currie would have done had there been no Preston and no Port Hope *Guide*. Would he have gone to his grave with the stigma of Hughes's attack on his name? 'Give a lie 24 hours start and the bells of eternity will ring before you catch up with it. Give it ten years and where are you?' Everyone knew that justice could be had before Parliament, and yet Currie had done nothing. On these grounds, Preston suggested, the blame attaching to the action had to rest on Currie's shoulders.

The tension in the courtroom became unbearable for some. An elderly gentleman, unable to find a seat and forced to stand, started to sob and covered his face with his hands. A group of women on the benches to the right of the jury allowed their tears to flow unrestrained. There was no apparent reason for their emotion to surface at this particular time, although Preston's voice had dropped to a funereal tone.

Preston then turned to Currie's conference with Horne and the decision to move on to Mons. 'I take the responsibility of saying that no more mad idea was ever conceived. We have evidence to show that Mons was infested with the enemy. [The Germans had] machine guns which fired six hundred shots a minute. I do not know of any words to suit the occasion. [It was] the most terrible proposition the Canadians had to face. When the defendants used the words "at the last hour, almost at the last minute," they [were] right. Was there ever such a miscarriage of judgment? One of his own colonels rebuked him in no uncertain terms when, in the box, he was asked what he did when he received the armistice message, and he replied that he had ordered his men to stop. If Colonel Ewing was wrong, there sits the one man [pointing to Currie] who could have brought him to book. Did he rebuke Colonel Ewing? If he had, I think there would have been evidence of it.'

Germany was defeated, and the Kaiser was fleeing for his life. 'And did General Currie not know all this and realize that the time had come to stop losing lives?' Of course, Currie did not know that the armistice had been signed, but he did know as certainly as day followed night that the armistice would be signed on the eleventh, and in spite of this he made for Mons. Currie's excuse of 'higher orders' did not suffice. The orders did not tell him to throw the great mass of Canadian troops against the German army, and Preston reminded the jury that Currie had said 'God! Would I not like to see the Canadians at them again!' Preston's tone became mocking. 'Would any British general or statesman have said such a thing?' With sarcasm that appalled the military spectators, he pointed his finger at Currie and called him 'this master tactician, this war lord trained in a real estate and insurance office,' who wanted to see his men 'at it' again.

Preston repeated the assertion that Sam Hughes had made years ago:

had Currie avoided the tragedies of Lens, Cambrai, Passchendaele, and other such places, the battalions could have been kept up to strength. Hughes had been in a position to know that there had been recklessness in the handling of the affairs of the Canadian army.

He concluded his address strong in voice and combative in tone: 'I say of General Currie, there should have been no life lost after he got information from General Horne on November 9th [regarding German envoys].' There were Canadian dead lying thick in the city, and Currie was the man responsible. 'I impeach Arthur Currie before this bar on behalf of the widows who lost their husbands, the mothers who lost their sons, the fathers who lost their support, the children who lost their fathers, in the needless, frightful, reckless loss of life in the attack on Mons.'

Preston was hissed by some as he sat down, but no one could deny that his address had been carefully planned and dramatically executed. As one reporter put it, it was 'full of eloquence with touches of oratory.'[1]

By the time Preston concluded his address to the jury, it was already 6:30 in the evening. Tilley had the unenviable task of making his address to a tired and emotionally drained jury. He began by mentioning Preston's failure to take the stand and face cross-examination and suggesting that Preston was more interested in making speeches than in uncovering the facts.

Tilley reminded the jury that they had to focus on a specific newspaper article and specific allegations. The trial was not an inquiry into the entire course of the war. The issue to be determined was whether Preston and Wilson should be excused on the grounds that what they said in their article was true in fact. What did the article say, what sources did the defendants rely on, and what efforts had they made to verify their statements? There was no basis for the article except for part of a speech made by Sir Sam Hughes under the protection of parliamentary privilege. Even Hughes's speech did not justify the article. Hughes had referred to Mons as a little one-horse town of no strategic value. It would be for the jury to say whether Mons had importance or not. In any event, its strategic value was a matter for the higher command to decide. The defendants could not escape what they had said in their article – that after he had received the armistice message, Currie had issued a mad order to attack. There was nothing in Hughes's speech, or in any of the evidence, to justify the statement that on Armistice Day Canadian troops were ready to attack their own general.

This, Tilley asserted, was 'the meanest thing that could be said by a mean man.'

The article alleged that there had been an appalling loss of life. But the only man killed, Tilley contended, was Price, who had been the victim of a sniper and who might have been killed no matter where he had been. 'There is absolutely not one sentence in this article that has a dirty sting to it that has been justified. There was nothing done for General Currie's glorification. He was a general carrying out orders.'

Currie knew nothing about the armistice beyond the fact that there were negotiations going on, and he had no choice but to obey the orders he received. The Allied strategy was to maintain maximum pressure on the Germans in order to obtain the most favourable terms in the negotiations. Decisive results were required, and the order Currie received on 9 November determined what was to happen. Currie had had nothing whatsoever to do with that decision; if it was wrong that men had been lost after 9 November, the blame rested elsewhere than on General Currie.

In essence, Tilley said, Wilson and Preston were telling the mothers and fathers of the fallen men that their sacrifice had been useless – that there had been a deliberate waste of life and that the general had sacrificed lives for his personal glory. What answer did Preston make to that? His answer was that of a coward – that Currie should have gone after someone else who had more money or who had said other things on other occasions. Preston should not be allowed to escape on such grounds. Currie's action had been properly brought; he had given the defendants the facts before the trial and had offered them a chance to retract, but they went on, to the very last instant, insisting that what they had said was true.

Tilley urged the jury not to be lenient in awarding damages. If the defendants were not punished, how easy it would be to scatter filth about, and then escape by referring to other gossip and rumours.

Tilley concluded his address shortly before eight o'clock: 'I am proud to suggest to you that General Currie did his part.' As he sat down, many of the spectators applauded.

The session adjourned, and Justice Rose returned to his hotel to prepare the jury charge he would deliver in the morning. Tilley returned to his office in Toronto, leaving Parmenter in charge. Regan remained in Cobourg, anxious to hear how Rose would put the case to the jury.

Hugh Rose began his charge to the jury promptly at 9:30 AM on Tuesday, 1 May 1928. He reminded the jurors of the oath they had taken to determine the issue before them solely on the basis of the evidence they heard in court. He explained that it was his duty to instruct them on the law, and that they were obliged to take the law as he stated it. The facts were for them to determine.

He then explained the basic elements of the law of libel. 'To libel a person is to write or print and publish, concerning him, a statement which exposes him to hatred, ridicule or contempt, or which tends to cause him to be shunned or avoided, or which has a tendency to injure him in his office, profession or trade.' A plaintiff makes out a case by proving the statement, by showing that it referred to him, and by showing that it had this hurtful tendency. It then falls to the defendants to put forth a defence. In General Currie's case, there were only two relevant defences. The first was that of truth or justification. It was not enough for the defendants to show that some aspect of their statements was true; they had to show 'that every material defamatory statement contained in [the] article is true in substance and in fact.'

The second defence was that of fair comment – that the material statements of fact were true and that comments made upon those facts were an expression of an opinion upon a matter of public importance which a reasonable and fair person might honestly make. The defence could succeed even if the comment had been extreme, but it was available only when the facts upon which the comment was made were shown to be true. It could not be disputed that the matter discussed in the article was one of public interest. The crux of the case really was whether or not the defendants had been able to establish the truth of what they had stated.

His Lordship then analysed the *Guide* article line by line, pointing out which statements were statements of fact and which were statements of comment or opinion, and instructing the jury on the manner in which they should apply the law to the particulars of the article. When he came to the passage that referred to 'common talk among the soldiers,' Rose said that the writer of the article had no right to repeat gossip. 'You do just as much harm by repeating gossip as by making an original statement of fact, and you do not, on a plea that your statement is true in substance and in fact, get off by showing that you were repeating and were only professing to repeat gossip. If you are going to repeat gossip, you have got to assume the responsibility when you are brought to task of showing that the gossip, if there was any, was true gossip.'

Although the judge phrased many of his remarks as questions, there could be no doubt about the answers he expected. Referring to the statement in the article, 'In less time than it takes to tell the story, headquarters got into their motors and were fleeing for their lives,' he asked pointedly: 'Have you heard any evidence adduced or even tendered, to show that headquarters, in less time than it takes to tell the story, got into their motors and were fleeing for their lives?'

Witnesses had been called by the defence to swear they had seen dead bodies in Mons on 11 November 1918. One could not, however, determine the number of dead Canadians in Mons by adding up the number of bodies mentioned by each of the witnesses; each of ten witnesses might have seen the same dead body.

In relating the arguments of counsel to the evidence presented, Justice Rose made no secret of his own assessment. 'Although I listened most attentively yesterday to the speech of counsel for one of the defendants, and to the speech of the other defendant, I find it very difficult to state shortly what the real contention of the defendants is as to the ... evidence ... which tends to support the plea set up in this record, the plea upon which you are trying the case.' The defendants had led a mass of evidence and made many suggestions, but he found these difficult to grasp. There was, for example, some evidence relating to loss of life on 9 and 10 November and to the rumours that an armistice was imminent. 'Now that would be a very interesting matter for discussion ... if the issue in the case were as to mistakes in judgment made on the 9th or 10th of November.' Rose was clearly intent upon confining the issue, as Tilley had urged, to the specific statements in the article.

The jury was cautioned about placing undue emphasis on the war diaries from which Regan had so often read. The diaries were, as one witness had observed, looked upon as a kind of necessary evil. 'The man who wrote them up no doubt did the best he could at the time. One man would be writing the diary for a battalion. He was writing, perhaps, with some haste, but necessarily he was writing a good deal of hearsay, and perhaps writing rather loosely.' Such evidence would not normally be admitted in a court of law.

The judge then explained the law of damages. The jury was entitled to consider not only the article itself but the conduct of the defendants since the suit had been brought. Under the law of libel, if an apology is made, damages are reduced. If the defendant insists upon the truth of the alleged libel, damages can be aggravated. 'They may persist, and they may set up their plea of truth ... They may conduct their trial when it comes to a trial in a moderate way, or they may be abusive or insulting, they may persist after the jury thinks the facts are against them, and that they ought to apologize. The jury [must] take all that into consideration in assessing the damages. The damages have not necessarily very much relation to any money loss of the plaintiff.'

Ordinarily, neither counsel nor judge refers to the amount claimed in the statement of claim. Justice Rose, however, cautioned the jury not to pay too much attention to the fact that $50,000 had been claimed. If they found for General Currie, they should 'consider what will more or less compensate the plaintiff and what will mark the extent of their disapproval of the conduct of the defendants if they think the conduct of the defendants is not to be approved.' The jury should not, he said, be concerned with the means of the defendants or with the fact that some other newspaper could also have been sued.

Although he had spoken only a little over two hours (a short time for so complex a trial), Justice Rose concluded by stating, 'I think that perhaps I have spoken at unnecessary length.' He invited the jury to return with questions if they were in doubt on any of the issues he had raised.

One juror immediately asked whether it would be appropriate for the jury to consider the impact of the costs. The judge answered that he would decide who should cover the costs, and that the jury should simply give a true verdict according to the evidence.

Justice Rose completed his remarks, and the jury retired. Parmenter had no objection to make; the charge was very favourable to Currie. Regan then rose to make several objections. He complained that the jury would conclude that Justice Rose's view was that the defendants had conducted their case in an abusive and insulting way. Regan also contended that more emphasis had been given to the plaintiff's evidence than to the defendants'. Justice Rose had named the officers who had testified for the plaintiff, whereas the defendants' witnesses were referred to merely as 'these men that were here some days ago.' Justice Rose's charge had also, according to Regan, failed to pay sufficient heed to the war diary accounts of the fighting, which contradicted the version given by the plaintiffs and their witnesses.

As Regan continued, repeating points he had made during the trial, Justice Rose became impatient. It was clear that Regan was getting nowhere. Rose refused to redirect the jury on any of the points Regan made, and court was adjourned.

Lunch was provided in the jury room. The judge, the lawyers, and the parties left the courthouse for lunch, but many spectators remained in their seats, eagerly awaiting the verdict. Some had arrived as early as seven o'clock that morning, and they were not about to give up their places now.

At two o'clock Justice Rose returned to the bench to hear a civil dispute between two brothers quarrelling over a family property. After only a few minutes, the litigants accepted the judge's suggestion that they should explore the possibility of settlement, and the case went no further.

By three o'clock there was still no verdict, and there was some speculation that the jury might be deadlocked. But at 3:27 PM, after three and a half hours, word came that a verdict had been reached. Led by the foreman, George Anderson, the jury filed in, and the sheriff went to call the judge. The courtroom was completely still. Currie and Preston were in their places. Wilson, unable to withstand the tension, did not return. According to one reporter, he was 'greatly fatigued and worn out by the long days in the courtroom.'[2] When Justice Rose entered, Regan was not present, and several more tense moments followed while the constable fetched him.

'Gentlemen of the jury, have you agreed upon your verdict?' asked the clerk. The foreman rose slowly. 'On behalf of the jury, I beg to submit the finding that the Defendants are guilty of libel, and that the award of five hundred dollars be given to the Plaintiff.' A moment of silence followed. It was broken by the applause of two or three spectators, who were quickly silenced by Sheriff Nesbitt. Neither Currie nor Preston showed any sign of emotion. The clerk repeated the finding: 'Gentlemen of the jury, hearken unto your verdict as the court has recorded it: you find a verdict for the Plaintiff, five hundred dollars damages.'

Regan demanded a poll of each member of the jury. Justice Rose seemed startled, but agreed. The clerk called out the names one by one. The first six assented. The seventh man was George A. Mouncey, one of two ex-servicemen on the jury. He was an artillery-man, and had been twice wounded. He had intently followed the evidence during the trial. When his name was called, he answered. 'No.' The clerk looked surprised, and repeated the question. 'No.' repeated Mouncey. The emphatic tone of his answer left no doubt that he dissented. The remaining five jurors answered 'Yes.' Despite Mouncey's dissent, Currie was entitled to a verdict in his favour: unanimity is required in criminal cases, but a civil jury of twelve could return a verdict even with two dissenters.[3]

Currie was immediately surrounded by well-wishers eager to shake his hand. Allan Magee reached him first, and congratulated him with an enthusiastic slap on the back. Currie was relieved by the verdict, but surprised by the amount of money he had been awarded. When asked by reporters for his reaction, he stated: 'The verdict is very satisfactory to me. I have really nothing to say about it other than it was vindication I sought rather than money.' With tears in his eyes, he shook hands with each juror, including Mouncey, the dissenter.

Preston left the courtroom smiling, apparently unperturbed by the result. 'I presume there will be an appeal, but I cannot say until I have consulted with Mr. Wilson.'

Currie was applauded by the crowd in the rotunda of Victoria Hall, and greeted with cheers as he walked along King Street. He returned to the Dunham Hotel, where that evening a number of local officers and men who had served under him gave a banquet. There were few formal speeches. As Currie rose to thank his commrades, tears streamed down his cheeks and he seemed hardly able to speak. He did, however, read to those assembled a telegram he had received earlier in the day before he knew what the verdict would be.

As father of George Lawrence Price, the only Canadian killed on Armistice Day, I wish to convey to you, Sir, my humble hope that you will succeed in bringing to justice those responsible for bringing this case before the public, because all this simply renews old wounds that are better forgotten. James Price, Fort William.

14

Appeal

A libel verdict for the plaintiff is not always received with enthusiasm by the press, but in Sir Arthur Currie's case the editorial writers warmly endorsed the jury's decision. The Toronto *Star* proclaimed that Currie had 'been completely vindicated, as everyone who shared his campaign must have known he would be.'[1] The Kingston *Whig-Standard* described Preston's charges as 'preposterous and astounding' and heartily approved the verdict as good for Currie and good for Canada.[2] The Montreal *Gazette* agreed that Currie had been vindicated, and congratulated him on having had the courage to bring the suit. Today journalists often contend that the law of defamation imposes undue restrictions on the freedom of the press and on the ability of the press to inform the public about sensitive matters of public concern.[3] The *Gazette*'s editorial, however, took a very different line. The result achieved by Currie was, it argued, an important one for all people engaged in public affairs:

Men of great ability who would have otherwise been available for posts of public responsibility, have been constrained to remain in private life because of the scurvy treatment which so many leaders receive. Much has been lost to the country in this way, but less will be lost in the future if, once in a while, exemplary action is taken and a just reparation is exacted. It is in this respect Sir Arthur Currie has rendered a new service to the Dominion, one which should have, and we believe will have, a broad and lasting influence.[4]

Currie's return to Montreal was a triumph, although, if one recalled the cool reception Currie received when he returned to Canada in 1919, there was more than a touch of unintended irony in the opening sentence of the Montreal *Gazette*'s report: 'Sir Arthur came back to town last night among some scenes that could hardly have been excelled in enthusiasm had he been returning from the War.'[5]

Currie had left for Montreal on the three o'clock train the day after the trial ended. A large crowd had gathered at Windsor Station, and most of those who surged against the police barriers in their eagerness to greet him were McGill students. A Royal Highlanders band piped him down the platform. The tune of 'Bonnie Dundee' was interspersed with the McGill yell and cheers for 'Sir Art' from the students. Currie, accompanied by his son Garner, paused to shake a few hands on his way to the safety of the car that awaited him. Even the streets were lined with well-wishers, and a band of the Royal Montreal Regiment stationed on the steps of St George's Church opposite the station played wartime tunes as the general and his son drove away. Some students jumped on top of the car and ordered the chauffeur to continue his drive. Many others followed along behind. The McGill yell was repeated over and over.

Currie was taken to the United Service Club. He spoke briefly from the steps of the club to those outside. He was visibly moved by the warmth of his reception, but made it clear that he could accept applause not for himself but for the soldiers who had fought valiantly under his command. He repeated the sentiment he had so often expressed before the trial – the fight and the victory belonged to the entire Canadian Corps, not just to Arthur Currie.

I don't know how we could have had the temerity to stop fighting on the 9th. We had done much, and we would have been the only Corps to lie down and quit. Canadians do not lie down and quit within two days of victory. Mothers wrote telling me that they understood and realized their sons had fallen doing their duty. Ten years have passed since we came home, and we have never been more united since the conflict ceased. Once more we have come through a dirty fight, and once more we have won. The Corps is once more united as it was in the fields of France and Flanders.

Loudspeakers had been installed in the club, and a crowd gathered to listen to Currie's speech. Special arrangements had been made so that his remarks could be broadcast to thousands of radio listeners throughout Canada. 'I have not felt happier for a long day,' he said.

'This wonderful demonstration of affection for the Commander of the famous Canadian Corps has done much to unite us once again.'

Currie received hundreds of congratulatory letters and telegrams.[6] They came from old friends, parents who had lost sons in the war, and returned soldiers of every rank. Local Canadian Legion presidents wrote in great numbers. Letters were received from colleagues at McGill, retired British generals, small-town newspaper editors, superior court judges, and fellow university presidents. The governor-general, Lord Willingdon, wrote, as did Sir Robert Borden, Arthur Meighen, Newton Rowell, Sir George Perley, and Sir Edward Kemp. From Australia came a terse telegram: 'Congratulations Monash.' Some correspondents complained that the damages were too low, and others pleaded with Currie to forget the whole affair once and for all.

Further celebrations, including a formal banquet, were proposed, but Frederick Wilson and W.T.R. Preston were already threatening to appeal the verdict. The two defendants had spent the morning after the trial with Frank Regan at the British Hotel in Cobourg, and announced publicly that an appeal would be filed. Wilson said that Regan would represent him again, and stated confidently, 'We consider that we have abundant points on which to make an appeal – the judge's unfair stand in regard to excluding our evidence, and his more than unfair charge to the jury.'[7]

Currie put on a brave face: 'Let them go ahead if they think they will get any consolation out of it.'[8] Parmenter told Currie not to worry, but also advised him to postpone any more celebrations until the time for filing an appeal had passed. Preston, he feared, might use such an occasion as an excuse for bursting into print again. Others told Currie that he could not expect the verdict to silence Preston, and that Preston was likely to strike again with a book 'more carefully libelous than heretofore and much more widely circulated.'[9]

The accuracy of these predictions was proved when Preston objected to an editorial in the Toronto *Globe* that welcomed the jury's verdict and proclaimed that Currie had been vindicated. Preston asserted on the front page of the Port Hope *Evening Guide* that 'a substantial number of the jury were opposed to giving a verdict' in Currie's favour, and suggested that the *Globe* should conduct a poll of its readers to determine whether the public wanted a full parliamentary investigation 'securing not only "the truth" but "the whole truth" about the frightful, unnecessary waste of human life, not only at Mons, but throughout the war, as was charged by the Port Hope *Guide*.'[10]

There is no doubt that the jury's low award and the dissent of the ex-serviceman juror qualified Currie's victory. He had always said that he was not after money, but the discrepancy between the $50,000 he claimed and the $500 he was awarded did not go unnoticed. The court reporter, Robert Dickson, himself a returned soldier who had finished the war just outside Mons, later referred to the award as 'comparatively trifling.'[11] Bovey was disturbed that 'the damages were so small' and in fact awards ten times as large for less serious libels were not uncommon.[12]

Currie was told by Judge E.T. Huycke in Peterborough, whose brother had been on the jury, that 'the reason for the small amount of the judgment apparently was their idea you might get that, but would fail to [collect] a larger amount' because Wilson simply did not have the money.[13] Preston claimed that several members of the jury had been opposed to giving a verdict in Currie's favour, although he did not explain why there was only one dissent when the jury was polled. There may have been some truth to his contention, however, for years later another juror said that the jury had been badly split: one faction wanted to give Currie a substantial award of damages while the other wanted to find for Wilson and Preston; the $500 verdict was nothing more than a compromise.[14]

Despite the low award, however, Currie was greatly relieved by the result of the trial. It is possible that he wrote to members of the jury to thank them – no letters have been found, but he did get the addresses from Roy Willmott, his Cobourg solicitor.[15] Still, he often described the trial as a 'distressing' and 'humiliating' experience.[16] He thought the conduct of the defendants 'mean,' and the trial itself 'sordid.'[17] None the less, he was convinced that it had been worth it: 'I had to do it. I could not die with such a charge unanswered. I wanted the people of Canada to know the truth, I wanted to prove Sam H. a liar and I wanted to suggest to the students of McGill that it is neither manly nor honourable to compromise with a lie.'[18] He felt that the Corps had been pulled together for another proud moment. 'It was a most bitter experience and yet it had to be endured.'[19]

There seems little doubt that the trial had been a much more stressful experience than Currie had expected. At times the result had seemed less than certain, and whatever vindication he had obtained had been dearly paid for in worry and humiliation. He had struggled at his adversaries' level for a victory he had thought before the trial to be inevitable. For weeks, every ounce of his energy had been consumed by the case. Although he was the principal combatant, he had to let his lawyers do the actual fighting. It was only when he stepped into the witness-box that he had any real control, and even then the unfamiliar rules and the very atmosphere of the courtroom seemed to give all the advantages to the lawyer he faced in cross-examination. By the time the trial ended, Currie was on the verge of a physical and nervous collapse. His doctor told him to stay away from his office and rest, but Currie was eager to return to his duties at McGill.

Despite the stated intentions of Wilson and Preston, an appeal seemed unlikely. The case was essentially a factual one, and it is extremely difficult to convince the Court of Appeal to reverse a jury finding. A few days after the trial, Roy Willmott, one of Currie's Cobourg solicitors, reported to his client that he had learned that Frank Regan was not encouraging an appeal, and that no steps had been taken to order a transcript of the evidence, which would be needed if an appeal was to be taken.[20]

Willmott's information proved unreliable. Preston was never one to give up easily, and Wilson was facing financial ruin. Although only $500 in damages had been awarded, he had to pay Currie's costs, which were going to be enormous. Filing a notice of appeal would automatically stay Currie's right to collect any money, and would at least buy some time. The appeal could not be heard until a complete transcript was prepared, which, because of the length of the trial, would take several months. Perhaps the fact that one juror had dissented gave the defendants some hope. Although they would have to come up with the money to pay for the transcript, the appeal probably would not take more than a day and would be far less costly than the trial.

Preston and Wilson themselves went to Osgoode Hall in Toronto to file the notice of appeal. Wilson was no longer represented by Frank Regan. He retained Robert Richard Hall, KC, of Peterborough, a fellow Liberal and former member of Parliament who had been defeated in the elections of 1911 and 1917.

Currie had first learned of the *Guide's* attack on him from Peter Brown, the rival Port Hope editor, and as soon as Brown heard of the decision to appeal, he wired Currie: 'Campbell solicitor Port Hope announced tonight that appeal would be filed tomorrow or Tuesday against jury's findings.'[21]

Currie received the message by telephone in his office on 13 May 1928. The strain was too much for him. He collapsed, and was later found unconscious. For a few days his friends and associates were pessimistic about his condition. He spent almost a month in hospital recuperating, and was still under a doctor's care in mid-June.

Currie's physician, Dr Martin, advised him to get away immediately so that he would be 'out of range of worry of the case.'[22] Currie took his doctor's advice. An acting principal was appointed, and Currie and his wife left for Europe at the end of June 1928. He did not return to Canada for almost a year.

Dr Martin urged Currie's lawyers to dispose of the appeal as soon as possible so that Currie could put the whole business behind him. The court reporter said that preparation of the transcript would take at least two months, which meant that the appeal would not be heard until well into the autumn. The court reporter was worried that he might not be paid for his work, and refused to begin the transcription until satisfactory arrangements were made.

Tilley and Parmenter were confident that the appeal would be disposed of in short order, and they tried to reassure Currie. To preserve the independence they had asserted at trial, Wilson and Preston had filed separate appeals. To initiate an appeal it was only necessary to file a notice setting out the grounds for the appeal in a general way.[23] In their notices of appeal, both Wilson and Preston contended that Justice Rose had erred in refusing to admit evidence, and that his charge to the jury was wrong. Neither the evidence that should have been admitted nor their precise complaints regarding the charge were specified. They contended that the verdict was contrary to the weight of the evidence and again raised the spectre of Currie's pre-war financial transgressions by alleging that the judge had erred in refusing to allow them to cross-examine the plaintiff 'on matters relevant to the issues.' They alleged that the judge had 'erred in commenting to the jury upon the conduct of the defendants.' Both appellants sought to rely on new evidence, something an appellate court will permit only in exceptional circumstances. Preston's notice of appeal claimed that his co-defendant Wilson had been allowed more than the proper number of expert witnesses; it is not clear why Preston thought that this would help him, even if it was true.

Nothing in the notices of appeal looked particularly threatening, and Parmenter even speculated that the defendants would abandon the appeal. It is next to impossible to reverse a jury verdict on factual issues, and, in the absence of any egregious legal mistakes, the Court of Appeal would recognize that the trial had been a long and difficult one and would allow a trial judge as able and experienced as Justice Rose a certain margin of error. Tilley was unusually categorical: 'There is no possible chance of the appeal succeeding.' In an attempt to reassure Currie, Tilley said that he was 'inclined to think the appeal would be a helpful matter from your standpoint because it will give the judges an opportunity of expressing their opinion with regard to the libel. I think we may expect them to comment unfavourably with regard to both Wilson and Preston.'[24]

The court reporter was paid $400 on account and given a personal guarantee by W.A.F. Campbell for the balance, but by the end of August he still had work left to do. Tilley left on the CPR board of directors' annual inspection trip to western Canada at the end of August, and did not return until 24 September. The appeal could not be heard until late October.

In mid-October, after the transcript had been completed and preparation for the appeal was well under way, a notice was served stating that the defendants were abandoning the appeal. It was signed 'W.A.F. Campbell, solicitor for the defendants, per Frank Regan.'[25] Wilson would say only that the appeal had been withdrawn 'on the advice of counsel.' Robert Richard Hall, speaking on Wilson's behalf, said that because the decision was essentially one for the jury, there was little that an appeal court could do. 'The difficulties in the way of my clients in regard to an appeal were almost unsurmountable ... In view of the difficulties, I finally decided with great reluctance that I could not advise my clients to proceed with an appeal, in view of the remoteness of hope of success. There will, therefore, be no appeal. The defence has contended, however, and still contends, that there has been a miscarriage of justice.'[26]

Preston immediately repudiated the suggestion that the appeal would not proceed, stating that he knew nothing of its abandonment. Preston, who was in Ottawa when the notice was served, was quoted as saying that 'since the trial at Cobourg a considerable amount of new evidence has come to light, disclosure of which will startle the country, and so far as I am concerned the fight is still on.'[27]

Within a few days both Wilson and Preston applied to the court to set aside the notice discontinuing the appeal, thereby resurrecting their right to proceed. Preston filed an affidavit stating that he had not been consulted and that Campbell had not signed the notice of discontinuance that had been served. Wilson swore that he had instructed Hall to proceed with the appeal, and denied having given instructions to abandon it.

Thomas F. Hall, KC, of Cobourg (unrelated to Robert Richard Hall), who had been co-counsel with Regan at the trial, appeared for Wilson and Preston on the application to the court to set aside the notice of discontinuance. Preston was as confident as ever. 'We do not know what the outcome of the proceedings will be, but this is not the only court. We intend to fight the thing right to the bitter end, and we are not going to be bamboozled out of it.'[28]

It is not known whether Thomas Hall made any reference in the hearing to the new evidence Preston claimed to have uncovered, but the court did decide to permit the appeal to go ahead. The judges insisted, however, that the case was to proceed immediately and fixed 29 October 1928 as the date on which the appeal would be heard. Parmenter's reaction was stoic; he reported to Currie that it would be more satisfactory to have the appeal dealt with on the merits than on a technicality.

Tilley and Parmenter hoped the case would be heard by the First Appellate Division, which counted among its members Chief Justice Mulock and Justice Magee, Alan Magee's father. In the end, however, it came on before the Second Appellate Division, with Chief Justice Latchford presiding over a court composed of Justices Riddell, Middleton, and Orde (the father of Reginald Orde, judge advocate-general, who had testified at the trial about departmental records).

Tilley remained supremely confident. He was in Ottawa arguing a case in the Supreme Court of Canada on the day the appeal was heard, and Parmenter represented Currie. Tilley thought that if the appellants got anywhere the case would take more than a day and that he could return to Toronto on the second day to respond.

Wilson and Preston were again represented by Thomas Hall. He argued until three o'clock in the afternoon, but with little success.[29] He was frequently interrupted by the judges, who made no secret of their disapproval of the attack that had been made upon Currie. Before he even started, Hall was met with 'This isn't R.R. Hall?' from Justice Orde, indicating that his Lordship had read the press report of Wilson's former counsel's explanation of why he had abandoned the appeal as being hopeless.

Some of the interventions from the bench were unusual, if not unjudicial. Chief Justice Latchford launched a tirade against the Ross rifle, which amounted to an attack on Sir Sam Hughes: 'I have it on good authority that many soldiers died with jammed Ross rifles in their hands, cursing the man who put them there ... The rifle might have been a good one for sniping, but it was utterly useless under the conditions. The men presented a helpless target because they were equipped with this rifle at the insistence of Sir Charles Ross and his friends in the House of Commons.'

Justices Riddell and Latchford both remarked pointedly that they had never heard of any unnecessary loss of life at Mons, and when Hall argued that the defence evidence suggested that men had indeed been killed there, Chief Justice Latchford replied bluntly, 'My son was there.' Justice Orde asserted that the article had slandered every officer of the Corps, rebutting Hall's objection to a speech made by General MacBrien during the trial urging all officers to stand together. Justice Riddell added, 'It is perfectly understandable. The chaps who were with him would stand by him. Why do you object?' Even if MacBrien's remarks were out of place, he added, the appropriate remedy would have been to ask the trial judge to make a finding of contempt rather than to complain now.

Hall argued that defence evidence had been improperly excluded, particularly Sam Hughes's House of Commons speeches. While these had been referred to in cross-examination, they had not been accepted as part of the defence case. Chief Justice Latchford quipped, 'A great many things that Sir Sam Hughes said in his time could not be regarded as evidence in the court,' to which Mr Justice Middleton added, 'Who cares what Sir Sam Hughes said.'

Hall contended that Justice Rose had failed to put the case fairly to the jury by placing insufficient weight on the testimony that dead Canadians were seen on 11 November 1918, but Chief Justice Latchford pointed out that even if dead men were seen it did not prove they had been killed that morning.

The startling new evidence Preston claimed to have found was an order from Canadian Corps headquarters dated 4:30 PM on 10 November 1918, which stated: 'All operations cancelled, hostilities cease 11th hour, 11th inst. Troops stand fast at the line reached. No fraternization with the enemy.' It is not clear where this document came from. If Currie did issue it, he could have used it himself to show that he had ordered an early cessation of operations. In the end, no serious effort was made by Hall to have it introduced, and Preston seems to have uncovered nothing else.

At the conclusion of Hall's argument, without even calling on Parmenter, Chief Justice Latchford delivered a brief oral judgment disposing of the case.

We are all of one opinion in regard to these appeals. No argument has been presented to this court that would lead us to think there has been any mistrial of the action, or that anything was improperly withheld from the jury in the judge's charge, or that anything that should not have been said was said. There was no improper rejection of evidence and no improper admission. The greatest latitude, it seems to me, was extended to counsel for the defendants by the trial judge, and the only error – and it is an error – is that the latitude was too wide.

15

Conclusion

The Currie libel action was an event of national significance. It is unusual for a lawsuit to capture the attention of the entire country, yet the trial was in the headlines for more than two weeks.[1] The major dailies carried extensive accounts of the trial, and although the law of contempt was thought to preclude any public statements passing judgment on the proceedings or predicting the outcome, few informed Canadians were without an opinion. Public opinion seems to have favoured Currie. But Wilson and Preston, the underdogs, unquestionably garnered support, particularly in their own community, where the trial was seen by many as a contest between a courageous small-town editor and the powerful and pompous military establishment.

There were many who regretted that the case had been brought at all. As the father of the unfortunate Price observed in his telegram to Currie, for some Canadians it reopened old wounds. The trial pitted the ordinary soldiers who testified for the defence against their former officers, and renewed feelings of frustration and resentment. For others, however, the experience of the trial was cathartic. Soldiers who had thought their effort forgotten or unappreciated were proud to see their commander 'go at' the cynics. As Currie had predicted, the trial represented more than a personal struggle to vindicate his name. It was a contest he fought with and for the comrades who joined him at Cobourg on behalf of all senior officers in the Canadian Corps.

In the minds of many, Mons was merely a symbol of the futility, false heroics, and human waste of the Great War. The trial put the credibility and integrity of the Corps command at issue. It became a part of the Canadian public's attempt to come to terms with the staggering cost of the war ten years after the armistice.

It was only as the case unfolded in the courtroom that Currie fully understood the risk he had taken. He was a straightforward man who expected straightforward solutions. He had little appreciation of the uncertainties of litigation until it was too late to retreat from his initial decision to sue. Although he had been warned of the risks, Currie was certain that by taking legal action he was taking charge of the situation, and that a verdict in his favour was inevitable. He was dismayed to find himself frequently on the defensive, caught up in a process he did not fully understand.

To deal in a court of law with questions such as those raised in the Currie case is extraordinary. The adversary trial process is designed to dissect and examine discrete events more modest in scale. Rules of evidence deliberately filter the flow of information. Argument and debate are closely constrained and controlled. Tilley fully understood – and brilliantly exploited – the rules of litigation. At every turn he resisted Regan's attempts to turn the trial into a no-holds-barred public inquiry, and succeeded in focusing the attention of the court on what happened within the city limits of Mons on Armistice Day. Even Currie admitted that Canadian losses in the final push at the end of the war were huge, and if the militarily unsophisticated jury had been allowed to examine a less confined issue, its verdict might well have been different.

Currie was praised for having had the courage to bring a libel action, and it was predicted that the result of the trial would have a healthy effect on public debate in Canada. But despite Preston's well-deserved reputation as a muckraker, some of the arguments he made deserve greater attention now than they received at the time. Currie's actions at Mons and throughout the war were a matter of public concern and a legitimate subject for public debate. As Currie knew so well, the desirability of unrestrained debate in Parliament means that members are given absolute immunity from suit for what they say within the confines of the House. A newspaper is faced with the other extreme – absolute liability – even when it comments on matters of public concern. Even if the newspaper has a reasonable basis for believing the truth of what it prints, it will be found liable unless it can prove that what it printed was true. As the Currie case demonstrates, the rules of evidence made adducing such proof in a court of law an exacting exercise. Those strict rules may be appropriate to determine a person's guilt or innocence of a serious criminal offence; near certainty is required where the liberty of the subject is at stake. But how appropriate is it to confine the press to those facts that can be proved in the same way and virtually to the same degree?[2] Is the common law protection afforded to personal reputation not bound to stifle debate on important public issues? The mere threat of litigation will dissuade many an editor from publishing a controversial story about a powerful figure. Should the press be excused from liability unless it knowingly or recklessly misstates the facts regarding a public official?[3] A public figure such as Sir Arthur Currie could clear his name and maintain his reputation in ways less costly and cumbersome and less intrusive on freedom of expression. Such questions were not seriously debated at the time of the Currie case, though the low damages award indicates that the jury did take into account the fact that the *Guide* had repeated, albeit with embellishment, the words uttered by Sam Hughes years earlier.

Currie, of course, might well have sued even if he had been faced with legal rules more protective of the press.[4] It seems unlikely that he would have been dissuaded from suing had the law required him to prove that the defendants were negligent in what they had written. Currie was convinced that his case was so clear that no one who made any effort to check the facts could have reached the conclusion expressed in the 'Mons' article. Currie frequently described the defendants as 'mean,' and he was convinced that old enemies were at work behind the scenes. He might have gone ahead even if he had been required to prove deliberate wrongdoing on the part of Wilson and Preston.

Although the formal rules favour the plaintiff in a libel case, an action like the Currie trial can be a bitter and gruelling experience for the participants. Currie did get a verdict in his favour, but he found the law less hospitable to his claim than he had expected. As he saw it, he had suffered a grievous wrong and was entitled to clear and decisive vindication. Many sympathized with that view, and were disturbed by the nastiness of the trial. But the legal process does not offer vindication without exacting a price. The Currie case had a profound effect on the lives of Currie and Wilson, and Regan's career was not helped by the persistently aggressive defence he afforded his clients. On the futures of Tilley, Rose, and Preston the case had far less impact.

Tilley conducted the case with masterly forensic precision. He was unrattled by Regan's antics, and though his style was neither dramatic nor exciting, his handling of the case was highly skilful and professional. For Tilley the case was an important one, but his reputation was already made and his career would have continued on its successful course without it. Three years after the Currie trial, in 1931, he was elected treasurer of the Law Society of Upper Canada, the highest office in the Ontario legal profession's governing body, a position he held until 1935. He argued many more important cases before his death in 1942 at the age of seventy-five. To this day he is remembered as one of Canada's great lawyers, and his conduct of the Currie case suggests that his reputation is well deserved.

For Justice Hugh Rose, the Currie trial was undoubtedly the most public case of his career. The firmness and coolness he demonstrated throughout the case were characteristic of this bachelor lawyer. Two years after the Currie trial, Hugh Rose was appointed chief justice of the High Court (the trial division of the Supreme Court of Ontario), a post he held until his death at the age of seventy-six in 1945.

W.T.R. Preston seems to have been little affected by the case. Indeed, he rather enjoyed the fight right up to the end. He revelled in controversy and relished the limelight. To have returned, however briefly, to a position of national prominence was far more important to him than whether he won or lost the case.

Preston's political activities had diminished by the time of the Currie case. Shortly after the trial he had a serious rift with Mackenzie King, and, although he always considered himself a Liberal, he could not follow a leader 'who does not understand the meaning of loyalty to Party principles, but prefers treachery to principles and friends.'[5] By the early 1930s Preston had moved to England. He came back to Canada in 1933 for yet another libel trial, this one the final chapter in his long struggle with the Ottawa *Journal* and its publisher P.D. Ross, whose memoirs, *Retrospects of a Newspaper Person*, contain many uncomplimentary references to Preston. Ross wrote, 'Mr. Preston's life story suggests an unfailing pugnacious, jealous and vindictive temper.' Preston, now in his eighties, sued again, claiming damages of $20,000. The case was tried before Justice Kerwin and a jury, and once again

Preston acted on his own behalf. The defendants were represented by an eminent counsel, D.L. McCarthy, KC. The trial was front-page news.[6] Preston claimed that his fight with Ross, which extended over thirty years and three previous actions, 'had no parallel in English jurisprudence,' and he urged the jury 'to lift the stigma from his name.'

During the trial much of Preston's controversial career was canvassed. He vehemently denied any wrongdoing in the West Elgin election, and even denied sending the telegram that had earned him the nickname 'Hug the Machine Preston,' though he could not explain why he had not disclaimed responsibility for the telegram earlier. George F. Henderson, KC, who had acted for the *Journal* in previous cases, corroborated the version Ross had given and which Preston disputed. According to Henderson, Preston was a 'stormy petrel' who had been 'in trouble all over the world ... He is of the opinion he is a hundred per cent right and every one else wrong.'

Preston's closing address to the jury was an emotional plea for vindication. He knew that this would probably be his last time in the public eye and his last chance to gain the respectability he coveted. 'I submit that I have the right to pass on to my children an honourable name clear of any doubt. I think I am claiming what I have a right to claim, a verdict vindicating my reputation.'

At the end of three days of trial, the case went to the jury. After deliberating for two hours, the jury returned an unusual verdict. Although the jurors found for the defendants, they added, 'We find that Mr. Preston has had an honourable public career.' Justice Kerwin dismissed Preston's action with costs. Preston returned to England, where he remained until his death in November 1942 at the age of ninety-two.

For Frederick Wilson, the Currie case was a disaster. He had clearly been under a great deal of stress during the trial, and though the jury had been lenient in awarding damages he still had to pay Currie's costs. He died on 13 October 1929, a year after the appeal, at the age of sixty-nine. His death was attributed to a breakdown 'brought on by the worry he had carried in recent years,'[7] unquestionably a direct result of the Currie libel action. His defence had put an enormous strain on Wilson's modest financial resources, and at the time of his death he had not paid his own lawyers. Four years after the trial Thomas F. Hall sued Wilson's estate, claiming $3,216 in fees and disbursements. Hall was represented by Frank Regan, who displayed questionable ethics in taking the brief against his old client. George N. Gordon, who had tried to extricate Wilson from the Currie affair before the trial, was called as a witness. Gordon testified that it had been understood that the legal services of Hall and Regan were to be rendered without fee as a political gesture to fellow Liberals. Regan disputed this, and he objected to Gordon's suggestion that he had lost the case. 'You say that I lost the case, yet the writ was for fifty thousand and judgment was only for five hundred. Still, you say we never had a chance to win the case.' Gordon replied that the case had been a 'complete vindication for Sir Arthur Currie,' but Regan disagreed – whether from conviction or in order to collect his fees, it is not clear: 'It was not a complete vindication.'[8]

The Currie trial certainly did not help Frank Regan's career. Before the trial many in the profession had thought him a counsel of some potential, and there can be little doubt that Regan himself hoped to make his name in the case. He made a name, but not the one he wanted. He was widely condemned for his conduct of the defence. Some lawyers felt that Regan had used the case for publicity, and disapproved heartily of his conduct.[9] Others thought that he had given 'an exhibition of how a law suit ought not to be conducted.'[10] Among those was Senator W.A. Griesbach, a former soldier, who thought that 'no other lawyer in Canada could have been found to conduct the case as Regan handled the defence.'[11] Another observer, admittedly a Currie supporter, thought that Regan was a 'joke' and a 'disgrace to the profession,' but allowed cynically that it could be said in his favour that his conduct had helped to win the case for Currie.[12] George N. Gordon was 'indignant' at Regan's conduct and thought that his client, Wilson, had been prompted to put up a 'useless defence' by Regan and Hall.[13]

Much of this criticism was unfair, and seems to have been based on nothing more than the fact that Regan had undertaken Wilson's defence in the first place. It goes very much against the ethics of the profession to identify the lawyer with the deeds or character of the client, though this is perhaps not well understood by the public at large. To criticize Regan simply because he defended his client against a man of Currie's stature and prominence would be wrong. Lawyers who take unpopular cases against powerful interests should be applauded, not condemned.

Regan's client lacked the resources to undertake a case of this magnitude, and Regan did the best he could with what he had. Indeed, given the evidence he had to work with, Regan performed remarkably well. He faced a formidable foe, and could not have been more stalwart in his client's defence; but his conduct does deserve some criticism. At times his strategy was ill-conceived and counter-productive. His treatment of witnesses sometimes went beyond forcefulness and was almost abusive. He tried to make up for the shortcomings in the evidence he had been able to collect by putting before the jury material he must have known to be inadmissible. An advocate can be aggressive in his client's defence while remaining fair and observing the rules; but Regan often failed to observe the limits of legitimate advocacy.

Regan had political aspirations, but he found that he was hindered by the reputation he had acquired from his conduct of the Currie case. Two years after the trial, apparently having changed his political stripe, he sought the Conservative nomination in a Toronto riding. When he met with the objection that as the man who attacked Sir Arthur Currie he was unsuitable as a candidate, he decided to approach Currie through P.L. Brown, the editor of the Port Hope *Times*.[14] Regan asked Currie to intimate in some public way that he found no fault with the manner in which Regan had defended Wilson's interests. Currie refused even to consider the request, and when pressed by Brown, who told him that Regan claimed to have treated Currie like a gentleman, Currie replied coldly that 'Regan might have thought so; but what constitutes a gentleman was not regarded in the same way by all people.'[15]

Five years after the Currie trial, Regan returned to public prominence in the 'Dorland affair.' This was a brief Regan must have relished. Largely because of Regan's digging and persistence, a commission of inquiry headed by Justice Kingstone found that several members of the Toronto police department had been guilty of serious misjudgment and misconduct. Regan's client, Dorland, had formed a plan to rob a bank, but his confederate went to the police. The police responded with a hair-raising scheme. It was decided at the highest level that Dorland should be encouraged to proceed with the robbery and that the police, heavily armed and hidden within the bank, should apprehend him when he entered. Dorland became suspicious and drove away, but was met with a barrage of gunfire from another contingent of police stationed nearby. No one was hurt, but the incident gave rise to a public outcry. The police tried to cover up the affair, but Regan was able to demonstrate police perjury and forging of police and court records. The chairman of the Police Commission was implicated and forced to resign.[16]

Regan continued to attract high-profile briefs. In 1936 he defended Harry O'Donnell, who had been charged with the murder of a young girl whose body was found in a Toronto ravine. O'Donnell was convicted and hanged for the crime. Regan later defended Elizabeth Tilford, who was convicted of the murder of her husband by poisoning, and he was retained to defend two brothers charged in the gangland slaying of a bookmaker called Jimmy Windsor. He was always on the lookout for an interesting brief, particularly one that would attract publicity.[17] As the years passed, his political affiliation changed again when he became an active supporter of the Co-operative Commonwealth Federation. Regan died of a heart attack at the age of fifty-four in June 1940.

Despite his victory, the case remained a bitter experience for Arthur Currie. When the appeal was argued he was still in England recuperating. He spent his time at golf and bridge, and made the occasional trip to Oxford and Cambridge to discuss matters of academic concern. But he was frustrated by the idleness forced upon him by his poor health. There can be no doubt that his illness was a direct result of the strain of the trial. He wrote to friends of his shame 'for letting the worries incident to the Cobourg trial bowl me over so completely.'[18] Even after his six months' vacation, his doctors ordered him to remain away from work, telling him that he needed more rest. Currie admitted that his 'recuperative powers are not what they were.' The trial, he said, was the final battle of the war, 'and not having been wounded in France it was my turn now.'[19] Three years after the trial Currie confided to an old friend that he had suffered 'a complete nervous breakdown caused largely by the harrowing thought that ten years after the war one was forced to fight another battle to retain hold of any good name one had.'[20] Currie never fully regained his health. When he was laid low by illness in the years following, he would deny that his condition had anything to do with the collapse the trial had caused, but there seems little doubt that it dealt him a severe blow.

Currie was not a wealthy man, and the cost of the trial was a major worry. Tilley's fee for the trial was $7,500, and another $500 was billed for the appeal.[21] These fees seem relatively modest in view of the length and complexity of the trial and Tilley's position as the leading counsel of the day. Duncan Chisholm's fees and disbursements came to $5,527. George Montgomery, Currie's Montreal solicitor, sent a bill for $276 in disbursements; when Currie asked him for a bill for his fees, Montgomery replied: 'As far as charges are concerned, the black eye which you gave Mr. W.T.R. Preston is sufficient compensation for me. I am afraid that I felt it was as much my fight as yours.'[22]

Still, Currie's legal bill was more than $14,000, in addition to the expenses incurred in Cobourg during the three weeks of trial by Currie himself and by the small army of witnesses he had summoned. Chisholm was able to collect the $500 damages award from Wilson.

Currie had also been awarded costs, but in a case like this the amount the winning party can collect from the loser by no means provides complete indemnity. To deal with the costs, Wilson retained John Wellington Pickup (later to become chief justice of Ontario), a member of Hugh Rose's old firm of Fasken, Robertson, Aitchison, Pickup and Calvin. Wilson pleaded that payment of anything more than $4,000 would bankrupt him, but Currie managed to get $5,000.

Vindication did not come cheaply. Currie would have been out of pocket well over $10,000 had it not been for the personal generosity of Edward Beatty, the president of the CPR and a governor of McGill, and a number of prominent Montrealers. Shortly after the trial, and after Currie's collapse, Beatty (who had advised against suing in the first place) wrote to Currie: 'It has occurred to some of the Governors of McGill University and a few of your more intimate friends that they could show their admiration and affection for you in a tangible way by defraying the cost of the Cobourg trial and providing you with a sufficient margin over these expenses to enable you to take a very much needed rest.'[23] In all, Beatty collected $30,300. The donors included George Montgomery, who had already given so generously of his time.

Currie returned from his convalescence abroad, and resumed his duties at McGill University in May 1929. He died on 30 November 1933, a few days short of his fifty-eighth birthday. His last years were devoted to McGill and to the cause of veterans' pensions. In 1930 he represented Canada at the ceremonies inaugurating New Delhi as the capital of India. He remained a prominent figure to the end, unveiling innumerable memorials, laying wreaths, and attending with remarkable sympathy and patience to the affairs of war veterans who had fallen on hard times.

Currie often worried that the work of the Canadian Corps was being forgotten. He complained when a newspaper feature, 'Today in History,' neglected to mention the anniversary of the battle that broke the Hindenburg line at the Drocourt-Quéant Switch on 2 September 1918.[24] When the writing of the government-commissioned history of the war was proceeding too slowly for his liking, Currie wrote Prime Minister R.B. Bennett urging speed: 'Soldiers fight battles, but historians make the history of them.'[25]

Shortly before his death he began to feel that another war was coming, and the thought depressed him deeply. Some of his old comrades thought that he had become a pacifist when he spoke out in favour of disarmament. Currie knew the suffering caused by war, and did not want to see it again. In his last Armistice Day address in 1933, he despaired of the 'bitterness and hate, selfishness and greed, [which] are still entrenched in our social and economic and political life.'[26] But there remained in his mind the ideals he thought emerged only in time of war – the spirit of a common effort, the pulling together for a higher cause. 'I know it can't be done, but if one could strip war of all its cruelty and sorrow it would be worthwhile; there is so much in it that makes one more proud of his brother man than he has occasion to be in his peace time efforts. It is the high spot in our lives.'[27]

Although Currie was revered by his friends and comrades he was disliked by many others, and he was denied formal public recognition until after his death. The remark he made on the death of an old friend proved prophetic with regard to his own reputation: 'So often a man has to die before the rest of the world lets it be known in what regard he is held.'[28] Currie's state funeral was said at the time to have been the most elaborate in Canadian history.[29]

Currie's estate was modest. He never changed his will from the one he signed in August 1914 before going overseas, and the net value of his estate produced an income of only $800 per annum for his widow.[30] Once again it was Edward Beatty who used his influence to provide some financial assistance. A year after Currie's death Beatty wrote to the prime minister, pointing out Lady Currie's financial plight and pleading that McGill University simply could not afford to continue to allow her a substantial portion of Sir Arthur's salary any longer.[31] Bennett decided that something had to be done and, with the support of the Liberal leader Mackenzie King, proposed that a grant be made to Currie's estate. There was opposition from within Bennett's own party, and from those outside who thought the payment inappropriate and an insult to the thousands of veterans who were struggling for the bare necessities of life.[32] But eighteen months after Currie's death, and almost seventeen years after the capture of Mons, the Parliament of Canada passed a resolution granting Currie's estate $50,000 'in recognition of the eminent service rendered to his country by the deceased general during the great war.'[33]

Notes

References to original documents are to the Currie Papers, Public Archives of Canada, MG 30 E 100, unless otherwise stated.

I   MONS

1 Information concerning the events following the liberation of Mons was collected at the city's war museum.
2 Currie diary, file 194
3 This passage from General Morrison's war memoirs was quoted at the trial. These memoirs, later published under the title *With the Canadians from Valcartier to the Rhine* (1928), appeared as a newspaper serial at about the time of the Currie trial: see Ottawa *Citizen*, commencing 30 March 1928. The extract quoted in the text was not published until after the trial: Ottawa *Citizen*, 13 May 1928.
4 Bovey to Currie, 20 August 1919, attaching a copy of *La Presse de Bruxelles* reporting the ceremony, file 7
5 Undated copy, Currie Papers, McGill University Archives
6 The Toronto *Globe* of 13 June 1927 provides a full account of the ceremony.
7 House of Commons Debates, 4 March 1919, 207. Hughes's attack on Currie is discussed in detail in chapter 3.
8 Currie to Lt-Col. O.F. Brothers, 30 March 1928, file 60
9 Currie to Dick Symons, 30 March 1928, file 61

10 Brown to Currie, 20 June 1927, file 62
11 See Stephen Legate *Stephen Leacock* (Toronto: Doubleday 1970) 187
12 Montgomery to Bovey, 25 July 1927, file 62
13 For a discussion of defamatory libel see John King *The Law of Criminal Libel* (Toronto: Carswell 1912); Law Commission (UK) 'Criminal Libel' Working Paper No. 84 (1982); Law Reform Commission of Canada 'Defamatory Libel' Working Paper No. 35 (1984).
14 See King, supra note 13, citing *R.* v. *Patteson* (1875) 36 UCQB 129.
15 Now section 273 (formerly section 324)
16 See now *Lord* v. *Ryan* (1976) 19 C. de D. 265 (Que.) upholding a reasonable-belief defence.
17 Chisholm to Montgomery, 25 June 1927, file 62
18 Currie to Ralston, 22 June 1927, file 60
19 Ibid.
20 Libel and Slander Act, RSO 1927, c. 101, sections 7, 13
21 Chisholm to Montgomery, 23 July 1927, file 62

2 ARTHUR CURRIE, THE GREAT WAR, AND THE CANADIAN CORPS

1 There are three biographies of Currie. The first, Hugh M. Urquhart *Arthur Currie: The Biography of a Great Canadian* (Toronto: Dent 1950) was sponsored by a group of Currie's friends from the Canadian Corps and McGill. I have used it as the primary source of information regarding Currie's early life. The second biography appeared after this book had already gone through early drafts, but has also been relied upon: Daniel G. Dancocks *Sir Arthur Currie: A Biography* (Toronto: Methuen 1985). The best source of information on Currie's military career is A.M.J. Hyatt *General Sir Arthur Currie: A Military Biography* (Toronto: University of Toronto Press 1987).
2 Urquhart 26
3 Ibid. 37
4 Hyatt 23
5 See G.W.L. Nicholson *Canadian Expeditionary Force, 1914–1919: The Official History of the Canadian Army in the First World War* (Ottawa: Queen's Printer 1962); John Swettenham *To Seize the Victory* (Toronto: Ryerson Press 1965).
6 Desmond Morton *A Peculiar Kind of Politics* (Toronto: University of Toronto Press 1982) 98
7 Ibid. 121
8 A.J.M. Hyatt 'Sir Arthur Currie and Conscription: A Soldier's View' (1969) 50 *Canadian Historical Review* 285

9 McInnes to Currie, 5 December 1917, file 3; Oliver to Currie, 6 December 1917, file 3
10 Currie to Perley, 10 December 1917, file 3
11 Currie to Creelman, 30 November 1917, file 1. See also Currie to Oliver, 30 November 1917, file 3
12 Currie to Loomis, 27 January 1918, file 2
13 Morton *Politics* 163
14 Currie to Borden, 26 November 1918, file 1
15 Montreal *Gazette* 4 October 1918
16 *Times* 12 October 1918
17 Montreal *Gazette* 17 October 1918
18 *Times* 17 October 1918
19 Montreal *Gazette* 23 October 1918
20 Currie to Kemp, 1 November 1918, file 2
21 Montreal *Gazette* 12 November 1918
22 Currie diary, 7 November 1918, file 194
23 *Times* 9 November 1918
24 A copy of the order was entered at the Currie trial as exhibit 25.
25 The text of this order was read many times at the trial.
26 Trial transcript
27 Horne to Currie, 11 November 1918, file 2
28 Ralph Hodder-Williams *Princess Patricia's Light Infantry 1914–1919* (London: Hodder and Stoughton 1923) 383
29 Currie to Borden, 26 November 1918, file 1
30 'A Story of Five Cities' in J. Castell Hopkins *Canada at War, 1914–1918* (Toronto: Canadian Annual Review 1919)
31 Toronto *Globe* 16 November 1918
32 Currie to B.E. Kelly, 17 August 1920, file 31
33 Currie to Clark, 21 May 1920, file 10
34 Currie to Lineham, 21 May 1920, file 12
35 Currie to Clark, 21 May 1920, file 10
36 Currie to W.W. Foster, 7 October 1924, file 24. Speculation that Currie had political ambitions was prompted by a speech he gave at the Civil Service Research Conference in September 1924, where he stated, 'Unfortunately many of our people have lost faith in the politician. We must try to restore faith in our country and elect only men whom we can trust.' Montreal *Star* 12 September 1924.
37 Currie to King, 7 December 1921, file 32
38 See, for example, Currie to Aukland Geddes, 2 March 1921, file 25.
39 Currie to Griesbach, 12 July 1926, file 28
40 Ibid.

41 Byng to Currie, 14 April 1927, file 19. For a fuller account of the Currie-Byng correspondence, see A.J.M. Hyatt 'The King-Byng Episode: A Footnote to History' (1963) 43 *Dalhousie Review* 469

3   SAM HUGHES: WAR OF RUMOURS

1 Toronto *Daily Star* 5 March 1919
2 House of Commons Debates, 4 March 1919, 199
3 Ibid. 206
4 Ibid. 207
5 There are now three biographies of Hughes. The first two are sympathetic rather than scholarly accounts: Charles F. Winter *Lt. Gen. the Hon. Sir Sam Hughes* (Toronto: Macmillan 1931); Alan R. Capon *His Faults Lie Gently* (Lindsay: Floyd W. Hall 1969). The most recent biography is a scholarly book: Ronald G. Haycock *Sam Hughes: The Public Career of a Controversial Canadian, 1885–1916* (Waterloo: Wilfrid Laurier University Press 1986). Morton *A Peculiar Kind of Politics* (1982) contains a considerable amount of material regarding Hughes.
6 Capon 24
7 Borden recorded several complaints he received as prime minister from the governor-general regarding Hughes's behaviour: Henry Borden (ed.): *Robert Laird Borden: His Memoirs* vol. 1 (Toronto: Macmillan 1938) 384–5, 459, 462, 493.
8 Winter 7
9 Borden *Memoirs* 330
10 Ibid.
11 Ibid.
12 Morton *Politics* 18. See House of Commons Debates, 1 June 1914, 4579–80, where Hugh Guthrie, later the minister of militia and defence, criticized Hughes for the 'grossest extravagance' and for needlessly raising a militia force of some 80,000 men. 'There is no reason for it; there is no emergency in sight, and there will be none in our day and generation.'
13 *Memoirs* 457
14 House of Commons Debates, 26 January 1916, 292
15 *Memoirs* 463–4
16 House of Commons Debates, 26 January 1916, 288
17 Morton *Politics* xi
18 Ibid.

19 Hughes to Aitken, 30 November 1915, Beaverbrook Papers, House of Lords, File E-1-1
20 Borden to Hughes, 1 December 1915, ibid.
21 Hughes to French, 6 December 1915, ibid.
22 Morton *Politics* 48
23 21 January 1916, quoted in Morton *Politics* 55
24 See, for example, Winter 101.
25 Morton *Politics* 60
26 Hughes to Borden, 24 March 1916, quoted in Morton *Politics* 63
27 Capon 73
28 *Memoirs* 472
29 Ibid. 522
30 Ibid. 559–60
31 Ibid. 567
32 Morton *Politics* 89
33 *Memoirs* 571
34 Foreword to Capon *His Faults Lie Gently*. See also Leslie Frost *Fighting Men* (Toronto: Clarke Irwin 1967) 64–5.
35 Morton *Politics* viii
36 *Memoirs* 463
37 Capon 17
38 Winter 12
39 House of Commons Debates, 30 January 1917, 253 et seq.; 6 May 1918, 1485 et seq.
40 Ibid. 6 May 1918, 1488
41 Beaverbrook Papers, file E-1-5
42 Currie to Borden, 26 November 1918, file 1
43 Morton *Politics* 74
44 13 June 1917, quoted in Hyatt 'Conscription' 290
45 Currie to McGillicudy, no date, quoted in Hyatt *Currie* 71
46 R. Craig Brown and Desmond Morton 'The Embarrassing Apotheosis of a "Great Canadian": Sir Arthur Currie's Personal Crisis in 1917' (1979) 60 *Canadian Historical Review* 41
47 Hyatt 'Conscription' 291. For Macdonell's account of the pressures brought to bear upon Currie at this time, see Macdonell to Borden, 14 December 1933, Borden Papers, PAC vol. 268, file 82.
48 Urquhart 164
49 Ibid. 198
50 Hughes to Aitken, 24 November 1917, Beaverbrook Papers, file E-1–file 7

51 Currie to Loomis, 27 January 1918, file 1
52 House of Commons Debates, 30 January 1917, 268
53 Quoted in House of Commons Debates, 4 March 1919, 204
54 Currie to Beaverbrook, 27 January 1918, file 1
55 Currie to Brewster, 27 January 1918, file 1
56 House of Commons Debates, 6 May 1918, 1488
57 Hughes to Borden, 1 October 1918, quoted in House of Commons Debates, 4 March 1918, 206
58 Hughes to Aitken, 8 October 1918, Beaverbrook Papers, file E-1-7
59 Currie to Alistair Fraser, 7 December 1918, file 60
60 Urquhart, 275
61 Currie to James Birchenough, 23 August 1919, file 6
62 Supra note 59
63 Message forwarded by Kemp to Currie for response, 26 February 1919, file 7
64 There is no record in Currie's papers of any reply, although Currie did later provide a report on various engagements, including Mons, where he stated: 'There was no assault on the city of Mons and there was no particular battle for it ... it would be absurd to say that any casualties suffered ... on November 10th and 11th were due to the capture of Mons': memorandum, n.d., file 7
65 5 March 1919
66 Ibid.
67 Toronto *Daily Star* 6 March 1919
68 Montreal *Gazette* 13 March 1919
69 London *Advertiser*, quoted in Toronto *Daily Star* 10 March 1919
70 Toronto *Telegram* March 1919
71 House of Commons Debates, 14 March 1919, 468
72 Toronto *Daily Star* 15 March 1919
73 House of Commons Debates, 27 May 1919, 2884
74 Ibid. 2857
75 Ibid. 7 July 1919, 4697
76 Urquhart 275–6
77 Currie diary, 17 November 1918
78 Urquhart 222. Dancocks seems to dispute this. See, for example, *Sir Arthur Currie* 66–7
79 See Dancocks 133–4; he agrees, however, that the message was not well received by the men in the ranks.
80 Urquhart 223
81 Ibid.
82 Ibid.

83 Will R. Bird *Ghosts Have Warm Hands* (Toronto: Clarke Irwin 1968) 220–1
84 Morton *Politics* xii
85 Ibid.
86 Urquhart 226–7; Dancocks 141–2; David Lloyd George *War Memoirs*, vol. 6 (London: Ivor Nicholson 1936) 3423–4, describes Currie as one of the war's few 'brilliant military leaders.'
87 Memorandum Respecting the late Sir Arthur Currie, 13 August 1934, Borden Papers, PAC MG 264, vol. 268, pt. 2
88 Urquhart 280
89 Toronto *Globe* 30 August 1919
90 30 August 1919
91 30 August 1919
92 House of Commons Debates, 29 September 1919, 635
93 Ibid. 642
94 Toronto *Telegram* 30 September 1919
95 30 September 1919
96 Currie to H.B. Mitchell, 13 October 1919, file 7
97 House of Commons Debates, 16 June 1920, 3656
98 Currie to Sclater, 29 June 1920, file 16. See also Currie to H.J. Young, 20 August 1920, file 16, referring to the possibility that Hughes might repeat his charges outside the House of Commons: 'I shall see what protection the law of Canada will give me against his malicious slanders.'

4   A CASE FOR THE DEFENCE?

1 Toronto *Mail and Empire* 18 April 1928
2 See Wilfred H. Kesterton *A History of Journalism in Canada* (Toronto: McClelland and Stewart 1967).
3 Toronto *Globe* 14 October 1929
4 Port Hope *Evening Guide* 29 June 1927
5 Gordon to Currie, 28 July 1927, file 62
6 Currie to Gordon, 10 September 1927, file 62
7 This was related to Currie by Gordon long after the trial: 9 June 1932, file 67
8 Gordon to Currie, 4 October 1927, file 62
9 Currie to Gordon, 17 October 1927, file 62
10 Gordon to Currie, 18 October 1927, file 62
11 The court file has not survived, and the pleadings are not in the Currie Papers. However, the full text of both documents was published in the Toronto *Telegram* on 3 March 1928.

12 The impact of the Charter on the law of defamation is still uncertain. For discussion, see Robert Sharpe 'The Charter and Defamation: Will the Courts Protect the Media' in Philip Anisman and Allen Linden (eds.) *The Media, the Courts and the Charter* (Toronto: Carswell 1986). The Supreme Court of Canada has held that the Charter does not apply to litigation between private parties where no government action is involved or relied upon: *Retail, Wholesale & Department Store Union, Local 580 et al.* v. *Dolphin Delivery Ltd.* [1986] 2 SCR 573. While this seems to preclude the Charter's application to the Currie case should it arise today, the court also held that the judiciary 'ought to apply and develop the principles of the common law in a manner consistent with the fundamental values enshrined in the Constitution' (at 603).

13 The issue is considered again in chapter 15.

14 The following account of the meeting is based upon evidence given at the trial.

15 See chapter 1.

16 Some prominent Liberals were enthusiastic about Preston's work. Samuel Jacobs, a Liberal MP, wrote: 'The circulation of a couple of hundred thousand [copies] would do the Liberal party inestimable good. It is well that incidents to which you refer should be kept before the electorate. The rigorous way in which you handle the subject is worthy of all commendation': Jacobs to Preston, 20 September 1928, PAC, Jacobs Papers, MG 27, III C.3, vol. 6.

17 *My Generation of Politics and Politicians* (Toronto: D.A. Rose 1927) 378

18 R. Craig Brown *Robert Laird Borden: A Biography* vol. 2 (Toronto: Macmillan 1980) 186–7

19 *My Generation* 344

20 Ibid. 324

21 'Taking Off the Lid: Startling Exposures of Overseas Military Election Frauds' pamphlet (1919) 5

22 House of Commons Debates, 26 July 1899, 8569 et seq.

23 *Report of Commissioners Re West Elgin Election Investigation*, Ontario Sessional Papers No. 46 (1900), 15

24 *My Generation* 453

25 *Encyclopedia Canadiana*, vol. 8 (1975) 299; *The Macmillan Dictionary of Canadian Biography* 4th ed. (Toronto: Macmillan 1978) 677

26 The trial is reported in the *Times* (11 and 12 May 1915), as is the appeal (26 February 1916).

27 A full report is contained in the *Times* 28 June to 1 July 1915. For Canadian coverage, see the Toronto *Globe, Star, Telegram,* and *Mail and Empire.*

28 The Laurier Papers, PSC MG 26 G, include a substantial volume of correspondence between Preston and Laurier commencing in 1887 and continuing until Laurier's death in 1919. The references in the following footnotes are to the Laurier Papers.

29 Preston to Laurier, 21 December 1916, vol. 704, 194165

30 Preston to Laurier, 2 April 1916, vol. 697, 191486

31 A good account of Preston's role is given in Morton *Politics* 139–48. See also Desmond Morton 'Polling the Soldier Vote: The Overseas Campaign in the Canadian General Election of 1917' (1975) 10 *Journal of Canadian Studies* 39. For Preston's own version, see *My Generation* 364–82.

32 Preston to Laurier, 11 September 1917, vol. 713, 196988

33 Preston to Laurier, 25 September 1917, vol. 713, 196990

34 Preston to Laurier, 30 May 1917, vol. 709, 195830

35 Preston to Laurier, 9 February 1918, vol. 721, 199653

36 Preston to Laurier, 29 October 1917, vol. 715, 197859

37 *Canadian Annual Review 1917* 634

38 Ibid. 635

39 *My Generation* 370

40 Preston to Laurier, 19 December 1917, vol. 717, 198985

41 Preston to Laurier, 1 January 1918, vol. 720, 199248

42 Two pamphlets published under Preston's name in 1919 provide lively examples: 'Taking Off the Lid: Startling Exposures of Overseas Military Election Frauds,' and 'The Prime Minister's Offence: Election Debauchery Overseas.' Preston told Laurier he would run in the first constituency to become available so that he could put the material he had collected to use: Preston to Laurier, 21 December 1917, vol. 718, 199080.

43 P.D. Ross *Retrospects of a Newspaper Person* (Toronto: Oxford 1931) 126–30

44 Preston to J.W. Dafoe, 15 and 16 November 1910; 22 December 1910; 1 February 1911, Dafoe Papers, PAC MG 30 D 45

45 Ananias was a biblical figure who fell dead after being rebuked for lying; to call someone 'Ananias' is to call him or her a liar.

46 *Retrospects* 131–6

47 For the final chapter in Preston's fight with the *Journal*, see chapter 15.

48 J.W. Dafoe (of the Manitoba *Free Press*), reviewing *My Generation*, quoted in Toronto *Mail and Empire* 18 April 1928

5 TO SUE OR NOT TO SUE?

1 Gordon to Montgomery, 14 December 1927, file 62

2 Currie to Montgomery, 21 December 1927, file 62

3 Tilley to Montgomery, 30 December 1927, file 62

4 Montgomery to Tilley, 31 December 1927, file 62

5 Ibid.

6 Currie to Montgomery, 18 January 1928, file 62

7 Ibid.

8 Tilley to Montgomery, 26 January 1928, file 62

9 Currie to Montgomery, 23 February 1928, file 62

10 Montgomery to Currie, 27 February 1928, file 62

11 *Cyclopaedia of Canadian Biography* (Toronto: Rose Publishing Co. 1919) 189

12 A brief biographical sketch of Tilley appears in (1968) 2 *Law Society of Upper Canada Gazette* 35

13 [1927] SCR 637

14 [1987] 1 SCR 1148

15 [1928] AC 363

16 Borden *Memoirs* 736; Borden diaries, 6 September 1917, quoted in David Williams *Duff: A Life in the Law* (Toronto: Osgoode Society 1984) 90

17 Gow to Currie, 7 April 1928, file 60

18 The case is fully reported in the *Times* 1 May to 5 June 1924

19 6 June 1924

20 *Times* 27 August 1924

21 The trial is fully reported in the *Times* 28 January to 3 February 1927. See also Joseph Dean *Hatred, Ridicule or Contempt* (London: Constable and Company 1953) 96–117.

22 4 February 1927

23 Referred to by Holt CJ in *Johnson* v. *Browning* (1705) 6 Mod. Rep. 216, at 217

24 H. Montgomery Hyde *The Trials of Oscar Wilde* (London: William Hodge and Company 1948)

25 Montreal *Gazette* 19 February 1927

26 Toronto *Daily Star* 16 March 1927

27 30 March 1927

28 Lt.-Col O.F. Brothers to Currie, 19 March 1928, file 60

29 Peck to Currie, 20 March 1928, file 61

30 The best study is Paul Fussell *The Great War and Modern Memory* (New York: Oxford 1975).

31 Ibid. See also B.I. Evans *English Literature Between the Wars* (London: Methuen 1948); M.S. Greicus *Prose Writers of World War 1* (London: Longman 1973).

32 Currie to Burton, 26 June 1930, file 19
33 Burton to Currie, 27 June 1930, file 19
34 Currie to Macdonell, 25 June 1930, file 33
35 Currie to George Gibson, 29 November 1926, file 25
36 9 April 1928, file 65
37 Currie to Maj.-Gen. Elmsley, 16 March 1928, file 60
38 Currie to Clark, 30 March 1928, file 64
39 An Act to Amend the Jurors Act, SO 1952, c. 46
40 Tilley to Montgomery, 30 December 1927, file 62
41 Ibid.
42 14 March 1928, file 61
43 Currie to Griesbach, 23 March 1928, file 60

6 PREPARING FOR TRIAL

1 Currie to Maj. Ten Broeke, 27 March 1928, file 60
2 Currie to Maj. H.W. McGill, 28 March 1928, file 65
3 Carson's recollection of the Currie case was published after his death: *Canadian Lawyer* (February 1981).
4 Montreal *Gazette* 24 May 1948
5 Ralston to Currie, 15 March 1928, file 60
6 Duguid to Currie, 15 March 1928, file 60
7 Desbarats to Currie, 3 April 1928, file 60
8 Desbarats to Currie, 10 April 1928, file 60
9 Toronto *Telegram* 10 March 1927
10 All of the quotations in this section have been taken from portions of the discovery included in the trial transcript.
11 Toronto *Telegram* 12 March 1928
12 Toronto *Telegram* 16 March 1928
13 Toronto *Telegram* 17 March 1928
14 Montreal *Gazette* 19 March 1928
15 Ibid.
16 Currie to Odlum, 5 April 1928, file 61
17 Parmenter to Currie, 23 March 1928, file 64
18 Currie's financial indiscretions are discussed in Brown and Morton, 'The Embarrassing Apotheosis of a "Great Canadian"'. The matter is well documented in a PAC file: 'Clothing and Equipment and Equipment Inspection Reports 50th Regiment,' PAC R 24, vol. 5871, HW 7-52-5.

19 Quoted in Brown and Morton, 57
20 Perley to Borden, 21 July 1917, quoted in Brown and Morton, 60. Borden himself later recorded: 'During [Currie's] command of the Canadian Corps I greatly feared that his default would become a public scandal and destroy his usefulness.' Memorandum, Borden Papers, PAC vol. 268, pt. 2.
21 Currie to Parmenter, 22 March 1928, file 62
22 J.H. Gillespie to Currie, 12 April 1928, file 61
23 Currie to Parmenter, 22 March 1928, file 62
24 Currie to E.E. Winslow, 30 March 1928, file 61
25 Currie to Macdonell, 20 March 1928, file 61
26 Currie to E.E. Winslow, 30 March 1928, file 61
27 Currie to Hayter, 22 March 1928, file 64
28 Currie to Parmenter, 22 March 1928, file 62
29 Currie to Clark, 30 March 1928, file 64
30 Ibid.
31 Currie to Odlum, 5 April 1928, file 61
32 Currie to Clark, 23 March 1928, file 60
33 Parmenter to Bovey, 31 March 1928, file 62
34 The St Julien incident is fully discussed in chapter 8.
35 Montreal *Gazette* 13 April 1927. The two questions were: 'Did you receive from the government of Canada the sum of $30,000 or any other amount in 1913 or 1914 or approximately within that time for the purpose of purchasing uniforms for the Highland regiment in Victoria of which you were an officer?' and 'Is that statement correct that Sir Sam Hughes made on the floor of the House of Commons on June 16, 1920, that it was you instead of Col. Jack Currie who was in the dug-out and by reason of which incident Col. Jack Currie was sent home from the front?'
36 Undated memorandum, file 63
37 Magee to Urquhart, 16 August 1934, file 63

7   THE TRIAL BEGINS

1 A biographical sketch of Hugh Rose is to be found in [1968] *Law Society of Upper Canada Gazette* 17.
2 Rose J's trial judgment is reported at (1926) 59 OLR 96.
3 Ottawa *Citizen* 27 April 1928
4 The details of the trial have been taken from the transcript, a copy of which has been preserved in the Currie Papers, and from the very complete newspaper accounts of the daily proceedings found in the Toronto *Star, Globe, Mail and Empire,* and *Telegram,* and the Montreal *Gazette.*

5 Gordon Reid (ed.) *Poor Bloody Murder* (Oakville: Mosaic Press 1980) 241–2
6 See Jurors and Juries Act, RSO 1927, c. 96, ss. 78–84.
7 Toronto *Telegram* 17 April 1928
8 Toronto *Globe* 5 May 1928
9 See Mark Orkin *Legal Ethics* (Toronto: Cartwright 1957) 44 et seq.

8   ANOTHER CURRIE

1 House of Commons Debates, 22 February 1916, 989 et seq.
2 Ibid. 1002.
3 Ibid.
4 House of Commons Debates, 23 February 1916, 1046
5 Currie to Hughes, 16 March, file 58
6 House of Commons Debates, 30 March 1916, 2351
7 House of Commons Debates, 29 September 1919, 634–6
8 House of Commons Debates, 16 June 1920, 3648
9 Ibid. 3655
10 Currie to E.F. Lynn, 10 May 1928, file 58
11 Toronto *Globe* 18 April 1928
12 Peterborough *Examiner* 20 April 1928

9   DEFENSIVE STRATEGIES

1 On this point, see *O'Sullivan* v. *Turk* [1947] 2 DLR 819 (Man. KB).
2 The Evidence Act, RSO 1927, c. 107, s. 9, permitted a party to call three expert witnesses. See now RSO 1980, c. 145, s. 12.
3 Toronto *Globe and Mail* 11 December 1968.
4 Montreal *Gazette* 21 April 1928
5 Toronto *Telegram* 24 April 1928
6 The content of the article is described in chapter 1.
7 It may well be that the basic rule is too strict, but it was unquestioned at the time of the Currie case. This point is discussed in chapters 4 and 15.

10   GENERAL CURRIE'S REPLY

1 *Reference re Meaning of the Word 'Persons' in s. 24 of the BNA Act* [1928] SCR 276. The decision was reversed on appeal to the Judicial Committee of the Privy Council: *Edwards* v. *AG Canada* [1930] AC 124.

2 25 April 1928
3 Toronto *Globe* 26 April 1928
4 The source of Morrison's account is cited in chapter 1, note 3.

II   THE GENERALS TAKE THE STAND

1 The painting was that reproduced as the frontispiece in this book, 'The Return to Mons' by I. Sheldon-Williams

12   GENERAL CURRIE UNDER FIRE

1 That evening, one headline proclaimed, 'COBOURG COURT CROWD APPLAUDS GENERAL CURRIE:' Ottawa *Citizen* 27 April 1928.
2 Southam to Currie, 2 May 1928, file 62
3 Ottawa *Journal* 29 June 1927
4 St Catharines *Standard* 2 July 1917

13   VERDICT

1 Peterborough *Examiner* 1 May 1928
2 Peterborough *Examiner* 2 May 1928
3 Judicature Act, RSO 1927, c. 88, s. 59(1). See now Courts of Justice Act, SO 1984, s. 121(b), permitting one dissent from a six-person jury.

14   APPEAL

1 Toronto Star 4 May 1928
2 2 May 1928
3 This point is taken up in greater detail in chapter 15.
4 Montreal *Gazette* 2 May 1928
5 Montreal *Gazette* 3 May 1928
6 Files 64, 65, 66, 67, 68, and 69
7 Toronto *Star* 2 May 1928
8 Toronto *Telegram* 2 May 1928
9 Brook Claxton to Currie, 3 May 1928, file 66
10 Quoted in Toronto *Globe* 5 May 1928
11 Reid (ed.) *Poor Bloody Murder* 242

12 Bovey to Parmenter, 4 May 1928, file 62. During the Currie trial, the Supreme Court of Canada allowed an appeal and restored a jury verdict for $6,000 damages in favour of the Woodstock *Sentinel Review* against the publisher of the Toronto *Telegram* for a story which insinuated that the Woodstock paper kept liquor on its premises despite its public prohibitionist stance: *Sentinel Review Co. Ltd.* v. *Robinson* [1928] SCR 258, reversing (1927) 61 OLR 62. (Tilley successfully argued the case for the defendants in the Court of Appeal, but did not appear in the Supreme Court of Canada when they lost.) In June 1927, a Montreal court awarded $5,000 against the Montreal *Standard* in favour of an alderman who complained of a story suggesting that he, along with the rest of the council, had acted improperly in the purchase of a public utility: Montreal *Gazette* 30 June 1927. The mayor of Toronto was awarded $5,000 for a libel which suggested that he had acted improperly in a street-widening, and the verdict was upheld on appeal to the Supreme Court of Canada: *Canadian Annual Review 1929*.

13 Huycke to Currie, 14 June 1928, file 64. Huycke had earlier written to Currie: 'It happened that a brother of mine, a decent and fairly progressive farmer, was a member of the jury and I never before wished to be guilty of "jury fixing" but I forebore.' 7 June 1928, file 64.

14 This information was given to me by Mrs Sally McCaig, the daughter of Thomas F. Hall, KC, who was told the story by a member of the jury years after the trial.

15 Willmott to Currie, 4 May 1928, file 62

16 See, for example, Currie to J.G. Brown, 18 June 1928, file 65

17 Currie to H. K. Betty, 14 June 1928, file 65; Currie to Gordon, 11 June 1932, file 67

18 Currie to Tait, 28 Demember 1928, file 61

19 Currie to J.M. Finlay, 26 August 1928, file 24

20 Willmott to Currie, 4 May 1928, file 62

21 Brown to Currie, 13 May 1928, file 62

22 Bovey to Parmenter, 17 May 1928, file 62

23 The text of the Notices of Appeal was reported in the Ottawa *Citizen* of 15 May 1928

24 Tilley to Currie, 19 May 1928, file 62

25 Montreal *Gazette* 17 October 1928

26 Toronto *Globe* 13 October 1928

27 Ibid.

28 Toronto *Star* 16 October 1928

29 Reports of the proceedings are to be found in the Toronto *Star* of 29 October 1928, the Toronto *Globe and Mail* and *Empire*, and the Montreal *Gazette* of 30 October 1928.

15   CONCLUSION

1   The Ottawa *Citizen* 2 May 1928 called it 'one of the most sensational litigations in the history of Canadian jurisprudence ... a lawsuit without parallel in any country, one that has been followed with an intensity of interest throughout Canada which perhaps no other litigation has attracted.'

2   In a criminal case, the proof must be beyond a reasonable doubt; in civil cases, it need only be on a balance of probabilities. However, the courts have held that even in civil cases, where allegations of fraud or criminal conduct are made, proof to 'a degree commensurate with the occasion' will be required: *Bater* v. *Bater* [1950] 2 All ER 458; *Continental Insurance* v. *Dalton Cartage Co. Ltd.* [1982] 1 SCR 164.

3   As in the United States: *New York Times* v. *Sullivan* 376 U.S. 254 (1964).

4   What follows is based upon my more extensive consideration in 'The Charter and Defamation: Will the Courts Protect the Media?'

5   Preston to Murphy, 21 July 1932, Murphy Papers, PAC MG 27 III B8, vol. 25, file 114. See also Preston to Murphy, 22 April 1930, ibid.

6   The following is based on the accounts of the trial in the Toronto *Star*, *Telegram*, *Globe*, and *Mail and Empire* of 6–9 February 1933.

7   Toronto *Globe* 14 October 1929

8   Toronto *Daily Star* 8 June 1932; Gordon to Currie, 9 June 1932, file 67

9   See for example, Fraser to Currie, 20 April 1928, file 60

10   Embury to Currie, n.d., file 67

11   Griesbach to Currie, 4 May 1928, file 67

12   W.E. Hodgins to Currie, 2 May 1928, file 67

13   Gordon to Currie, 9 June 1932, file 67

14   Brown surfaced behind the scenes at several points in the story of the Currie case, and when he came to see Sir Arthur on Regan's behalf, he related his own unfortunate circumstances. He claimed to have been encouraged to secure control of the Port Hope *Times* by R.B. Bennett in order to publicize Bennett and the Conservative party. He had been promised a substantial sum of party money, but was paid only a fraction. By 1930, the bank was pressing him on a loan, and he had to suspend publication of the *Times*: memorandum, Currie to file, 9 February 1930, file 64. He later moved to Toronto and in 1932 published on his own behalf *The Conservative Blue Book*, a 'who's who' of the Conservative party.

15   Ibid.

16   For a full account of the Dorland affair, see Charles W. Bell *Who Said Murder* (Toronto: Macmillan 1935).

17 In May 1935 a royal commission was appointed to investigate charges made in the House of Commons by Agnes MacPhail regarding the inspector of Kingston penitentiary. Regan wrote to her (addressing her as 'Dear Agnes'), urging upon her the necessity of having her own counsel and offering her his own services free of charge. Regan to MacPhail, 3 May 1935, MacPhail Papers, PAC MG 27 III C4, vol. 1.

18 Currie to Macdonell, 16 June 1928, file 33

19 Currie to Tait, 28 December 1928, file 61

20 Currie to Ada Gordon, 10 August 1931, file 25

21 Tilley to Currie, 15 June 1928; file 72; Tilley to Bovey, 1 November 1928, file 63

22 Montgomery to Currie, 14 June 1928, file 72

23 Beatty to Currie, 6 June 1928, file 64

24 Currie to Bassett, 2 September 1932, file 18

25 Currie to Bennett, 24 March 1933, file 18

26 Pamphlet, 'Armistice Night, 1933: University Veterans Dinner Toronto,' Borden papers, PAC, vol. 268, pt. 2 Currie wrote the address but was too ill to give it, and it was read by Allan Magee.

27 Currie to Macdonell, 11 December 1931, file 33

28 Currie to J.E. Winslow, 14 November 1931, file 40, commenting on the death of Currie's old Victoria business associate, Matson.

29 Robert L. Borden Letters to Limbo (Toronto: University of Toronto Press 1971) 263

30 A copy of Currie's will and details about his financial affairs are to be found in the Bennett papers, PAC MG 26K, vol. 971.

31 Beatty to Bennett, 4 December 1934, ibid., 615902

32 See F.-J. Lafleche to Bennett, 26 June 1935, ibid., 615921. The grant was opposed by several members led by the CCF leader, J.S. Woodsworth: 'I think of the large numbers of the rank and file who have had no such tribute paid to them although they are sadly in need of it ... We say we do not stand for class distinction in this country, but in passing a grant of this kind we are setting up certain class distinctions that in my judgment are injurious to the best interests of this country.' House of Commons Debates, 28 June 1935, 4109–10. One correspondent objected in the most vehement language, and, without crediting his source, quoted lengthy extracts from the Port Hope Guide's 'Mons' editorial: Andrew McFarland to Bennett, 17 July 1935, ibid., 615927.

33 House of Commons Debates, 28 June 1935, 4901; 5 July 1935, 4308

Index

PUBLICATIONS OF THE OSGOODE SOCIETY